Prophetic Charisma

Prophetic Charisma

The Psychology

of Revolutionary

Religious Personalities

Len Oakes

With a Foreword by
Sarah Hamilton-Byrne

Syracuse University Press

Copyright © 1997 by Syracuse University Press
Syracuse, New York 13244-5160
All Rights Reserved

First Edition 1997
97 98 99 00 01 02   6 5 4 3 2 1

The paper used in this publication meets the minimum requirements of
American National Standard for Information Sciences—Permanence of
Paper for Printed Library Materials, ANSI Z39.48-1984. ∞™

Library of Congress Cataloging-in-Publication Data
Oakes, Len.
    Prophetic charisma : the psychology of revolutionary religious
personalities / Len Oakes ; with a foreword by Sarah Hamilton-Byrne.
—1st ed.
        p.   cm.
    Includes bibliographical references and index.
    ISBN 0-8156-2700-9 (cloth : alk. paper).—ISBN 0-8156-0398-3
(pbk. : alk. paper)
        1. Prophets—Psychology.   2. Charisma (Personality trait)
3. Religious leaders—Psychology.   4. Cults—Psychology.   I. Title.
BL633.O24   1997
291.6'1'019—dc21   97-20929

Manufactured in the United States of America

To

Larry Constantine, Barry Kirkwood, and Lawrence Foster

—for their support.

If we understood the function of cults we would probably understand the function of cultures. Every established ecclesia of the majority began as a minority crisis cult of one, in historic, not supernatural time; and his cult spread and diffused historically, sometimes until it became the Established Religion, whose priests (as opposed to visionary shamans) are merely the nonecstatic journeyman officiants of routinized established cults.

—Weston La Barre,

Culture in Context: Selected Writings of Weston La Barre

Len Oakes is a senior consultant psychologist with the Cairnmillar Institute of Melbourne, Australia, and completed his doctoral dissertation on the psychology of charisma at the University of Auckland, New Zealand. He is a member of the Australian Psychological Society, the New Zealand Psychological Society, and the International Society for Hypnosis and has published articles on communal studies, the psychology of religion, and counselling issues associated with new religious movements. He is associate editor of the journal *Psychotherapy in Australia*.

Contents

Foreword

In this unique contribution to our understanding of the social phenomenon of charismatic groups and those who lead them, Dr. Len Oakes explores the psychology of charisma and proposes his own theory of the five-stage life cycle of two types of prophets—the messianic and the charismatic—from their primitive narcissistic beginnings to their ultimately inevitable implosion or demise. The central premise of Dr. Oakes's thesis is that the core of the cult leader's distinctiveness, and the basis of any subsequent psychopathology, is the narcissistic personality—characterized by grandiosity, manipulativeness, a need for control of others and inner congruence, but also by paranormal empathy, confidence, memory, autonomy, detachment, and islands of social and personal insight. Hidden under these defenses is an empty core, a terror of weakness, and a secret sense of shame that leads to a compensatory grandiosity. As with any personality type, cult leaders' expressions of their preexisting narcissistic dispositions can lie anywhere along a continuum from normal to borderline to frankly psychotic; Oakes has met and talked to numerous leaders who together exemplify all of these states. He also explores the psychology of apostates and proposes a life cycle of individual involvement in charismatic groups.

The phenomenon of the religious cult continues to attract and mystify us. The attraction is partly that of the exotic and the unknown, the taboo, the promise of Foucaultian "limit experiences" normally denied the sober citizen of the outside world, socialized so neatly into repressing the urge to ecstasy; who, trapped in the nine-to-five paradigm, has almost forgotten what it is to put life on the line for a belief, to gamble one's own destiny for the promise of something not generally accessible in the gray and boring outside world.

Len Oakes talks, as I do, as a former insider. He lived inside a charismatic cult; he knew at first hand the seduction of surrender to a guru. He has paid the personal price for that, but he has also had the wisdom and courage not only to achieve a personal understanding of the psychology of the experience by putting to use his academic strength and skills, but also to develop the language to convey in an accessible way some of the conclusions and insights he has achieved by this study. The intimate knowledge and experience of the workings of cults give his thesis an authority that goes beyond mere intellectual analysis. More important, it affords his work a dignity; by trying to make sense of a literally life-shattering and often intensely painful set of experiences, he converts the past into something productive and meaningful. Thus from his own personal suffering he derives meaning, not necessarily from a renunciation or overcoming of the past, but from an acknowledgment that it serves as a unique part of his life story, something that affords and enhances his insight. Hence he achieves a victory consistent with that of those whose greatest revenge is to live well; he manages to turn his past into a source of strength instead of despair.

Because of my experiences, I follow the popular and academic literature on cults with some interest. There tend to be two broad categories: frankly uninformed, sensationalist, popular accounts, often with a pronounced hysterical undertone of Christian moralistic indignation, written by those who have no understanding and no will to understand; and the testaments of ex-members trapped in incoherent rage at the losses they have endured, each with an ax to grind and without any attempt to come to terms with, or gain anything from, their experiences. Both sets of writers have a vested interest in painting such a world as black and white, and they generally fail to acknowledge the complexity of the legacy of the cult experience or to discuss it in any meaningful way. Because they cannot acknowledge any positives, they fail to pick up the lessons of the shades of gray, and thus do not impart any understanding of the phenomenon.

In addition, it is often very difficult to begin to convey to those who haven't had the experience of being part of a charismatic group, an insight into such a culture. That world is too far removed from their own—it is like another planet, another dimension of reality, whose existence often can be approached only on an intuitive rather than a rational level. This is not adequate for academia. Hence there is a dearth of psychologically sophisticated commentary about either the cult experience or the psychology of cult leaders. In this book Dr. Oakes takes on that challenge and begins with great clarity of insight to fill the gap between the two worlds, as only someone with direct human experience could do, so as to make that world a little more intellectually intelligible. In doing so, he gains and communicates an academic understanding that can potentially be translated into concrete therapeutic approaches for those whose lives have been changed by cult involvement.

In this book Dr. Oakes goes a long way toward answering his central questions: Why would anyone become a prophet? How does one do so? By postulating the origin, further development, and crises of the narcissistic personality style, as well as the manifestly creative subsequent defenses that these people characteristically employ, he gives us insight into their often bizarre and otherwise inexplicable behaviors, and achieves a credible theory of charisma. This is a compassionate as well as a knowledgeable account. It turns the cult leader into a human being instead of a mysterious ogre. It brings us to some sort of empathy with the sort of person who is literally a "legend in their own mind"—an exceptionally resourceful person who is both saner and crazier than normal, someone "larger than life" from whom we may learn fundamental lessons about our own nature, and the basis of social and spiritual morality. As such, I would recommend it as essential reading for those who seek an appreciation of the charismatic leader. And it will indeed resonate with the ring of truthful and courageous insight for those who have had any personal involvement and for those who seek to understand or counsel apostates.

Sarah Hamilton-Byrne

Author of *Unseen, Unheard, Unknown: My Life Inside the Family of Anne Hamilton-Byrne*

Prophetic Charisma

Introduction

When a superior intellect and a psychopathic temperament coalesce — as in the endless permutations and combinations of human faculty they are bound to coalesce often enough — in the same individual, we have the best possible condition for the kind of effective genius that gets into the biographical dictionaries. Such men do not remain mere critics and understanders with their intellect. Their ideas possess them, they inflict them, for better or for worse, upon their companions or their age.

—William James
Varieties of Religious Experience

All cultures have their heroes, and no hero is more mysterious, or more extraordinary, than God's messenger—the prophet. Whether called messiahs or saviors, gurus or avatars, such figures continue to fascinate us, whether for their truths or their absurdities, for the adulation of their followers or the hatred of their enemies. Hardly a week goes by without some bizarre or sensational item appearing in the media about a wild-eyed preacher or an exotic cult coming into conflict with the authorities; the public appetite for such stories is endless.

It is strange, therefore, that we know so little about such figures. While there are biographies of individual leaders, there are few studies of revolutionary religious leaders as a group or as a personality type. Prophets appear suddenly, as if from nowhere, and take the world by surprise; we seem unable to pigeonhole them, to ignore them, or even to describe them other than in superficial ways.

This seems especially peculiar given that Western culture—nominally Christian and still rooted in Christian values—has as its central myth the story of Jesus of Nazareth. One might think that the comparative study of revolutionary religious leaders would be a priority for scholars wishing to shed light on the person of Jesus, or for anyone

1

trying to understand the psychology of religion. But such studies are seldom undertaken, and rarely from a psychological perspective. Perhaps it is time to look more closely at these figures and what they are trying to tell us.

What all prophets have in common is their opposition to convention and their ability to inspire others with their visions. Hence, a key assumption of this study is that charismatic prophets really are, in important ways, different from ordinary people. This will be obvious to anyone who has had prolonged exposure to such a leader. It is not merely that their followers believe them to be extraordinary people—as Max Weber has argued (Weber 1968a, 242)—suggesting the possibility that prophets may in fact be quite ordinary individuals who, for some reason, become the objects of charismatic "construction" by groups (Wallis 1982). It simply beggars the imagination to suggest that men such as L. Ron Hubbard, Fritz Perls, Werner Erhard, Bhagwan Shree Rajneesh and Sun Myung Moon are not really, objectively, unusual people possessing exceptional abilities to inspire the kinds of mass followings they have achieved. Of course all behavior occurs in a social context, and this needs to be considered when attempting to explain conduct, but the aim herein is to understand the personalities of these unusual beings in the contexts of their social environments.

For the purposes of this book a prophet is defined as one who (a) espouses a message of salvation that is opposed to conventional values, and (b) attracts a following of people who look to him for guidance in their daily lives. By this definition such figures as Madame Blavatsky, founder of the Theosophical Society; Prabhupada Bhaktivedanta, founder of the International Society for Krishna Consciousness (the Hare Krishnas); Ann Lee, founder of the Shakers, Joseph Smith, founder of the Mormons; and Father Divine, founder of the Peace Mission, may be fairly considered to be modern prophets (as they are considered by their followers), as may the many less famous founders of communes and new religious movements who also gain followings for their revolutionary personal visions.

Prophets come in a stunning variety of forms. Some are extroverts, some are introverts. Some are humorous, some are humorless. Some seem frankly disturbed, and others appear to be models of good mental health. Some are modest about their achievements, others are megalomaniacal. This diversity must be grasped in order to perceive the underlying similarities. The many factors that complicate the picture include the great variety of the personal circumstances, life histories, and social-psychological, economic, historical, and cultural influences that shape each individual leader. Then there are the differing belief systems of prophets, especially whether they work within a supernatural or a naturalistic worldview, and also the kinds of leadership claims permitted by these ideologies. Some prophets espouse beliefs that limit their claims to leadership—for example, anarchism. In addition, prophets have different goals; not all aspire to change the world or even to attract a large following. Nor are they all equally successful at inspiring converts, although a small following may be intensely devoted and achieve much. Last, there are factors to do with the life of the cult: how wealthy and powerful it has grown; whether the prophet has adopted other roles, such as lawgiver, military leader, or chief executive of an international empire; and whether or not the cult is in conflict with the outside world. In sum, we may find so many differences between prophets that their common features elude us.

Nevertheless, the study of revolutionary religious personalities has much to recommend it, especially for what it may teach us of the human heart and contemporary life. Prophets typically highlight repressed impulses in human nature, and charismatic movements often exaggerate neglected trends in society, carrying to their extreme logical conclusion certain ideas and passions from which others recoil. Because of this, we may come to understand ourselves and our society better by understanding why prophets are the way they are, and why they and their followers do the things they do.

This study evolved in three phases. The first began in 1972 when I attended an encounter group run by a charismatic psychotherapist. At that time the Human Potential movement was in full swing and I was twenty-four years old. That group experience so impressed me that I moved into the leader's home, which he shared with a small group of other "followers" (we did not call ourselves that then, but in effect it is what we were). We helped the leader to run workshops and supported him in various ways. This relationship ended in 1975 when I moved on. Three years later this leader founded a rural commune. In 1980 I visited this community, partly for personal reasons and partly from curiosity. At this time I was enrolled to study psychology at the local university. During my visit the leader invited me to join his group and to document its history, adding, "This will be the greatest social laboratory in the world. There's enough research to be done here to keep you busy for the rest of your life." It was an offer I could not pass up.

For the next decade I lived as an inside outsider in the community. It supported my studies and my life. My position in the group was somewhat privileged in that, because of my role as historian-researcher, I was exempted from some of the responsibilities of membership. Although I could never again see the leader as my personal guru in the way I once had and as the other members did now, and although I never became a legal "trustee" of the group (the outward sign of admission to the inner circle of policy makers and spokespersons), I entered into the communal life as fully as I could. I married there and my children were born there. There were times when I defended the group passionately to outside critics, and other occasions when I flatly opposed the leader's directives.

My work in the community led to a book and several studies. I also conducted questionnaire surveys of the members at yearly intervals; I intend to publish this research someday as a case study of the theory put forward here. The goal of this work was to attempt to understand, as far as one is able, the mind of a charismatic prophet. Of course it was also an effort to understand my own motives for my original involvement with him. Hence my time with the group became a unique historical opportunity when a trusted sympathizer witnessed the development of a new religious movement from its inception. In this study I treat this group as a "critical case" in the manner of Patton (1980).

The results of this stage of the inquiry emerged as an understanding of several overlapping domains. Much personal knowledge and information about the group was gained, but how much of this was specific to myself and the milieu I was immersed in, and how much could be generalized to similar movements, was unclear. Of one thing I was sure: the leader whom I had known for sixteen years, having closely observed all aspects of his life and having come to know him as closely as anyone else in his life—and, I suspect, as closely as anyone ever gets to know a charismatic leader—remained as inexplicable to me as ever. I was convinced that he was as different from "normal" people as they were from such distinctively different categories as psychotics, psychopaths, geniuses, mystics, and saints, and that he represented a distinctive personality constellation that was as radically different in essence from those of his peers as adults are from children or women from men.

Hence the main tasks emerging from the first phase of the inquiry, and which were pursued in the second stage, were (a) to discover how much of what I knew about the group was unique to it and how much could be generalized to similar groups, and (b) to develop a theory about the natures of charismatic religious leaders and their movements.

The second phase of this research began in 1988 when I started work for my doctorate on the psychology of charisma. This involved several field trips within New Zealand to study charismatic groups and their leaders, and it resulted in my doctoral dissertation.

The technical aspects of the theory and method used in this phase of the study are discussed in Appendix A. To briefly summarize what was done, the study used structured interviews and a psychometric test, the Adjective Checklist (ACL), to investigate the personalities of eighteen leaders of communes and new religious movements in New Zealand.

Considering first the psychometric component of this stage, the ACL is a measure of personality comprising a list of three hundred commonly used adjectives that research has shown to be sufficient to comprehensively describe the main dimensions of an individual's personality (Gough and Heilbrun 1983). To describe themselves or some target individual, respondents check those adjectives they feel are appropriate. When the results are analyzed, a personality profile is assembled that comprises thirty-seven subscales measuring a range of personality traits such as dominance, creativity, self-confidence, aggressiveness, and the like. These scores may then be interpreted by using the standardized descriptions in the scoring manual. The ACL is a very widely used test with good reliability (Gough and Heilbrun 1983, 31). Norms have been calculated for the most commonly cited categories of subjects,[1] and it has been used in a variety of psychobiographical and observer-rating studies (Gough and Heilbrun 1983, 39–

---

1. Because only one subject in the quantitative component of the study was female, the interpretations for males provided in the ACL handbook (Gough and Heilbrun 1983, 15) are used, despite the existence of slight differences in the scoring and interpretation of one of the subscales. Calculation of standard deviations was derived from normative subgroup "D" (Gough and Heilbrun 1983, 15). The norms used for comparison in this study were those for adults, published by Gough and Heilbrun (1983, 109–10). They were drawn from heterogeneous samples of 1,986 males and 2,092 females tested during field surveys of population psychology, voting patterns, political participation, and similar research projects in the United States.

44), as well as in at least one other major study of a charismatic group (Richardson, Stewart, and Simmonds 1979). The ACL is also a very user-friendly personality test; to complete it, one merely checks a range of familiar words; this takes about five minutes. Hence it is especially appropriate and convenient for research into the personalities of charismatic leaders.

The ACL was administered to eleven of the leaders in this study. The results were intriguing. There was no particular cluster of traits, nor even a single trait developed to an extreme, that was in any way distinctive. Indeed, a healthier, more normal-looking profile would be hard to find. On thirty-four of the thirty-seven subscales the leaders were "average" (that is, they scored within one standard deviation of the mean), and on only three subscales did they differ significantly from the general population (scoring within two standard deviations of the mean). These were for the subscales "Deference," "Creative Personality," and "Free Child."

On the Deference subscale the leaders scored significantly lower than the general population, that is, they were less deferential than most people. The ACL manual advises that such persons delight in competition, taking risks, and defeating their rivals. Their behavior tends to be headstrong and compulsive, and it frequently leads to conflict. They also are talkative, assertive, interesting and arresting, rebellious and nonconforming. They push limits to see what they can get away with, express their hostile feelings directly, value their independence and autonomy, and prefer not to delay gratification (Gough and Heilbrun 1983, 15).

On the Creative Personality subscale, the leaders scored significantly higher than the general population, that is, they were more creative than most. The ACL manual describes them as venturesome, clever, and quick to respond. They have broad interests and think in unusual ways. They are sensual, enjoy the arts, and can express their ideas well (Gough and Heilbrun 1983, 18).

On the Free Child subscale the leaders scored significantly higher than the general population. The manual advises that this scale describes a willful, carefree child or an adult who retains childish self-indulgence, spontaneity, and enjoyment of life. Such adults are ebullient and enterprising, and lack self-restraint. They are humorous, expressive, and gregarious but also self-dramatizing and histrionic. Those around them are likely to be swept along, whether they like it or not, in a rush toward enjoyment. Others see such people as entertaining but aggressive (Gough and Heilbrun 1983, 23). The leaders in this study scored higher on this trait than most of the population, but again the difference was not extreme.

This apparent ordinariness of the leaders as a group is striking. Doubtless there were some individuals who had a few extreme traits, but as a group they were undistinguished. They did tend toward a creative and independent turn of mind, but they were not, despite their adventurousness, given to wildly erratic behaviors. Yet this was a group of people who had inspired others to follow them, often at great personal cost, in pursuit of impossible dreams. The ACL results, while in some ways disappointing, make an explanation of the leadership abilities of these figures seem even more mysterious than before.

Next the qualitative data were examined. This material included the results of systematic observation of the behaviors of the leaders, tape-recorded structured interviews with them and their followers, and discussions with defectors and others who had had contact with the movements. The leaders' beliefs about themselves, their worldviews, and their relationships with their followers were explored. Analysis of this material led to a tentative theory of two types of prophets—messianic and charismatic—and of six life stages through which they pass. This "natural history" of the prophet comprised the bulk of my doctoral dissertation.

The third phase of the study developed slowly from my reading of literally hundreds of books and articles on prophets, gurus, messiahs, saviors, and the like. In this reading I concentrated mainly on biographies and the accounts of followers, apostates, scholars, and the leaders themselves. The goal of this phase was to apply the theory developed in the second phase to several widely known leaders of cults and communes. Overall, the theory accurately described both the leaders studied firsthand and the better-known figures studied through biographical sources. Despite some modifications (the six life stages were eventually reduced to five), eventually a pattern emerged that seemed to fit most of the leaders most of the time. In addition, a description of the essence of charisma, what Max Weber called "pure" charisma—an ecstatic experience when eyes meet, hearts stop, and minds merge, which lies at the heart of the leader-follower relationship —was developed.

In 1991, during a period of crisis in the commune, I and my family left to travel to Melbourne (my wife's hometown), where I completed my dissertation. After gaining my degree, I continued my research in Australia, studying charismatic leaders and new religious movements there. To date I have interviewed fifteen such prophets and almost two hundred of their followers, and have studied several other leaders who were absent or deceased but whose followers provided me with extensive material on them. I also have attended dozens of public meetings with visiting teachers, healers, and evangelists.

Before presenting the findings in detail, descriptions of some of the leaders and groups in the study are provided in order to convey an idea of who they were. The following vignettes, with fictionalized names,[2] are representative.

Fred Thomson. A working-class man from a small New Zealand town, Fred joined the army and briefly saw action in World War II. On his return he took advantage of a government program for ex-servicemen to attend a university, and four years later graduated with a bachelor's degree in English. He married and worked for several years as a public servant, but found he could make far better money as a salesman. In time he started a sales training school that made him rich and widely respected in the business world. However, after he was divorced, he began to rethink his life. He was now fifty years old. He tried psychedelic drugs, journeyed to California to attend growth groups, and went to India to investigate gurus. While there, he discovered that he was God. He returned and set up a commune that he called Humanitas and that in time grew to over two hundred residents.

2. The identities of the leaders and groups studied are disguised because the only way that several of them could be persuaded to cooperate was by providing comprehensive guarantees of anonymity. Further, because New Zealand has a small population, to identify some of the leaders would be effectively to identify them all. In fact, local specialists may well recognize some of the people involved despite my efforts. There is a second reason for secrecy. It is that at this writing (1996) three of the leaders studied are in jail for major criminal offenses. These leaders were prosecuted during the time of this study, and I have been approached several times by journalists seeking information about them. In order to safeguard confidentiality during this period, my doctoral dissertation was embargoed by the University of Auckland library for three years after completion. It is hoped that such precautions may reduce the likelihood of sensationalist accounts appearing in the media about these jailed leaders who now have no way of defending themselves.

However, growing hostility to his role as a "sex guru" led to a series of police actions that ended his career.

Mary Spencer. Born to a poor rural family, Mary had an early life that was harsh and narrow. She grew up poorly educated, and worked as a waitress and a cleaner. She had two failed marriages behind her and few prospects ahead when, at the age of thirty, she experienced an ecstatic spiritual awakening. She set up as a New Age teacher and within a decade had recruited a large following. Her movement, named simply The Tribe, combined yoga, utopianism, and innovative psychotherapy techniques. Mary now claimed to be the reincarnation of Jesus Christ and other historical prophets, and she trained her followers in esoteric practices. Then a bizarre series of scandals enmeshed the group and, although no major crimes were ever conclusively linked to her, Mary fled the country and now lives in wealthy semiretirement.

Leo Haley. Born and raised in a large, poor family in Jamaica, Leo became a Rastafarian while still a youngster. He held no leadership aspirations for himself, happily fitting in with the crowd while hustling for a living in whatever way he could. At twenty-eight Leo's life changed when he married an educated white woman visiting Jamaica to study. He returned with her to Australia, where he met local blacks who, despite a commitment to Rastafarian beliefs, were hungry for a deeper understanding of the meanings of these beliefs. Leo now found himself in the role of a teacher and began to form a group around himself. In time his following grew to over a hundred people who looked to him for guidance in spiritual matters, and also for practical advice about their daily lives. He equipped himself for his leadership role by an intensive program of study and work. His talents as a musician helped him spread the word through record and tape sales. Looking back, Leo feels that his arrival in Australia was the result of God's calling him to do His work and to lead others to Him.

Swami Joe. Jewish by birth, Joe experienced a series of visions in his childhood that he was unable to explain. Later he attended a prestigious American university and earned a master's degree in theology, then journeyed to India to become a devotee of the Hindu teacher Swami Satchitananda. After studying meditation for nine years, Joe returned to the United States with a commission to set up ashrams there to spread the guru's message. Following the death of Satchitananda two years later, Joe claimed these groups as his own and began some radical changes, renaming the movement Elysium. He felt that a more informal flavor was appropriate, and he adopted the name Swami Joe. He also introduced nonyoga techniques to assist the more actively minded Westerners with their meditations. In time Joe became very fashionable as an international guru, and attracted much controversy for his provocative statements. Currently he operates five centers, three in America one in Europe, and one in Australia.

Dr. Paul Clavell. Raised in a middle-class Catholic family, the young Paul entered the Cistercian order to train as a priest. However, he began to harbor grave doubts about his faith. These led, at the age of thirty, to a mental collapse in which he was forced to the conclusion that "All that I believed in, my life, the church, and God, was bullshit." Paul left the monastery (although he remained a priest) and began a painful period of self-searching. The study of psychology, for which he was eventually awarded a doctorate, provided some answers, but in time he developed his own form of self-therapy that he began to use on others in his work as a counselor. Although he had success in this, the church hierarchy opposed his work and he was moved to the radio evangelical service. Here he also enjoyed success as an innovative broadcaster and again the church barred his way forward, feeling that he was threatening traditional beliefs. Finally, totally disillusioned with the church, Paul set up the Orgone Centre, training others in the deep therapy techniques he believes are the only real answer to the world's problems. A powerful speaker at public meetings and a charismatic therapist, he has a loyal following of several dozen graduates of his academy who recognize him as the leading voice for progress in their part of the world.

Typical groups studied include the following:

The Karma Centre. This is an urban ashram run by Swami Divyananda, a fifty-year-old American ex-university professor and convert to the Hindu religion. Meetings are held several times each week at which thirty to forty devotees turn out to hear Swamiji talk. Teachings are mostly traditional Hindu beliefs, and meditation practices are modified for the Western audience. Most members live and work in the city, coming together only at meetings and on occasional retreats. A form of yoga therapy has been developed that bears some similarities to Primal Therapy.

The Church of Christian Love. This breakaway branch of a large Pentecostal denomination was founded in 1973 by the Reverend William

Hart. It is a radical "last days" group that has developed some novel teachings including "divine love"—a form of group marriage—and "Hartening"—a type of evangelical self-criticism. There are about one hundred adults and children in the church. Members live communally on several properties located in a rural enclave. Some members have jobs in nearby towns, but most work on their properties at cottage industries of an arts-and-crafts nature. The church operates its own school and tries to have as little contact with the outside world as possible. Since the death of Reverend Hart in 1984, the group has suffered schism and is currently in decline.

The Brotherhood of Strangers. This is an occult group that was founded in 1965 by Wolf Schubart, a German immigrant with links to ancient occult traditions. Thirty-five members (all male) meet weekly for occult rituals, the only collective activity they share. Members are mostly self-employed tradespeople and professional people, well-educated and successful. One of the main aims of the group is to influence politics by using magical means. The group is extremely secretive; members take ritual names and swear allegiance to the leader.

Other leaders studied, along with the groups they founded, were Joshua Einstein, a thirty-seven-year-old growth movement entrepreneur with about one hundred informal followers; Harry Huntington, founder of the Oceanville Christian pacifist commune with approximately ninety residents; Suzie Shiva, a fifty-year-old female psychotherapist and yoga teacher; Kit van Voon, the fifty-seven-year-old male leader of Leeholm, a radical back-to-the-land pacifist commune of about thirty members; Charlie Tantra, a forty-year-old white male American tantra teacher with a following of about fifty; "Bro" John, the founder of a forty-member hippie commune called New Ecstasy; Arnold Harper, the seventy-year-old head of a two-hundred-member unnamed fundamentalist Christian community; Frank Jansen, the forty-four-year-old, white middle-class pastor of a controversial Pentecostal church; "Free-Love" Farley, the dominant member of a forty-strong (allegedly leaderless) anarchist commune named Sunshine Hill; and Lindsey Amherst, the deceased leader of a fifty-member rural commune called Tao. In addition, less complete information was gathered on two other leaders and their groups who are included in this study. These are Gary Melsop, the founder of a breakaway New Age Christian group called the Church of the New Christ, and Golden Tara, a forty-two-year-old female naturopath and leader of the New Age group Anima. Although followers of these two leaders were interviewed, they themselves declined to be interviewed. A summary of the leaders and groups studied is presented in Appendix B.

Besides these twenty leaders and their groups, several well-known and dozens of lesser-known prophets were studied. These included Jim Jones, Bhagwan Shree Rajneesh, L. Ron Hubbard, Chuck Dederich, Werner Erhard, Fritz Perls, David "Moses" Berg, Kathryn Kuhlman, Father Divine, and J. H. Noyes. Much of the material in this book is taken from biographies of these figures. Occasionally, to illustrate a principle, some material from the lives of charismatic political leaders is included; the many books about Adolf Hitler, Winston Churchill, and Mohandas Gandhi are too good and too numerous, and their subjects are too closely related to the subjects of this study, to ignore.

The pattern of results that eventually emerged from the analysis of the qualitative data, and that can be used to explain many of the behaviors of prophets, includes, first, a more finely grained description of the basic behaviors of the leaders—that is, a list of specific traits unlikely to be measured by a standardized psychological test—and, second, a developmental sequence of life stages—a kind of "natural history of prophetic development"—that accounts for the development of these traits and behaviors. Concerning the first, while there are exceptions and some individual differences—for that is the way of human nature—nevertheless it is likely that a list of about a dozen traits may broadly characterize the prophetic personality type. These are discussed below.

Without ever appearing frenetic, prophets show enormous *energy* for life and the goals they set. Most need only a few hours of sleep each night. Some work tirelessly for the welfare of others, perhaps even dying from exhaustion, as did Phineas Quimby, the metaphysical healer and founder of New Thought. Others, such as Bhagwan Shree Rajneesh and Sri Chinmoy, compose enormous literatures of philosophy, poetry, or music. Or consider Prabhupada Bhaktivedanta, the founder of the Hare Krishnas, who began his mission to America when in his seventies. The extraordinary energy of these figures seems to accompany an inner clarity. They are not beset by the fears, shame, and guilt that limit others. This in turn makes them especially attractive because of the "infectiousness of the unconflicted personality" (Redl 1942, 582). Their energy flows freely and feeds their enormous *self-confidence*.

The grandiose self-confidence of charismatic leaders is legendary. It shows in their claims to special powers as God's Son or His chosen messenger, or whatever. Examples may be found among the tent evangelists who practice faith healing. These leaders have to cope with failure on a daily basis—no glass eyes or wooden legs are ever replaced during their services—yet they are sustained by a faith in themselves and their God that verges on the deranged. In the mid-1950s evangelist and healer A. A. Allen launched his "Raise the Dead" campaign. Several of his followers refused to bury their dead, sending them to Allen's headquarters in Arizona. Allen was forced to discontinue this mission, but he was not alone in his efforts; other healers also specialized in resurrections. When replying to critics, one such evangelist shrugged. "There's three and a half billion people in the world. Why should I worry about a billion that hates our guts ... there's two and a half billion more" (Harrell 1975, 101). Other historical examples reveal just how extreme this self-confidence may become. Simon Magus was, according to Hippolytus, buried alive at his own request, so confident was he that he would arise on the third day. And in the twelfth century an Arab messiah offered to have his head cut off to prove his authenticity. He was obliged. In neither case did the promised resurrection occur (Wallis 1943, 181–82).

This grandiosity underlies the optimism and positivity of prophets. Even those preaching the end of the world usually describe it as a time of glorious salvation when sinners will be punished. A fearlessness goes along with this confidence that makes everything they say seem authoritative. Yet this may cause problems; their confidence may become a kind of mania, a defensive certainty that is unable to question. Delusions of omnipotence and refusal to compromise or hear criticisms may appear as a dogmatic need always to be right and an inability to admit error, to apologize, or to recognize the hurtful effects their behaviors have on others. Such leaders are difficult to work with because they must always get their own way. They may not harbor evil motives; it is just that they genuinely cannot see that others have an equal claim in life. For the grandiosity of the prophet is in part a blindness to others, and a fixation on a *revolutionary vision*.

The prophet has a message that comes to dominate. As St. Paul said, "It is no longer I who live, but Christ who lives in me" (Galatians 2:20); or, as one of the leaders of the study said, "I've become the message now." This vision is opposed to convention and is focused on ultimate concerns and the reordering of the world. Hence it often leads the prophet into conflict with the law. David "Moses" Berg, founder of the Children of God, is a "last days" prophet (Davis and Davis 1984). His revelation contains the message that in this end time the faithful are free from the restraints of the law. In the early years of his mission, his followers lived like gypsies and were forbidden to hold secular jobs. Berg proclaimed, "If the truth kills, let it kill." Sexual inhibitions were loosened, and members offered sex to potential converts. Eventually Berg was accused by his daughter of incest and forced to flee to Europe (Davis and Davis 1984). He is, it seems, driven by his vision to the extent that all else, perhaps even survival itself, is of secondary importance to him. Because of his vision, his followers have suffered greatly, yet he retains their loyalty through his *inspirational rhetoric*.

The rhetorical skill of charismatic prophets can be phenomenal. Benjamin Franklin was once obliged to attend the service of a tent revivalist of whom he was deeply suspicious. Yet such was the inspirational power of the preacher that when the collection plate was passed, Franklin eagerly emptied his pockets into it. Of course rhetoric may be used for good or evil purposes, but when it is used by a prophet, certain themes tend to recur. These include the use of moral absolutes to amplify a sense of crisis in which the sinfulness of the world is described in absolute terms, while relative terms are used to describe the leader's work; as one leader in the study said, "This world is evil. It is of the Devil. Here we try to live God's will. We're not perfect but we do our best. We do okay, really." The prophet also may imply that he has been to the depths and the heights of the moral universe; has glimpsed heaven and hell—however these are defined—and returned with privileged insight.

And every prophet's message contains two parts. The first or "negative revelation" is an account of all that is bad in the world and of the road to hell. "Positive revelation" describes the path to salvation and the prophet's special role as guide. Deep human wants for unconditional love and life after death are implied to lie within the grasp of the faithful. Moral guidelines for successful living are embedded along with answers to existential questions such as "Who am I?" Such a heady brew may the rhetoric become that the prophet also may fall under its spell, believing his own propaganda and alienating his friends and family with a compulsive fanaticism. Such leaders appear to be "on stage" the entire time, seeming to derive sustenance from endlessly repeating their own rhetoric, which has become for them a "beautiful lie you can live in" (Rapp 1972). At such moments they may seem quite grotesque, but they are saved from total loss of credibility by their extreme *manipulativeness*.

The prophet's manipulative skills are acquired over many years of practice and are highly refined. At a personal level he can be charming and warm, speaking frankly but supportively. Prophets have an unpredictability that is exciting. They use the extremes of their personalities to gently keep others off guard; for instance, in the years I knew one leader, he was only once heard to tell an off-color joke, but it was one of the most offensive I have ever heard, and it was told not for a belly laugh but with a teasing smile. Prophets are natural actors, with the odd corollary that when they publicly try acting, their performance may be uncharacteristically hammy or wooden. The leader appears sensitive and concerned, usually remembering the names of people he has met; others find him nourishing to be around. Yet the leader astutely registers the needs and vulnerabilities of the people he meets, subtly implying that he can fulfill these needs. The cult is set up (at least in part) to satisfy the wants and exploit the vulnerabilities of the followers, who find, once they have joined, that it is hard to challenge the leader because of the large number of needy members who depend for their well-being on him.

The prophet communicates very early that there are topics that are taboo for discussion. These include his need to control others and the dependency and hero worship that are encouraged. Yes-men (or, more frequently, yes-women) are installed in key positions in the group; they will be demoted if their affections lapse. The prophet may collectivize guilt by implying, as apostates of Stephen Gaskin of the Farm put it, that unless the followers work and sacrifice for the great vision, the movement—perhaps the whole world—is doomed. Two leaders in this study gave striking examples of this, one by stating that "Anyone here who is not all the way happy is actively sabotaging the whole group," and the other by telling his followers that "To the degree that you do not love any person here, you are refusing to love everyone, including me, for we are all one." The leader may also claim to have a unique quality of love that the followers need for their salvation and that they could never find elsewhere; Jim Jones and Charles Manson used this ploy to mesmerize recruits (Lindholm 1990).

The prophet's organization abounds with mechanisms that disempower the followers, as the books by Stewart Lamont and Kate Strelley show for the Scientology and Rajneesh movements (Lamont 1986; Strelley and San Souci 1987). The leader never acknowledges this manipulativeness and, when it is pointed out, may bluster and deny any ill effects. To the inner circle the prophet may be quite frank about some motives, but to the world beyond and to most of the followers he is *aloof*.

Prophets are self-contained and autonomous, seeming to need little or nothing from others. Disciplined and self-controlled, they manage in even the most intimate encounters to signify something greater than what they are. The prophet always holds himself slightly apart from others, revealing little of his true feelings and seeming to be something of a mystery even to his long-term followers. This may mean that he is unable to have close friendships—as L. Ron Hubbard admitted he was unable to do (Miller 1987)—but it can also mean that he doesn't take his conflicts with others personally. Provided miscreants show contrition, and the cost of the conflict has not been too great, the leader can be very indulgent and forgiving. For he sees himself as above his charges in the way a lion tamer is above his beasts; they may turn on him from time to time in misguided rebellion, but he is not like them. There is a subtle difference and a great *strength*.

Prophets go to great lengths to prove their strength. This strength lies not just in their superior intellect and other talents. It also shows in their endurance, robustness of character, and strong will. A major strength is a willingness to apply 100 percent of oneself to some task. Most of us give 100 percent only when we have to, when we are desperate or threatened, but the leader is able to go all out for an ideal. However, he may also come to see each encounter as a battleground; as one said, "You have to win every time." This need to appear strong can be successful only if the prophet really is strong; in his need to keep up appearances, he may lose sight of his real strengths and fall victim to an image. At such moments he appears hollow and grotesque, unable to show softness or genuineness. This undermines the impression he most strives to make, of a profound *congruence*.

In many of the leader's actions there is a simplicity and an immediacy, an economy of movement and a directness of response, with an absence of pretense, flourish, or style, that creates a seemingly divine aura. This congruence may be apparent only to the long-term followers, and may not be noticed by those whose values are different from the leader's. But to those in tune with the prophet's vision, he seems to express its essence in all he does. Even the way the leader moves and talks is subtly different from others. Prophets seem to immerse themselves within their ideals so totally, to subordinate themselves to —and identify themselves with—the Good so completely, that they appear to abandon all superfluous functions and to become the living, realized human forms of their truths; in short, the incarnate God. For those who share their values there is something just right—even perfect—about the leader's behavior, and this quality does not merely exist in the followers' minds. Whatever the prophet does, he seems to do appropriately, striking a golden mean in his actions. His merest movements seem to point to something more; to contain a reassuring message. This is especially true of four aspects of daily behavior: his sense of humor, which may be Puckish and warm; a native curiosity, which finds all things interesting; a tendency to reflect other people's behaviors back to them in a gently mocking yet acutely revealing and disarming way; and what will be described in more detail below as the "giving" orientation, a personal style that others find nourishing. In all of this the prophet displays a centeredness that most of us feel within ourselves only at rare moments, but that adds up to an awesome, even ecstatic presence. It is as if, deep down, the leader really "knows."

This congruence inspires an easy sense of play among the followers (Sennett 1975, 179) and a euphoria well described by Hugh Milne, a devotee of Bhagwan Shree Rajneesh:

Many people have asked me how a sensible, independent person could be mesmerised by someone like Bhagwan. The answer, as many sanyasis would agree, is that once you had been affected by his energy and experienced the sensation of being touched by it, you knew there was nothing like it, no bliss to compare with it. Once you had experienced it, you had to go back for more, to try and regain that feeling of harmony and being at one with the universe. It is similar to a drug-induced high, except that there is no artificial chemical at work. Bhagwan's touch could be just as addictive as the strongest drug. (Milne 1986, 179)

Rajneesh has reportedly said that "authenticity *is* morality." Ignoring the wild implications of this statement, the sense is like that of the Zen notion that even in the way the master ties his shoelaces, there is beauty, balance, and truth.

Now sometimes prophets may in fact display nothing of the sort. Often they miss the mark, but others seem to miss the mark more frequently, so by comparison the prophet still seems special. Also, the prophet's congruence exists only with his own values; people who do not share these values, or who meet him for the first time, may be unmoved because they do not understand how he is expressing his ideals even in his most mundane behaviors. Yet the surprising thing is that even in the leader's lapses there is often a kind of logic, a human approximation of the divine that is "good enough." Equally surprising is that many outsiders who do not know the prophet well or share his values do detect this quality, and they may agree that in all sorts of little ways he really does live what he teaches. This parsimony of the prophet's total being is nowhere sharper than in his *social insight*.

Of all the prophet's talents, his social insight is the most remarkable, verging at times on the paranormal. The ability of charismatic figures to read their audience, to say precisely those things which strike a chord, and to see into the hearts of others gives rise to tales of telepathy (quietly encouraged by the prophet). Fortunately we have some accounts by expert psychotherapists of how this is done. Milton Erickson has described how, as a child stricken by polio, he was forced to spend all his time lying in bed, watching his family through a mirror placed above him. By being unable to interact with them, yet forced to watch them for long periods, he gained an understanding of the patterns and nuances of his family's behaviors, and a detached overview of how they went about their lives. In time he was able to predict their actions. As an adult therapist he used the same strategy to read the inner states of his patients, with a finesse that became legendary (Bandler and Grinder 1975). Similarly, Fritz Perls once went around a group of psychiatrists he had just met and gave each a reading of his personality and life that was astonishingly accurate. He had developed this skill through a lifetime of practice, and he has described it in his writings (Sheppard 1976; Gaines 1979).

Likewise, a follower of J. H. Noyes, founder of the Oneida community, related the effect that Noyes's "criticisms" had on him, saying that even years after Noyes's death he still yearned for the intimacy and wisdom of these insights, describing them as "the greatest blessings that have been conferred upon me" (Thomas 1977; Parker 1935). This wisdom is partly the result of the "centeredness" of the prophet; when attending to others, he does not project his own fears or desires, nor is he distracted by pretenses and defenses. Like the way the Zen master ties his shoelaces, the prophet's perceptions are refined to the essence, seldom becoming confused by the games and manipulations of others. This is because of a unique property of personal attention, a *detached availability.*

The followers often describe the prophet as having a stillness or serenity, an inner calm that is detached from the external world yet attentive to it. There is an inner clarity that allows the leader to see details others fail to notice. One follower told me, "When our eyes meet, she holds nothing back but is totally there for me. I get a sense of her special knowledge of me, as if I am the most important person in the world to her at that moment."

This quality of attention is especially a quality of attending to whatever it is that the other is attending to, an attending to their attention, a preparedness to follow that attention, and a readiness for greater depth and transcendence in the encounter. The followers learn that they can trust the leader as a sounding board for even their most secret or absurd thoughts and not be judged harshly. Even on topics about which the prophet knows little, he often manages to find some new insight that, when described, seems obvious, though others have previously overlooked it. There is an innocent quality to these observations, as of someone seeing a thing for the first time. The leader seems to observe without prejudice or motive, and this impresses as a great *acceptance of others.*

Some prophets hate certain groups, so it is not the case that all prophets accept others universally or unconditionally, but with most people the prophet seems free from, or rises above, the petty—often unconscious—prejudices and judgments that blind others. "Is this person stupid?" we might wonder, or "Should I be seen mixing with these people?" The prophet has none of this. The best exemplar of this acceptance was Jesus, who felt no rogue, leper, or prostitute was beneath his notice. The prophet has preferences—he values loyalty and is happiest among happy people—and is not above cultivating those who may prove useful, but he does not recoil from the wretched, nor is he rejecting of the sometimes horrific life stories he hears. The prophet seems almost classless, having an *unrefined quality.*

Practical, earthy, ordinary to the point of being *extra*ordinary, the prophet gives the impression of one who has no excess baggage and no pretense. With a simple, direct speaking style, and given to homilies and folksy oversimplifications, the prophet may be seen by some as "common." He has a knack for naive explanatory metaphors of the "If-this-beach-ball-were-the-Sun-then-our-Earth-would-be-a-grain-of-sand-at-the-North-Pole" variety. Scholars have described this as "infantilism" (Hiden and Farquharson 1988, 15–16) or an "archaic" quality (Kohut 1971). It is a hangover from childhood that is part innocence and part defiance—prophets do not accommodate themselves to change in society or technology very well. The leader has the common touch, but more than that; his personal style is unsophisticated and goes straight to the core. The prophet has mastered the codes of dominance, yet signals power and class incompletely, as if to say "I reject these values" (although never so much as to risk ostracism). It is a style devoid of style.

In all of this it is crucial not to dismiss the "magic" of the prophet as merely a figment of the followers' imaginations. Nor should we attempt to explain it as an illusion wrought by deceit, or try to reduce it to something mundane. It *does* exist and it *can* be understood. Scholars working in other contexts have mentioned it. Ruth Willner, in her study of charismatic political leaders, has described the "magnetic" eyes these men have (Willner 1984). James Walter, in his biography of Australian Prime Minister Gough Whitlam, has mentioned the strange "glow" surrounding Whitlam (Walter 1985). Weston La Barre, discussing shamans, has spoken of charisma as "streaming" from the shaman (La Barre 1980).

In the above text the odd presence of the prophet—a deep congruence and an uncanny quality of attention, an ability to be totally attentive and involved—has been described. All this adds up to a profound sense of the utter *otherness* of the prophet, almost as if he had been raised on another planet. One gets the feeling that all the prophet's life experiences must have been in some way quite different from one's own, and that nothing one has experienced has prepared one to encounter him.

This magical quality is charisma, a fascinating effect of the leader's presence. In Chapter 2 the leading theories of charisma, those of Max Weber and Heinz Kohut, are discussed in order to provide a base for this study. The approach herein will be to attempt to explain charisma in a naturalistic way, taking into account the varying explanations and motivations of the informants of this study, and treating charisma as a genuine phenomenon—in Weber's terms, an extraordinary emotional seizure—endowed with unique properties and processes not reducible to other, more fundamental, entities or processes.

The second pattern to emerge from the data is that of a sequence of life stages, a kind of "natural history" of the prophet. Five stages are described.

1. Early narcissism. The childhoods of charismatic leaders invariably include relationships of a markedly narcissistic character, usually with an excessively devoted yet conflicted parent or some other overly involved member of the extended family. This relationship inappropriately defends the child against external reality, trapping him in an infantile mode of thought, while it provides a flawed model for subsequent social development. It is likely that such a relationship forms a template from which relationships in later life are patterned. The prophet may become driven to re-create the dynamics of this early narcissistic relationship in which only the utmost devotion by others is recognized as worthy of him. As an adult the prophet assumes a "divine" role in order to get love from others, but the only love he can recognize is the kind of uncritical devotion that echoes his earliest attachment. In Chapter 3, examples of how this may occur are provided by using case studies of Bhagwan Shree Rajneesh, Werner Erhard, and Swami Vivekananda.

2. Incubation. The emerging narcissistic adult is at first perplexed by the indifference shown toward him by others. In trying to understand this, he may conclude that there is "something special" about him and "something wrong" with the world. This experience may drive him to develop a revelation of salvation that recruits others and explains his failure to get the love he assumes is his right. Hence this is a time of testing and trial, of searching and confusion, of a "wandering in the wilderness." Six themes characterize this stage: (a) a sense of not belonging to any group, (b) construction of a personal "myth of calling," (c) splitting of the personality, (d) radical autonomy, (e) conflicts with authorities, and (f) the acquisition of practical skills appropriate to a later prophetic career. In Chapter 4 this stage of development is described in detail, and several examples are provided from the material collected in this study and from other sources concerning better-known prophets.

3. Awakening. Several scholars have pointed to the centrality of mystical or quasi-religious experiences in the lives of prophets. When it is studied closely, an "awakening" usually turns out to be a series of

interconnected events rather than a single life-changing transformation. Awakening solves some problems for the prophet—it changes his view of himself and the world—but it may cause others. As a result of awakening, the prophet assumes the mantle of God's messenger—a burden from which many initially recoil, asking aloud, "Why me, Lord?" However, awakening is not permanent, nor has it any ontological significance. Also, it is not related to morality, and there is unlikely to be any hierarchy of ever higher "enlightenment" states. Hence, awakening is less important than is sometimes thought. Chapter 5 analyzes an account of one such awakening sequence collected in this study, and critiques conventional notions of such experiences.

4. Mission. After awakening, the prophet's mission becomes clear. To recruit followers, the leader advances a bold claim to be the source of ultimate good for others. The boldness of this claim induces a fascinating effect, arousing faith, hope, and love in the hearts of those who become his followers. In pursuing his mission the leader heads an organization dedicated to supporting him and spreading his truth. Now he functions somewhat as a manager, relying on whatever managerial skills he possesses and certain qualities of being that induce compliance with his wishes. He adopts a double strategy to retain and expand his following, first by ensuring that the daily lives and mundane concerns of his followers are adequately taken care of, and second by devising rituals that allow for the experience of transcendence. In Chapter 6 this is described in detail.

Because we cannot really understand the prophet without understanding something of the followers and the peculiar bond they share with their leader, discussions are presented in chapters 7 and 8 of the followers and their quest, and also of charismatic rituals. Of particular interest is the question of why so many charismatic movements seem to end in disaster; some suggestions concerning this are included in Chapter 8. In Chapter 9 the consciousness of the prophet and the development of some of his most extraordinary abilities are discussed. These, it is argued, result from a unique psychological makeup that has properties in some ways analogous to the traits of mystics (Batson and Ventis 1982)—a creative freedom, a turbulence of thought, and a wildness of mood—and that leads to novel perceptions and experiences. An account of some of these attributes in the mind of a disturbed patient in psychiatric treatment is presented.

5. Decline or fall. It seems that there are two distinct kinds of proph-

ets with divergent career trajectories that may be identified retrospectively. For the first kind, the messianic prophets, the final stage is marked by an acceptance of the decline in their influence and power, of their limitations and their inevitable demise, in a pragmatic way. Such figures are fairly realistic in their dealings with society and may never come into major conflict with the law. In contrast, the careers of the charismatic prophets are punctuated by conflicts with society that may result in their being jailed or assassinated. Even if they aren't, they tend to cling to power as long as they can, leaving behind a power vacuum and schismatic groups after they die. Chapter 10 summarizes the arguments for this distinction between messianic and charismatic personality types.

The concluding chapter evaluates the role of the prophet. It suggests that the prophet's power lies in his challenge to the most fundamental values and beliefs we hold about ourselves and the world we live in, and that therein lie a danger and also a hope. For in explaining the mind of the prophet, we must be careful not to use one set of information as a defense against another. Throughout history men and women have chosen these leaders for special tasks. No doubt they will again. As in all things, an informed choice can only work for our greater good. While not providing the last word on the subject of charismatic prophets, this study, I hope, will go some way toward making such informed choices possible.

To conclude this introduction, a brief note on language usage may be helpful. Despite my intention to study female charismatic leaders, they proved difficult to find; only four of the leaders in this study are women. Such figures do exist, as a perusal of Gordon Melton's *Encyclopedia of American Religions* (Melton 1987) reveals; almost one-third of the minority religious groups of America were founded or cofounded by women, but at the time and locale of this study they were few. This is consistent with other studies that have found few female charismatics (Willner 1984; Zablocki 1980). Further, many of the female leaders mentioned by Melton were associated with very small or ephemeral groups. This posed some problems when attempting to write in a gender-neutral way about a group that was mostly male but might have included more females. The following approach was adopted. In each chapter the first mention of charismatic leadership takes the form "he or she." Subsequently, "they" and "their" are frequently used as gender-neutral substitutes. However, when this becomes overworked or grotesque, more traditional usage "he" is reverted to unless a female leader is being discussed. This represents a compromise between several poor solutions and follows the usage of leading scholars such as Ruth Willner and Eileen Barker (Willner 1984; Barker 1984).

Similarly, in describing the early development of charismatic leaders, it is the relationship of a child with its mother that is mostly spoken of, acknowledging that in fact this is what is usually involved, although in exceptional cases such as Bhagwan Shree Rajneesh, a different early relationship is involved. This is simpler than the awkward term "primary caregiver." However, this usage is absolutely not intended to imply unwarranted generalizations about either women or men.

In addition, although many of the leaders were Christian, some were not. For sake of simplicity, all worldviews are treated as equal in principle, whether they be Christian, atheistic, Oriental, or whatever. Similarly, the term "God" is used in a variety of metaphorical ways that will be familiar to the reader and do not necessarily invoke a literal God concept. Generally, the word "God" may be freely translated as "ultimate concern" in the manner of Paul Tillich (Tillich 1949). Occasionally terms like "heaven," "hell," and "devil" are also treated in this way or used metaphorically.

2

Charisma

See me, feel me, touch me, heal me . . .
Following you . . . I get excitement at your feet.

—Pete Townshend
Tommy

Charisma, the magnetic ability of some people to inspire and lead others, is an enigma that most of us have experienced yet find hard to explain. The concept seems inherently mysterious and indefinable, but the power of a Churchill or a Hitler to dominate others is obvious. What is this thing called charisma?

Although our era has been called the "age of charisma" (Schweitzer 1984), the idea of a divinely inspired power or talent is as old as mankind. The oldest surviving work of fiction, the Epic of Gilgamesh, tells of a warrior-king, part god and part man, who quests for the secret of eternal life. He has many adventures in the lands of the gods, and even attains that which he seeks, only to have it torn from his grasp at the last moment. He returns home convinced of the futility of his quest and knowing that "the central fact of my life is my death" (Kopp 1972, 31; Heidel 1968).

The word "charisma" comes from the name of the Greek goddess Charis, who personified grace, beauty, purity, and altruism. Possession of these faculties came to be known as charisma.[1] Later usages derive

---

1. The Greek word is *charizesthai,* and it means favor or gift of divine origin. The Greeks do not seem to have associated this with the kind of demagogic and irrational leadership of which Plato wrote in his *Gorgias,* although they were well aware of the rhapsodic "Dionysian" aspect of life; Plato was a member of the Elysian mystery cult. For Aristotle the *megalopsychos* was the great man who dares to live alone in secret worship of his own soul. The Romans called the hero's charismatic power *facilitas* and believed it was derived from the gods.

from St. Paul, who saw it as a gift of grace from God: "To one there is given through the spirit the message of wisdom, to another the message of knowledge by means of the same spirit, to another faith by the same spirit, to another gifts of healing by that one spirit, to another miraculous powers, to another prophecy" (1 Corinthians 12:8–10).

The most primitive form of charisma occurs in shamanism. This is the religion of the small tribal unit and the witch doctor. The shaman—"one who is excited, moved, raised" (Lindholm 1990, 158)—becomes master of the "techniques of ecstasy" (Eliade 1964). Typically he (or she, for among the !Kung fully 10 percent of women become shamans; Lindholm 1990, 163) is identified early as one with a "shadowed heart." The shaman is not psychotic but is disturbed in some way—the "disease of God," as the Koreans put it (La Barre 1980, 58)—showing peculiar behaviors from birth and experiencing spirit possession, trance, and epileptic seizures while a youth. Such a youth is apprenticed to a senior shaman, who trains him in occult practices. After hearing a call from a god or a spirit, the trainee withdraws into the desert or the woods to meditate in solitude, often undergoing some kind of spiritual test, such as a journey to the underworld. This culminates in a spiritual rebirth from which the shaman emerges with an inner strength and an uncanny sensitivity, emotional intensity, and detachment. Transformed, the graduate shaman returns to the tribe to claim his place as tribal witch doctor (Kopp 1972, 31–32).

Thus the shaman is a "wounded healer" who has conquered a sickness and learned to use it as a vehicle for the benefit of others. He or she is able to explore sacred realms and mediate with the spirit world on behalf of the tribe (Ellwood and Partin 1988, 12). Allied with this are the skills of psychopharmacology, healing, and the mastery of trance states. The shaman presides over the ceremonies, ritual functions, and crises of the tribe.

The shaman is unpredictable and fearless, holding office by virtue of personal spiritual attainment—his "psychological voltage" (La Barre 1980, 52)—and having mysterious, dangerous, supernatural powers. The shaman's peculiar disturbance and training enable him to "pierce the vanity of the conventional wisdom of the group" (Kopp 1972, 5), to diagnose its ills and prescribe social cures for the members. Anthropologist Weston La Barre described "the eerily supernatural omniscience and compelling power of charisma, streaming from the shaman like irresistible magnetic mana," and said that it comes from an ability to discern his clients' unconscious wish-fantasies, adding that the shaman "is so unerringly right because he so pinpoints these wishes" (La Barre 1980, 275). It is this power that earns the shaman his place, for he is feared rather than loved.

Modern usage of the term "charisma" derives from Max Weber (1864–1920), one of the founders of sociology.[2] Weber used both religious and economic factors to explain society. He saw Western civilization as moving toward greater and greater rationalization of all aspects of life. This, he feared, made modern life an "iron cage," turning daily existence into an alienated, mechanical, meaningless routine. But Weber also believed that ideas—especially religious ideas—can profoundly influence society, and that they cannot simply be dismissed as a function of underlying social processes (Jones and Anservitz 1975, 1098). One source of new ideas is the periodic emergence of charismatic prophets.

Weber defined charisma as "a certain quality of an individual personality by virtue of which he is considered extraordinary and treated as endowed with supernatural, superhuman, or at least specifically exceptional powers . . . [that] are regarded as of divine origin." Weber added, however, that the leader's disciples—those who see him as divine—are as much a source of his power as are his personal talents, for without them he is nothing (Weber 1968a, 241–42).

Describing the varieties of charismatic experience, Weber spoke of a continuum ranging from "pure" to "routinized" charisma. Pure charisma is rare (Weber 1968a, 1002) and is usually found only in the very beginning of a social movement when a "charismatic community" coalesces around a leader. This community is characterized by a belief in the special talents of its leader, an intense emotional bonding of the followers to him, financial support from sympathizers, rejection of normal work activities, and estrangement from the world as a whole (Schweitzer 1984, 18; Weber 1968a, 1121). Pure charisma thus is personal and is based on face-to-face contact and feelings of trust, duty, and love on the part of the followers (Schweitzer 1984, 33). It is creative and revolutionary, for "in its pure form charisma . . . may be said to exist only in the process of originating" (Weber 1964, 364). At the other

2. Weber 1946, 1958, 1964, 1968a, 1968b. Criticisms of Weber's theory have led to significant modifications of some aspects (e.g., Sennett 1975; Berger 1963) but little change in his key concepts (Blau 1963; S. C. Olin 1980).

end of the continuum, routinized charisma describes what happens when a leader's charisma is thinly dispersed throughout the followers who act in the leader's name, typically after he has died. It may survive many generations and underlie a stable social order, but it is conservative and is not a force for social change (Miyahara 1983, 370).

Along this continuum lie the variants of magical and prophetic charisma. Magical charisma is attached to the shaman or magician who is "permanently endowed with charisma" (Weber 1968a, 401). Such charisma is basically conservative, supporting the customs of the tribe. Prophetic charisma occurs in more complex societies and adheres to the prophet who proclaims a divine mission or radical political doctrine. This form of charisma leads to revolution and social change. Weber regarded the prophet as the prototype for other kinds of charismatic leaders (Schweitzer 1984, 32).

Weber added two crucial components to this. First, charisma is fundamentally a religious concept; although in his usage it need not involve a notion of the divine, nevertheless it remains a form of spiritual energy oriented to otherworldly ideals. Second, the charismatic process is one of intense emotional arousal and great pathos; charismatic belief revolutionizes people from within. In sum, charisma is a revolutionary spiritual power.

The charismatic prophet claims authority by sheer force of personality. He points to some mission outside or beyond his self that he embodies, and his mission involves the radical change of current values. Before receiving his calling, the leader must have some germ of charisma latent in him (Weber 1968a, 400), but later he maintains power solely by proving his strength in life; to be a prophet, he must perform miracles (Weber 1946, 248–49).

Weber wondered whether charisma might arise from some mental illness, but he rejected the notion (Weber 1968a, 499). Instead, he spoke of an "emotional seizure" that originates in the unconscious of the leader and results in three "extraordinary" emotions: ecstasy, euphoria, and political passions. These emotions arouse similar feelings in others, who become followers (Weber 1968b, 273–74); the greater the leader's emotional depth and belief in his calling, the greater is his appeal and the more intense is his following (Weber 1968a, 539). Weber also associated a particular calling with each extraordinary emotion. The first involves two kinds of leaders—the shaman and the "exemplary" prophet—who use ecstasy as a tool of salvation and self-deification. To produce ecstasy they may use alcohol and other drugs, music and dance, sexuality, or some combination of these; in short, orgies (Weber 1968b, 273). They also may provoke hysterical or epileptoid seizures (Weber 1968b, 273). This may seem like a mental disturbance or possession.

The second calling is what Weber described as the "ethical" prophet. This figure uses milder forms of euphoria, such as dreamlike mystical illumination and religious conversion, to create a realm of blessedness upon the earth, purged of violence and hate, fear and need (Schweitzer 1984, 35; Weber 1968a, 527; 1968b, 274). Such a prophet has a divine ethical mission, and powerful orgiastic release actually stands in the way of the systematic ethical remodeling of life that he requires (Weber 1968a, 274). For him, the goal of sanctification is ethical conduct oriented to the world beyond, and his aim is not to become like God but to become God's instrument and to be spiritually suffused by the deity (Weber 1968b, 275).

The third calling is the politician, associated with political passions. Examples include Churchill, Gandhi, and Hitler. A charismatic politician is able to arouse the passions of the followers and to channel them toward good or evil ends.

In using charisma to explain social change and heroic leaders, Weber did not intend merely to invent a dry academic term. Rather, he saw charisma as representing the incarnate life force itself, "the thrust of the sap in the tree and the blood in the veins," an elemental or daemonic power (Dow 1978). By linking charisma to ecstasy, Weber emphasized release from social, psychological, and economic restraint —being beyond reason and self-control. The leader is a model of release and the divine power that makes freedom possible. The followers surrender not to the person of the leader but to the power manifest in him, and they will desert him if his power fails. The followers attain freedom from routine and the commonplace by surrendering to the leader and—through him—to their own emotional depths. This is their Good, not in some ethical or conventional sense but in a primordial or instinctual way. Ecstasy comes from breaking down inhibitions, from the experience of carefree power, and from the abandonment of conventional morality. Charisma is an emotional life force opposed to the law, conformity, repression, and dreariness of an ordered life.

Weber thus comes close to Freud's theory of society (Freud 1930), in which repression is seen as necessary for civilized life. To Freud's basic scheme Weber adds the Dionysian element of charisma, most typically through a leader who calls the followers to a new life, a new vision, and a new freedom when society breaks down or becomes too repressive to bear. This tension between release and restraint, between the call of one's deeper nature and the demands of one's social group, is at the center of Weber's theory. Charisma "rejects all external order," "transforms all values," and compels "the surrender of the faithful to the extraordinary and the unheard of, to what is alien to all regulation and tradition, and therefore is viewed as divine" (Weber 1968a, 1115–17). The smoldering passion for freedom, for release from all restraint —including the restraint of one's own conscience—may lie latent in us all. But Weber did not celebrate charisma as a solution to the emotional emptiness of conformity. He saw its value as a tool for social progress, but he felt that it was too wild, irrational, and dangerous to lead to responsible leadership or a stable social order. Charisma could only be the revolutionary spark—the "process of originating"—and no more. In evaluating charisma he sought some way to combine the grace of charisma with an ethic of responsibility. He ended by inviting his students to test and explore their own ultimate values through engagement with it (Dow 1978).

Despite Weber's work, charisma remained a mysterious, even mystical, concept until Heinz Kohut and other psychoanalytic theorists began to study it. In a series of articles and books published during the 1970s, described by one writer as "breathtakingly unreadable,"[3] Kohut emerged as a leader of the psychoanalytic avant-garde that reshaped modern psychoanalysis (Sass 1988). His contribution has been said to "represent psychoanalysis catching up with 'being and nothingness', with the world of Sartre and Beckett, indeed, with the modern sensibility and the 'crisis of authority' " (Little 1980, 15).

Kohut studied a difficult class of disturbed patients with what is known as narcissistic disorders. As he studied them, he noticed simi-

3. Malcolm 1980, 136. See Kohut 1959, 1960, 1966, 1971, 1972, 1976, 1977, 1980, 1985. There are, of course, problems with Kohut's theory, especially in the context of this study. For example, he uses the term "true religion," which few theologians would accept and which he does not define. Further, Kohut's metapsychology relies heavily on the reenactment of hypothetical early ego states (Hanly and Masson 1976). However, the actual observations Kohut made are no doubt accurate. Throughout his voluminous writings on narcissism he has described so many behaviors typical of charismatic leadership that the connection is virtually indisputable.

larities between them and charismatic leaders. Kohut spoke of charismatic personalities rather than leaders because most of his patients were not leaders—indeed, some were barely able to function—but they possessed many of the traits of charismatic leaders.

What was it among his narcissistic patients that made Kohut think of charismatic leaders? He initially noticed that when they presented for therapy, they showed grandiose self-confidence and—unlike most patients—an extraordinary lack of self-doubt. Often they would be quite clear-headed and perceptive; Kohut recounts how one such patient accurately diagnosed his (Kohut's) shortcomings while in therapy. In addition, they could be very persuasive and accusative. These obvious strengths made them quite distinctive as a group; they did not present in the demoralized, anxious manner of most patients.

However, in time this facade of competence became less stable. Their confidence began to give way to vain boasting and a naive sense of invincibility. Unrealistic, grandiose fantasies appeared in their conversations, along with a streak of exhibitionism. So "brittle" did their confidence and self-certainty become that they were sometimes unable to admit to a gap in their knowledge; their need to appear strong was so shallow as to render them unable to ask for information, assistance, or advice. They were reluctant to seek therapy but had been forced to do so because of having been compromised by various fraudulent or sexually perverse behaviors.

As therapy progressed, these patients became increasingly unrealistic, hypochondriacal, and self-pitying. The nearer Kohut approached to the core of their disturbance, the more catastrophic were their reactions. They were also revealed to have little or no conscience or sense of guilt. Their relations with others were characterized by a sense that others were merely extensions of their (the patients') own egos. Sometimes these relationships were reduced to dominance of one individual who was all that was left in an otherwise empty reality.

In sum, these patients appeared to be both happy and healthy until one looked a little deeper. Then a profound emptiness was revealed, an emptiness that coexisted quite functionally with their superficial health and wisdom. They appeared to be able to accommodate this paradox—and other contradictions—because of an "all-or-nothing" quality of their personality that was so committed to an appearance of strength as to have split off all awareness of their deeper emptiness. Their extreme self-containment and self-absorption, along with their confident social manner, made them very appealing to others, who seemed to warm to some part of themselves that they recognized in these figures. This "mirroring" process in which a strong figure sees others as parts of his self, while the others see themselves in him, alerted Kohut to a narcissistic explanation of charisma.

Narcissism begins with the infant's early attachment to the mother and the accompanying sense that they form a unified whole. This is a carryover from life in the womb, when baby and mother were one. In this early period of "oneness" (Mahler, Pine, and Bergman 1967), a dialogue of mutual cuing and empathy, of quiet gesture and molding, develops for both mother and infant. Through the mother's holding and feeding the baby, a choreography develops in which their boundaries seem to melt away. It is as if the mother and child merge, the being of one dissolving into the being of the other (Kaplan 1979, 100).

At this time the child feels exalted in its mother's eyes, omnipotent in its childish world, and grandiose in its uninhibited egoism. The baby is a conqueror who seemingly creates magic without understanding how or why. The rising nipple finds the hungry mouth, and a warm, yielding softness that feels and smells just like the child molds itself around him. From this comes the illusion that his feelings and gestures have created the nipple, the mother's body, and the rest of the world (Kaplan 1979, 92). The child feels like "an angel baby held in the sumptuous lap of a saintly Madonna" (Kaplan 1979, 116), his love coming from a sense of shared perfection with the mother.

In normal development this "primary narcissism" (Freud 1914) soon gives way to the discovery that the world does not revolve around one's ego, and painful adjustment must be made to accept reality. This means recognizing one's aloneness and helplessness in the face of an indifferent universe, and rising to the challenge of reality. This occurs through "optimally failing parents" (Kohut 1977, 237) and optimal frustration of the infant in a secure family environment where the mother can coach her child toward separateness and autonomy. The gleam in her eye mirrors the infant's exhibitionistic display, and her participation in the baby's egotistical enjoyment confirms the child's self-esteem, despite whatever painful encounters with the world occur. By gradually increasing the selectivity of her responses, the mother channels the baby's behaviors in realistic directions and the sense of oneness slowly breaks down (Kohut 1977, 188). This in turn leads to the consolidation of the child's self. The store of self-confidence and self-esteem that sustains one through life derives from these early difficult but ultimately successful struggles (Kohut 1971, 116).

However, for some this development remains incomplete. This may happen when an extremely devoted and idealizing mother, whose "baby worship" (Kohut 1971, 124) has created a child with very high self-esteem, suddenly and unpredictably withdraws her empathy and support. If this is not so traumatic as to impair the child, and if the child is exceptionally talented and adaptable, he may compensate for the loss of the mother by taking on her "filter" mechanisms (my term) as part of his self (Kohut 1976, 414). Normally the mother filters reality in such a way that the child is not exposed to dangers or unpleasant events beyond its capacity to cope. When painful or confusing events occur, she interprets and evaluates them for the child in a positive manner. Perhaps the narcissistic child learns to mimic the mother's filter mechanisms when failures of rapport occur or when she isn't around for protection. The child may adopt her strategies, incorporating them as part of its own self, and so, rather than falling from grace with her, blends closer (emotionally) with her and retains, or even increases, the sense of oneness.

Now, instead of surrendering his narcissism, the child draws on all his resources. He learns to charm, manipulate, bully, and calculate his way through situations that defeat others. Alone he denies his aloneness and defies the world, yet without understanding the significance of his actions. As one who refuses to grow up, the child somehow avoids the "reality principle"—compromise with an indifferent and dangerous world—and his egocentric view of life remains substantially intact. As part of this, Kohut says, he becomes "superempathic" with his self and with his own needs.[4] The result is a remarkable autonomy in which the narcissistic child asserts his own perfection yet uses others to regulate his self-esteem, demanding full control over them without regard for their rights as independent peo-

4. Kohut doesn't go deeply into quite how this happens, but we can make some intelligent guesses. Personality is largely socially constructed, but if one regards the social world as merely an extension of one's ego—a part of oneself—major areas of psychic functioning change their meanings drastically (e.g., defense mechanisms). What would such a person be defending himself against? Himself? We need not dwell on this point except to observe in passing that seeing the external world as a part of oneself changes utterly the inner relations of the psyche.

ple. This leads to a severe reduction in the educational power of the environment (Kohut 1976, 414–15) . The narcissistic child lives in a psychological world of his own creation, beyond or outside "normal" reality, and virtually unreachable at depth.

Such a person grows up behaving normally, for he has learned the appropriate behaviors to get rewards and avoid punishment. But deep down, he still views the world as an extension of his ego in the way he originally saw the mother, and his early relationship with her remains the model for all subsequent relationships. Perhaps we all do this to some extent, and have varying degrees of insight into ourselves, but for the narcissist these insights remain purely intellectual. Deep down, he "knows" the world revolves around him, and his adult life is an attempt to perpetuate his childish egocentrism.

Adult forms of narcissism vary, and sometimes there are pathological elements (Kohut [1976] spoke of Hitler as having a "healed-over psychosis"), but the result is a person who sees the world in a radically different way from others. He is likely to be enormously confident and fearless. (How can one be afraid of anything in a world that is merely an extension of oneself? It would be like being afraid of one's leg.) He may seem, superficially, to be a product of the society he grew up in, but really he is his own universe and only his body, needs, thoughts, and feelings are experienced as truly real. Others are perceived intellectually but without emotional weight and color, without substance. Perhaps they are experienced in a manner analogous to how we experience our internal organs; we know they exist and are real, but we never actually encounter them.

Such a person is detached from the "real" world (although his world is real enough to him). By always being a little bit inside yet a little bit outside the world, he is well placed to diagnose its problems and devise solutions. His insights will seem to be profound truths to those who share his values and background. The talents he has developed in order to survive with his narcissistic worldview intact now give him an uncanny resonance with his times and with those who will become his followers. In addition, other key traits associated with childhood (to be discussed in the next chapter) are developed to an extreme. Perhaps this really does give the prophet a "truth" that others lack.

Eventually the successful adult narcissist stands ready for the call to leadership. He fits in well with those who seek a new life or are in crisis. In return for their love and devotion, he leads them to the promised land, and in so doing he re-creates the ego-reflecting universe he knew as a child. The followers appreciate his vision and wisdom because he keeps his head in a crisis; he is above the fray (which is why narcissistic patients are so hard to treat—they can't be reached).

Kohut gives us two images of the charismatic personality. In the first and less flattering, he discusses Wilhelm Fliess's relationship with Sigmund Freud (Kohut 1976). During Freud's most creative period— his self-analysis that preceded *The Interpretation of Dreams* in 1900—he became weak and needy in the throes of a supreme creative act. Many thinkers and artists need support during periods of intense creativity, especially when their creativity leads them into lonely areas not previously explored by others. Such isolation may prove terrifying because it repeats an early traumatic childhood fear of being alone and abandoned. At such times even a genius like Freud may attach himself to someone whom he sees as wise and all-powerful, with whom he temporarily bonds in order to draw support (Kohut 1976, 404). Fliess and others like him, with their unshakable self-confidence and certainty, lend themselves to this role (Kohut 1971, 316).

The Fliess type is similar to charismatic leaders like Hitler and Napoleon (Strozier 1980, 403), who have enormous yet brittle self-esteem. Lacking self-doubts, they set themselves up as leaders. Their absolute certainty makes possible great leadership but also risks total failure, for such people lack flexibility and have an all-or-nothing quality with only two options: success through strength, or destruction through defeat, suicide, or psychosis (Kohut 1976, 404; Strozier 1980, 403). Such leaders may be quite paranoid, but what fits them for their role is the fact that their self-esteem depends on their incessant use of certain mental functions. They continually judge others and point out their moral flaws, then—without shame or hesitation—they set themselves up as leaders and demand obedience. Yet they depend on their followers; Freud took up with Fliess when he needed him but dropped him soon afterward. Some of Kohut's patients behaved similarly (Kohut 1976, 404). Kohut insists that although such relationships are opportunistic, they are not pathological. Anyone who is in need of support will tend to be drawn to charisma (Kohut 1971, 317; 1976; 1980, 393, 493; 1985, 219).

Charismatic personalities come in all shades and degrees. A few are almost psychotic—dogmatic, blind fanatics possessing only an unusual cunning—yet others are quite different. To illustrate this, Kohut discusses Winston Churchill.

Churchill and other leaders of his type seem to have transformed their primary narcissism into a "cosmic narcissism" that is basically pro-social. In addition to his talent for inspirational leadership, Churchill was capable of wit and wisdom, qualities that Kohut argues are rare in charismatic personalities. Yet Churchill also had an inflated sense of his self. Kohut speculated that he may have retained the infantile delusion that he could fly; some passages in his autobiography, certain childhood escapades, his escape during the Boer war, and his leadership of Britain during World War II suggest this.[5]

Between the extremes of Fliess and Churchill there are many possible types of charismatic personalities. Their common features are extreme narcissism in which they identify others—and perhaps the entire universe—as parts of their own ego, an unshakable conviction of their own rightness and virtue, and a stunted empathy for others. Such traits may be expressed in a pro-or antisocial manner.

An important difference between charismatic personalities and ordinary folk is that most people attempt to fulfill their ambitions in a realistic way—that is, they take account of the needs and feelings of others. And normal people accept their limitations, their flawed yet "near enough" approximations of success in their attempts to live up to their ideals. For most of us, our ideals and values are mere direction-setting standards that we try to live up to. We feel good when we measure up and we feel bad when we fall short. Empathy with others shows us that nobody is perfect, and this prevents the development of a sense of absolute moral superiority. Hence no unrealistic feeling develops that we are perfect while others are corrupt. The charismatic, however, lacks empathy. He identifies totally with his ideals and no longer measures his behavior against them. He and his God are one, and there can be no half measures (Kohut 1976).

Such leaders pay a price. Their relationships are shallow because they have a double standard of reality; they relate with genuine concern to others at the same time as they see them as objects to manipulate. Further, the leader's ego-reflecting worldview is always under threat

5. "Dreams of flying are an extension of the aspirations of man's grandiose self, the carrier and instigator of his ambitions" (Kohut 1977, 113).

because people behave differently from how he wills them to behave. Although this difference can be excused—one's stomach sometimes behaves differently from how one wills it—the logical implication is that the leader is not really in control, that there is an objective reality beyond his ego. But to recognize this is to admit the original trauma that produced the flight into narcissism. This is avoided at all cost.

What the charismatic leader most lacks is a sense of the humanity of other people. He may accurately diagnose their problems and brilliantly solve them, he may even genuinely love the followers—loving them quite literally as he loves himself—yet they remain unreal to him because he must not acknowledge what it means to be a fellow sufferer, to feel alone and to have to adjust to an indifferent world, to have to reach out in trust to another for help. He may have actually been alone and had to trust and adjust, but he is rigidly fortified against the meanings of such events. They occur to him as strange, inexplicable interludes on a continuum of mastery and dominance, of self-sufficiency and control; he is "phobic" about recognizing any emotional vulnerability. Any outright opposition is countered with vociferous energy—what Kohut calls "narcissistic rage"—a rage that shows by its extremity and persistence that he is more deeply wounded by injuries to his worldview than by any physical injury (Kohut 1972). Hence he is fondest of the true believers who enthusiastically mirror his ego; those who don't are resented. Despite the leader's wisdom, his acceptance of others exists only as long as his own needs are being fulfilled. When they behave contrary to his wishes, he may respond with incomprehension or even paranoia. For what he really empathizes with is shades of himself, and he attracts only those who are in tune with him. He is unable to empathize with people who are indifferent to him, whose needs do not mesh with his own. His inability to experience himself as vulnerable is like a chasm between himself and others. For vulnerability is a vital part of human reality—we are not gods—and anyone who cannot experience it remains fundamentally out of rapport with ordinary people, no matter how successful his manipulations and wisdom may appear. Because of this lack the leader is not a great man; he is a great actor playing the role of a great man.

As for the followers, Kohut suggests that they are attempting to draw strength from a powerful figure in order to perform some profound creative change. This may take the form of a regressive psychic merger with an evil Hitler figure, in which case the relationship is based as much on shared hates as on mutual love. Or it may, as in the case of Freud's relationship with Fliess, be an opportunistic and temporary relationship aimed at discovering some deep truth about oneself or the world. It may involve aspects of the parent-child relationship, as well as "regression in the service of the ego," that is, creative acts that can seem bizarre or dangerous to outsiders (Kris 1952). Invariably courage is needed in order to give up the defenses and illusions carried over from childhood, and to surrender to the leader (Kohut 1976, 424).

One well-studied example of such a relationship is that between analyst and analysand. Kohut has written of the patient's temporary need to identify with the analyst (Kohut 1985, 47), and has argued that the key to understanding such relationships lies in creativity. The follower or analysand is seeking to fulfill some aspect of his or her self, while the leader or analyst is seeking to shape the world closer to his or her needs. The follower helps the leader to realize his or her vision while using the leader for his or her own personal transformation. But it is something of a hit-and-miss, blind-following-the-blind process. Just as a charismatic analyst with a quasi-religious fervor may cure a patient with love (albeit a somewhat narcissistic love; Kohut 1971, 222–23), so the prophet may help the followers yet be blindly unaware of their true needs. Perhaps neither ever really encounters the other. There may be pathological factors in both the follower's and the leader's creative efforts (Kohut 1985, 7, 249), but these need not detract from their worth. Despite even severe disturbance, many creative people manage to live fulfilling and significant lives, perhaps more so than most "normals" who, despite the absence of neurosis, often seem to lead empty, shallow, narrow existences (Kohut 1985, 48).

Both Weber and Kohut distinguished two kinds of leaders. Weber began by noting three main features that distinguish the prophet from other figures: (a) prophets do not receive their mission from any human authority—they simply seize it; (b) the prophet has a "vital emotional preaching" typical of prophecy; and (c) the prophet proclaims a path of salvation through personal revelation (Weber 1968b, 258–61). Weber then distinguished between "ethical" and "exemplary" prophets. The ethical prophet, as typified by Moses, believes he is an instrument of God. Such figures arise where there is belief in a personal, transcendent, ethical God. Preaching as one who has received a commission from God, the ethical prophet demands obedience as an ethical duty (Weber 1968b, 263). The exemplary prophet arises where belief in superdivine, impersonal forces and the concept of a rationally regulated world dominates. Teaching by example in the manner of Jesus and Buddha, he shows the way of salvation. His example appeals to those who crave salvation, recommending to them the same path he has traversed (Weber 1968b, 263–64).

Kohut distinguished between messianic and charismatic personalities, but added that mixed cases are likely to be most common (Kohut 1976, 415). He speculated freely about these constructs (Kohut 1976) and provided several practical distinctions. The messianic personality identifies its self with what Kohut calls the "idealized superego"—in effect, God or one's ultimate concern. Because the superego has "object qualities"—that is, it seems to be an entity of some sort—the messianic leader can envisage and describe, and even enter into a (dissociated) dialogue with, this God. Because of the nature of his early conflicts, he experiences this God as outside and above, and he receives his revelation from this heavenly external source. Thus he is led by his ideals in the manner of Moses or Muhammad (Kohut 1966, 250). Kohut suggests that a particular fantasy may sustain him—an unconscious belief that "You [the mother, parent, primary caregiver, or deity] are perfect and I am part of you." Thus there is a fundamental shifting aside of the self and a subsequent identification and union with God.

The charismatic personality, on the other hand, identifies with what Kohut calls the "grandiose self" in the form of some symbol of omnipotence—God—located within the self. Unlike the idealized superego, the grandiose self is not perceived by the mind as an object. Kohut likens it to the eye, a part of the organism that is involved in perception and hence cannot perceive itself; the grandiose self is the most primitive and essential "organ" of being and cannot apprehend or observe itself. Thus the charismatic prophet senses his God more vaguely, as a peculiar sensation within his being, a pressure coming from below, and he is driven by his ambitions rather than pulled by his ideals (Kohut 1966, 250). Kohut suggests that the unconscious fantasy sustaining this type is "I am God" (or perhaps "I and the mother [or father] are one"; Hanly and Masson 1976). In sum, the messianic prophet gazes up in awe at his God, whom he tries to emulate and follow, whereas the charismatic prophet feels God stirring within and tries to express and get recognition for his deity.

In concluding this brief overview of Kohut's theory, it is important to clarify some technical points in order to avoid misconceptions. In his account of the development of the infant, Kohut argues that the self is "bipolar," that it has two extremities—the "grandiose self" and the "idealized superego." The grandiose self is nurtured by the "mirroring self-object" and the idealized superego is nourished by the "idealizing self-object." In some discussions (typically in Kohut's case studies) the term "mirroring self-object" is loosely translated as "mother," for in the external world it is most often the mother who performs this function. Further, regardless of who the mirroring self-object is, the child's grandiose self will develop, for better or for worse, in response not just to the actual deeds of an external mother (or father) but also in response to the perceived and felt deeds of an internalized image of this person, and in accordance with how the infant construes these deeds, images, feelings, and perceptions. Kohut is emphasizing psychological processes within the child in response to actions by external agents, rather than the actions and external agents in themselves. This is because in the child's mind, its parents are not experienced as wholly external. Hence Kohut's coining of the term "self-object"—the mother (or father) is an object all right, but remains identified as part of the child's self. Similarly, in the external world the father often performs the functions of the idealizing self-object. If the real father is absent, the developmental process of construing an idealizing self-object and developing an idealized superego goes on.

In this book some modifications to Kohut's jargon are necessary, and they result from a stark choice. His precise terms are so unwieldy that even his fellow analysts have, on occasion, had difficulty understanding him. Yet to substitute "mother" and "father" annihilates the accuracy of his technical meanings. The justification for doing so is to retain a thread—a connection—with ordinary experience. No unwarranted assumptions about gender, or about the roles of mothers or fathers in narcissistic development, are intended. It is the psychological "mother"—the mirroring self-object—and the psychological "father" —the idealizing self-object—entities in the developing infant's mind, that are intended, even though actual mothers and fathers usually correspond to these entities. Nevertheless, the child remains the agent of his own processes, and may construe neglectful, abusive, or even absent parents as positive self-objects if driven to do so by the needs of the developing self.

In presenting the theory of prophetic development proposed herein, Kohut's term "self-object" will sometimes be used to designate a psychological parent or caregiver in the child's mind (the idealizing and mirroring self-objects), and sometimes to indicate actual parents (the mother or the father) or caregivers in the child's external world when it is useful to do so. This both simplifies and distorts the subtleties and complexities of Kohut's theory, but it allows for an easier discussion of the main issues. The terms "mother," "father," "carer," and "primary caregiver" will also be used in case studies and when traditional roles and relationships are likely to be involved. The more cumbersome technical jargon will be avoided wherever possible. In sum, these labels will be used as much for their convenience as for their technical accuracy.

To add to Weber and Kohut, Erich Fromm distinguishes between two kinds of narcissism—benign and malign. In the benign form— corresponding to Weber's ethical prophet and Kohut's messianic personality—the goal of the leader's efforts is something he produces, achieves, or does; that is, it is something external to himself. For the messianic prophet this includes doing God's will by saving souls, building up the church, serving others, preaching the gospel, or whatever. Consequently this form of narcissism is self-checking. To do God's work, the prophet must be related to reality; this constantly curbs his narcissism and keeps it within bounds (Fromm 1964, 77). In contrast, the goal of malignant narcissism—corresponding to Weber's exemplary prophet and Kohut's charismatic personality—is not something the prophet does or produces, but something he has or is. He draws closer to God not because of something he achieves but because of some inner quality. In maintaining this belief he does not need to be related to anyone or anything. Such figures may remove themselves more and more from reality and inflate their delusions to huge proportions in order to avoid discovering that their divinity is merely a product of their imagination. Thus malignant narcissism lacks the corrective element that is present in the benign form. It is not self-limiting but is crudely solipsistic and xenophobic (Fromm 1964, 77).

Combining the relevant components of Weber's, Kohut's, and Fromm's theories, we may achieve a fairly useful description of the two types of prophets. This description is outlined in Chapter 10. However, the picture remains complex. What is needed is to fit these theories together in some systematic way. This can be done by describing the developmental stages through which prophets progress. In doing this, we find that Weber's and Kohut's theories best describe different stages in this sequence, while Fromm's comments furnish useful background. This "natural history" of the prophet may be described as a five-stage sequence.

1. Early narcissism. Some process similar to, if not identical with, Heinz Kohut's description of the early life experiences of the charismatic personality must occur. To spend time with prophets is to discover that there really *is* something different about how they see the world. This "something" seems at first hard to define, and an attempt to locate its infantile origins has to be a speculative exercise. Chapter 3 will attempt to describe it and to retrace its likely development.

2. Incubation. This covers a period roughly following the onset of puberty and leading up to the adoption of the prophetic role. It is a time of struggle and uncertainty for the narcissistic personality as he attempts to reconcile his uniqueness with the demands of adult life. If he can negotiate this period safely, he is led to the discovery that he can never live as other people do, either because of some special truth he must express or because God has called him.

3. Awakening. This signals the adoption of the prophetic role. It may be a dramatic mystical experience or a more mundane realization of some important truth. There may also be several minor awakenings and false starts. In all, there is most likely to be a series of events culminating in some kind of crisis in the life of the developing narcissistic adult that is solved by taking on the role of the prophetic leader.

4. Mission. It is here that Max Weber's theory is most applicable. At this point the prophet heads an organization dedicated to supporting him and spreading his truth. However, it is also during this stage that the prophet interacts with the world on a grander scale than before, and many of his actions are responses to situations arising within his movement or from his leadership. Hence, in order to understand his behavior, we need to understand the unique features of his context and his movement, and the needs of his followers, as well as his own agenda.

5. Decline or fall. Some prophets grow old gracefully, and these tend to be messianic types. Those who fall from grace in the eyes of their followers and end their days in disgrace, or who are destroyed by external forces, tend to be charismatic personalities. These latter are more often unstable, power-seeking, and antisocial. This last stage in

the natural history of the prophet enables us to evaluate his life—and to identify more clearly the processes that drove him—in the light of Weber's and Kohut's theories.

In sum, charisma was traditionally seen as a supernatural phenomenon, a gift from God. However, Max Weber argued that while charisma may rest on some attribute of a leader, it needs to be recognized by others in order to be effective. In this study charisma is defined as an attribute of one whom we associate with our ultimate concern or, if we ourselves do not, others do. This definition substitutes the phrase "ultimate concern" for God in the manner suggested by theologian Paul Tillich (Tillich 1949), but some problems remain. Weber speaks about three social roles—the shaman, the politician, and the prophet —while Kohut speaks of two personality types—the messianic and the charismatic. Both treat the prophet as a prototype for other kinds of charismatic leaders, and agree that psychology alone cannot explain why some people become leaders and others do not.

The following chapters describe the natural history of prophets and attempt to explain their charisma. Because of the complexity of the subject, this account has to be somewhat selective, focusing at times more on messianic or charismatic personality types, though as both Weber and Kohut note, pure types are seldom found. The hope is that we may develop the tools to unravel the particular blend of factors that have combined to create the charisma of a specific individual.

3

Stage One | Early Narcissism

He who has been the undisputed darling of his mother retains throughout life that victorious feeling, that confidence in ultimate success, which not seldom brings actual success with it.

—Sigmund Freud
A Childhood Recollection from *Dictung und Wahrheit.*

How much can we say—*really*—about the inner life of another person? Some things we may safely assume; for example, that John felt hurt when Mary rejected him. But when we try to explain more complex behaviors such as leadership, we are much more speculative. It is possible, of course, by drawing on different sources and with the benefit of hindsight, to suggest credible reasons why Joan became a leader and Bill a follower, why Anne became an artist and Bruce a criminal. But to spell out, in a step-by-step way, all the processes and events that led up to the adoption of a particular role is, it must be frankly admitted, impossible, given the present state of our knowledge. Some heroic efforts to do this have been made, but an irreducible ambiguity remains (Runyon 1984). There is always some part of a person that cannot be known, no matter how hard we try. That is their dignity, and our humility.

The theories used herein come from depth psychology and the social sciences. At certain points these two approaches conflict, but both stress the early life of the child as crucially formative for later development (Conger and Kanungo 1988). The theory to be advanced herein begins with Heinz Kohut's work on the narcissistic personality, and then describes how such a person may become a focus for charismatic affections in others. The two key questions are *Why* would anyone become a prophet? *How* does one do so?

In Kohut's theory, the mother acts as a filter between the developing

44

child and the external world, so that the period of primary narcissism is extended far beyond its usual time and becomes deepened and crystallized within the child's mind as his or her basic view of life. The mother protects the child in such a way that the full significance of external reality is not recognized by the child. This is achieved by her devotion to, and support of, the child (mirroring, pacing, modeling, and so on), which is extended throughout the child's infancy and into later life. Kohut speculates that at some point in the later stages of this relationship there is a failure of rapport by the mother. In order to defend himself against the painful discovery that the world does not exist for him alone, the child may protect himself by incorporating the mother's filter mechanisms into his self. Thus the child retains the illusion of oneness with the mother and deals with the world in a way similar to hers.

Several points need to be emphasized about this scenario. First, although in perhaps a majority of cases it is the nurturing role of the mother that prepares the ground for subsequent development, there is no intrinsic reason why this should be so. In the case of Bhagwan Shree Rajneesh (described below) his grandfather was his primary love attachment. When considering this theory, we must remain aware that it is the child's constructed inner parent, the "self-object" derived from the relationship with an actual carer, that is crucial in narcissistic development.

Second, such a child has experienced a history of "baby worship" (Kohut 1971, 124), with all the heightened self-esteem and background of security that go along with it. Hence this is already a very secure, robust child. This corresponds with the facts of charismatic leaders; they seem to be fundamentally strong and secure people, their self-confidence impresses one as real, not mere bombast. The leaders in this study were not mere actors; they were men and women who probably could have succeeded at almost anything they tried (including acting as impressive figures). Prophets are not weak people. For an infamous example consider Jim Jones, who, in his last days in Guyana, despite being sick with fever, unable to stand, and incoherent much of the time, nevertheless still inspired love, fear, and loyalty among his followers (Reiterman and Jacobs 1982).

Further, the failure of rapport by the carer is not the failure of an "optimally failing parent" (Kohut 1977, 237) who ushers in maturity in an age-appropriate manner. The failure is delayed long past the time when such failures would usually occur, and comes at a time—perhaps the crucial time—when the worldview of the child is crystallizing in important ways. Hence the failure of rapport is not the optimal failure that is necessary for the healthy development of a realistic worldview. Rather, it is a delayed failure that occurs when the child is much stronger and more advanced in terms of ego development. Such a child may be able to cope with this failure in some way that denies or diminishes a full recognition of the reality of the universe, allowing the child to cling to an egocentric view of the world.

Furthermore, although the failure of rapport is delayed, the child's attempted solution to this problem when it does occur is extremely precocious, for it involves taking over the mature guidance strategies of the carer and incorporating them into the childish ego. This may seem like an impossible task, but we are dealing with an extraordinary child. Further, the carer's failure of rapport need not be total; it may occur initially only for brief periods, partially, and in a generally supportive environment. If successful (and it is a big *if*; Kohut's patients were mostly failed attempts), the child becomes an odd mixture of the immature and the premature, the infantile and the parental. This unusual blend of diverse elements of adjustment is typical of many prophets who are said to combine childlike innocence with ageless wisdom.

In order to adapt in this manner, the child will need unusual natural endowment, an extraordinary talent of some kind, or great native intelligence. For what the child is attempting to do is to live in a belief system that is fundamentally at odds with how the world is; that is, to retain an egocentric worldview in the face of an indifferent universe. The tension thus created probably would defeat most people (it creates problems for the prophet throughout his life), but perhaps, for an exceptional child, it may just be possible.

Last, in incorporating into his personality some of the carer's parental strategies, the child identifies with the self-object in a particularly intimate way, and this in a relationship that already has indistinct boundaries. It is appropriate to speak of "oneness" here and to examine the benefits derived by the child. In a series of studies, Lloyd Silverman and others have argued that unconscious fantasies of fusion with the mother can enhance performance and adaptation (provided that certain other conditions exist that we need not discuss here; Silverman, Lachmann, and Milich 1982, 1). Silverman claimed to have demonstrated this in research subjects through successful psychotherapy outcomes, improved performance in exams, and increased self-esteem and personal security (Silverman and Weinberger 1988; Balay and Shevrin 1988). The narcissistic development described above involves just such a fantasy of oneness, as large chunks of the parental behavioral repertoire are internalized as parts of the self. The benefit should be to boost the child's already burgeoning self-esteem to grandiose levels, and this is what we find among charismatic leaders.[1]

But what is the nature of the "unpredictable failure of rapport" that, Kohut argues, turns the developmental stream toward grandiose narcissism? Kohut's theory provides a credible account of how the child develops a mix of behavioral repertoires and experiential categories characteristic of charismatic leaders. But his theory also veers toward "eventism"; that is, the kind of "primal scene" theory that emphasizes a single event or series of events as determining all subsequent developments (Runyon 1984). It is, of course, entirely possible that some such imprinting is involved in the growth of charismatic personalities, but if the nature of the early carer-child relationship is explored further, it reveals other possibilities that enable us to avoid the postulate of a single determining event.

To begin with, the primary caregiver's baby worship is in effect the creation and daily re-creation of a god—the sacred infant. Typically, a mother invests her ultimate concerns in her child, who becomes the main source of her feelings of self-worth. The child's behaviors and worldview become more and more "divine," that is, magnificent, grandiose, and aloof. The challenge for the child in later life is to adapt these behaviors and worldview to a less indulgent audience.

This much of the theory is straightforward; cases of unhealthy over-identification by devoted mothers, of the Jocasta complex and similar neuroses, and of "son-and-heir" idealizing by emotionally blunted fathers are well known (Olden 1958; Chaplin 1968, 257). Further, there are well-documented accounts of such relationships in the lives of some charismatic leaders, for example, Adolf Hitler and Bhagwan Shree Rajneesh (Waite 1977; Gordon 1987). In addition, several of the leaders in this study agreed that their early relationships with their primary caregivers had been especially close and idyllic, as far as

---

1. As Rose (1972, 186) has argued, "The sense of identity [of narcissistic individuals] depends on the persistence of unconscious fantasies of fusion with objects."

they could remember. However, the motive for such involvement is probably some kind of insecurity. A mother's long-term self-sacrificial devotion to her child at the expense of other attachments and investments suggests some kind of compensation for deficits that we can only guess at (and that are probably different in each case). It seems unlikely that a mother who had the opportunity to nourish her self-esteem from more usual creative outlets, such as other family relationships, work, and leisure activities, would involve herself so totally in the development of a child. We do not need to know quite what drives her to do so, but we can assume that such mothers give their children a double message. On the one hand there is the totally involved, attentive, patient, supportive, mirroring and pacing that exists on the surface and that the child mostly sees. But beneath this loving exterior we can expect the child sooner or later (and it may take some time) to glimpse something of the mother's insecurities.

This is most likely to happen at those moments when the child falls out of role, that is, when he departs markedly from the pattern of interactions most satisfying to the carer. This is unlikely to occur in the first few years because of the predictability and simplicity of the baby's needs. But as the child becomes more complex and autonomous, its psychic fusion with the primary caregiver and the synchrony of their behaviors come under increasing strain. At such times several things may happen. Some children may prefer to stay within the warm glow of the mother's smile rather than risk provoking her anxieties. Others may enjoy disturbing her. But what is common to most possibilities is the sense that the child faces a clear choice between, on the one hand, infant-godlike behaviors that elicit the mother's love and, on the other hand, ungodly behavior that elicits the mother's insecurities. Given that there has been a long history of oneness between them, the child probably will not understand the nature of the mother's newly exposed insecurity (which she has taken great pains to hide or deny). Rather, the most salient experience that the child has at such moments is of the loss of fusion, the "fall from grace" into jarring, anxious interaction. Seen from the child's position, the experience is primarily of the loss of mother love. The reason for this loss—the carer's underlying insecurity—is unlikely to be seen or understood.

Hence the child receives a double message, albeit not consciously and never in words. The baby worship aspect of the relationship may be characterized by the phrase "Mommy and I are one" (from Silverman's research), but the times of loss of rapport may be felt as "Mommy will not love me unless I am God."[2] Note that it is not the mere occurrence of the failure of rapport that is important, but how it is construed by the child, typically as unconscious fantasies about its relationship with the mother or other self-object. Of course there may well be children whose responses to such problems are quite different from the line proposed here, but they will, it seems, be less likely to become charismatic leaders.

There are two things to notice about these messages. First, "Mommy will not love me unless I am God" may act as a limit on "Mommy and I are one," tending to lock in place the godly role. For God does not question His own behavior or motives, the more so if to do this is to risk losing Mommy's love. Hence the role of adored and worshiped god may become rigidly crystallized in the mind of the child as the prototype for all subsequent relationships; to question or momentarily suspend the role is to expose the most terrifying conflict any child can face: rejection by the mother (or other primary love attachment).

Second, the fantasy "Mommy will not love me unless I am God" is very likely to produce hostility toward the mother and, in later life, toward the world. The charismatic leader is "opposed to all rules of morality" (Weber 1946), and this opposition is likely to be rooted in an early hostility toward the mother, made clearer if we alter the phrase slightly to "Only being God is good enough for Mommy" (or "I must be God for Mommy"), plainly an impossible demand. Hence, despite the prophet's later claim to speak for a loving God, this element of hostility may pervade all his relationships, particularly with those who follow and worship him. (We can reflect, in passing, on all those charis-

2. The statements "Mommy and I are one" and "Mommy will not love me unless I am God" may appear to be typical of the wild oversimplifications of some ill-conceived psychoanalytic thought (Frosh 1989, 6). Such formulations are convenient descriptive devices, useful for translating descriptions of subtle and complex psychological states into easily understood terms. According to Stein (1956), there may be a hierarchy of such primitive fantasy states, beginning with the most basic "The breast and I are the same and cannot be separated," leading to slightly less primitive fantasies such as "Those I love are part of me" and, in later life, to the unconscious beliefs that motivate much of our behavior. In Stein's (1956) work on the marriage bond, this included such fantasies as "My wife is my phallus" (and corollary fantasy states about husbands). The aim of such phrases is to expose the unconscious significance of complex behaviors and to indicate issues that—especially in clinical work—need to be examined in order to understand the underlying motivations influencing these behaviors.

matic leaders who have ultimately led their followers to destruction, including Jim Jones, whose mother told him at an early age that he was destined to be the savior; Abse and Ulman 1977; Ulman and Abse 1983).

To summarize thus far, the pattern of early relationships most likely to predispose a child toward narcissistic, and ultimately charismatic, development includes an especially close but inappropriate relationship with a primary love attachment who teaches and models for the child the necessary elements for such development. This includes protecting the child in an unrealistic manner from learning about the reality of reality, while inducting him or her into a semidivine social role. At some time such a relationship breaks down. This may occur suddenly and dramatically or slowly and gently, but when the break occurs, the child struggles on as best he can with the elements of this early relationship fixed in his mind as the basic matrix for all future relationships. Some children may be damaged permanently by such an environment, but for those with peculiar talents and intelligence, some adaptation may be made that both accommodates and denies reality. What this is most likely to involve will be discussed soon.

This theory is sketched here in simple terms in order to avoid delving into psychoanalytic jargon and metapsychology, which is "experience distant" (Kohut 1976) and involves some extremely difficult concepts. Plain language and striking terms are preferred in order to clarify a complex subject. But obviously things are seldom quite so simple in real life. What has been presented herein are some key metaphors that try to give a good-enough guide to the phenomenon (which varies in each instance and is near the limit of our intellectual ability to conceptualize). We should not demand greater clarity than the subject permits, and charisma is an elusive subject indeed. If we impose upon the sequence outlined above the usual tapestry of developmental complexities that occur at such periods—that is, language and social development, the influence of socioeconomic and cultural factors, other family events, and so on and on—the particular strand of development described may well seem obscured and modified virtually out of existence. The simple terms used are not measuring instruments but tools to dig out what is buried. And it does seem that something like the above sequence, albeit distorted greatly by other influences, occurs in the early lives of prophets. Given the paucity of reliable data, it is surprising just how often stories of events like those outlined above do crop up. Three examples follow.

Werner Erhard, the founder of "est" and the Forum Seminars, was born John Paul Rosenberg in Philadelphia in 1935. His formal education finished at high school and he married young. At age twenty-five he abandoned his wife and four children and went to live with a woman who later became his second wife. After changing his name to Werner Erhard, he earned a living selling encyclopedias, and later by training salesmen. He dabbled in Scientology and other new religious movements. In 1963 he had a spiritual experience that led him to formulate the basic teachings of the "est" (Latin for "it is") workshops, later to become the Forum Seminars, a renowned worldwide experiential course in personal growth.

In a biography of him (Bartley 1978), Erhard described a major turning point in his life that occurred when his mother became pregnant with her second child. He returned home one afternoon with a broken, bloodied nose, received while playing lacrosse. He burst into his mother's bedroom, where she was lying ill in bed. She, following traditional belief that a woman who becomes upset while pregnant may harm her baby, resolved to react calmly. Without rising from her bed she told Werner tersely, "You know where the doctor is. Why don't you go to the doctor yourself?"

Until this point Erhard had enjoyed a particularly close relationship with his mother. She had been dissatisfied in her marriage and had turned to her son to fill her emotional needs (Bartley 1978, 20). She was devoted to him, and he recalled her in later years as "my guru, almost a Zen master" (Bartley 1978, 9). The sudden, unexpected withdrawal of her support wounded him deeply. Their close communication evaporated and they began to quarrel. Erhard described his emerging reality at that time:

After the Lacrosse incident a pattern of conflict was established in my life . . . It was a conflict between three expressions—"I want your love and support . . ." [and] "I'll show you . . ." I became stuck in proving myself . . . two inconsistent points of view lay there together, festering in my unconscious. They produced the command: In order to survive I must be dependent on my mother, but in order to survive I must be independent of my mother. This reduces to: In order to be dependent I must be independent, and in order to be independent I must be dependent. (Bartley 1978, 22)

It is likely that this is what psychoanalysts call a "cover memory," that is, a memory that condenses into a single dramatic scene a continuing and pervasive childhood conflict (Kakar 1981, 169). This is because the event occurred when Erhard was aged twelve and thus lies beyond the crucial first few years of life so important for Kohut's theory. However, it fulfills closely what Kohut described as the "unpredictable failure of rapport" between the child and the devoted mother, and in Erhard's own estimation it set up the basic dynamics of his later development. It also shows how torn and driven Erhard became through his complicated relationship with his mother. The story fits the theory, but things are rarely so simple. Kohut speaks of "forms and transformations of narcissism," implying a variety of scenarios (Kohut 1966). One can imagine dozens of variations on the theme. For example, some primary figure other than the mother may be involved. Or, rather than picking up such narcissistic tendencies from a single person, the child may develop them in a more ambiguous manner from diffuse elements in the family culture or, conceivably, from other relationships or culture generally.

Only passing mention has been made of the father's role because the theory is complex and simplicity is sought. Kohut says little of the father, and this may be significant. Among the sample of leaders in this study there seemed to be an almost complete lack of concern with their fathers. They seldom spontaneously mentioned their fathers, and several said that they had not cried when their father died, nor thereafter. Their fathers seem not to have been significant people to them. In Erhard's case, too, his father seems to have been emotionally distant from him and not to have played a major role in his life.

Furthermore, overlaying the narcissistic trend is the usual gamut of neuroses, complexes, and hang-ups that infect us all. In fact, rather than narcissism being the result of favorable—albeit distorted—conditions, it may result from awful conditions, as the only refuge of a child beset with problems. The carer's devoted empathy may in fact be something else. It may seem like empathy to an observer; it may be the nearest thing to empathy that those involved know; but there is something amiss with it. The guilty, cloying dependency of Hitler's mother (Waite 1977) is an example, but other forms also occur. In such cases the child's narcissism may exist as a kind of fantasy world to which he withdraws to generate self-esteem. This may become his main sense of reality, and all subsequent development may evolve from the emotional tones and experiences of this fantasy. A twisted, sadistic, paranoid version of "cosmic narcissism" may result. Or—another possibility suggested by Kohut (1976)—rather than narcissism pervading the entire personality, it may be restricted to only one sector, a sector that becomes increasingly dominant through life. This may be a fairly common thing. If we think of our own creative efforts, we may notice the tremendous sense of freedom and power that comes from creating an ego-reflecting miniworld of the imagination, free from conflict and anxiety. In fact a lot of one's inner world, from creativity to sexual fantasies, seems highly narcissistic. The two accounts that follow involve some of these permutations.

The case of Bhagwan Shree Rajneesh is notable because his primary caregiver was his grandfather. This example suggests that once a narcissistic developmental stream is set up, it may become conflicted with other influences that both open up and close off possibilities for growth. An intense empathic relationship may bestow great confidence and power, but its removal by death may be the ultimate form of a "sudden and unpredictable failure of rapport." What effect could this have?

Through the 1970s and most of the 1980s Rajneesh was the most visible of all Indian gurus, the most iconoclastic, entertaining, and sophisticated of them all. He was the intellectual's guru, with a thorough arts and humanities education. He dictated over three hundred books, all couched in accessible, everyday language. His followers were among the best-educated members of the alternative reality traditions, numbering about a quarter of a million worldwide at their peak.

Rajneesh was born in 1931 to a family of the Jain faith. He claimed to have first reached enlightenment while still a child. Later, while studying for his master's degree in 1953, he experienced a more complete enlightenment (Laxmi 1980). However, an earlier experience also influenced him greatly. This was the death of his grandfather, his closest love attachment, who raised him as his own son and refused to allow Rajneesh to visit his real parents, at one point telling him, "When

I die, only then can you go [to visit them]." The grandfather died, slowly and painfully, when Rajneesh was seven. Rajneesh witnessed this death and in later years recalled it:

> His final dying became very deeply engraved on my memory . . . he was [my] only love object, and because of his death perhaps, I have not been able to feel attached to anyone else much. Since then I have been alone . . . aloneness became my nature. His death freed me forever from all relationships. His death became for me the death of all attachments. Thereafter I could not establish a bond of relationship with anyone. Whenever my relationship with anyone began to become intimate, that death stared at me. For me love invariably became associated with death. . . . Afterwards I came to feel that this close observation of death at a tender age became a blessing in disguise for me. If such a death had occurred at a later age, perhaps I would have found other substitutes for my grandfather. If I had become interested in the other I would have lost the opportunity to journey towards the self. I became a sort of stranger to others. Generally it is at this age that we become related to the other—when we are admitted into society. That is the age when we are initiated, so to speak, by the society which wants to absorb us. But I have never been initiated into society. I entered as an individual and I have remained aloof and separate like an island. (Laxmi 1980, 12–13)

This "journey towards the self" gave Rajneesh a central focus within his own mind, an inner audience that enthusiastically applauded his dreams and victories. From it he drew the strength to follow his inner light, independent of the judgments of others as to the value or realism of his actions. By holding on to a belief in his own specialness, and by ignoring external obstacles, he became able to project his vision with an intellectual power that struck a responsive chord in his followers. But this same mind-set limited his ability to enter into relationships with others, and in the end it led to his downfall at Rajneeshpuram in Oregon.

A final example, that of Swami Vivekananda, shows the narcissistic developmental stream interacting with cultural and familial conflicts in such a way as almost to cripple the aspiring prophet, yet spurring him on to great achievement. It is a classic tale of prophetic failure.

Born Narendranath Dutt in 1863, Vivekananda was the favorite disciple of Ramakrishna. He popularized yoga in the West, founding the

Vedanta Society in New York in 1895. He produced four popular book-
lets on yoga, and his career became the model that many later gurus
followed. He also became a leading thinker of the Hindu Renaissance,
a modernized, nationalistic, version of Hinduism aimed at educated,
urbanized Indians and also at Westerners.

Vivekananda was the sixth child of an upper-caste Calcutta family.
Before his birth his only brother and two of his four sisters had died
in infancy. While pregnant, his mother dreamed that the god Shiva
agreed to be born as her son, a dream that suggests her emotional
investment in her child. She became extremely devoted to the boy,
whose brilliance at school and dominance of his peers suggest the
"conquistador feeling" of one who is the "undisputed darling" of his
mother.

Vivekananda's father was educated and Westernized, but his
mother was a traditional Hindu. He was born at a time of cultural
conflict between traditional and Western values. These conflicts seem
to have overlaid Vivekananda's grandiosity. While some elements of
his environment reinforced his sense of being "chosen"—most especially his closeness and striking resemblance to his grandfather, who
had renounced the world to become a monk—nevertheless he remained throughout his life torn between competing worldviews: traditional and Western, masculine and feminine.

As a prophet, Vivekananda's message asserted the "manly" values
of activism and radical social change, as against the conservatism and
tradition of the "nation of women," which was how he characterized
India at that time. This mission closely paralleled his struggle for autonomy and potency against his dependence on—and emotional attachment to—his mother. When a boy's early life experience is of a
deep identification and bonding to his mother, he has to struggle
harder than most to become a free individual in his own right (Kakar
1981, 170). In Vivekananda's struggle, played out in the arena of Indian
nationalism and the Hindu Renaissance, he alternated between passions of omnipotence and impotence, between vivid fantasies of isolation and fusion, between the elation of "I am All" and the despair of
"I am Nothing," between masculine and feminine sensibilities (Kakar
1981, 176). At his most extreme he would say, "The older I grow the
more everything seems to me to lie in manliness. This is my new
gospel. Do even evil like a man! Be wicked if you must, on a grand
scale. . . . I want the strength, manhood, kshatravirya or the virility of

a warrior . . . take away my weakness, take away my unmanliness, and Make me a Man!" (Kakar 1981, 175).

In 1897, at the peak of his success as a reformer, Vivekananda experienced a deep personal crisis and recanted, declaring that his ideas of progress and activism were delusions; things never got better, they remained the same. "It is all 'Mother' [Kali, the mother goddess] now," he said. "All my patriotism is gone. Everything is gone. Now it's only 'Mother, Mother,' I have been wrong" (Nivedita 1910, 168). In a letter to a friend he wrote, "I am free. I am mother's child. She works. She plays. . . . We are Her automata. She is the wire-puller" (Kakar 1981, 164).

Vivekananda showed this ambivalent leadership often in his career. He seems to have lived simultaneously in several different personae, moving from activist leader to ecstatic mystic, from rebellious son to one who follows his grandfather's lead, from guru to perennial guru seeker, struggling between active and passive, modern and traditional, male and female, yet never achieving synthesis (Kakar 1981, 179). He failed in his mission because he remained conflicted in ways that, while they gave him his unique strengths, also limited his effectiveness as a leader. He seems never to have reconciled the grandiosity of "Mommy and I are one" with his need to achieve a secure masculine identity. The struggle propelled him to great heights, but it also tore him apart psychically; he died in 1902 at the age of thirty-nine.

These examples do not prove the theory of prophetic development put forward here; they are not genuine case studies in the psychoanalytic sense. (Narcissistic people seldom seek therapy, preferring to focus on problems in the world rather than in themselves.) Rather, they are snapshots that indicate that something like the theory proposed herein may be true. For further support, some recent research on child development will be considered.

The work of John Bowlby (1969, 1973, 1980) and others on childhood attachment parallels the argument above. Although the attachment relationship occurs between two persons—the carer and the child—the attachment system exists within the mind of the attached person. It is an internal model of the world, relationships, attachment figures, and the self that guides the child's development, molding its mind and feeding its self-esteem, and it remains a powerful influence throughout life.

The attachment system has been studied by using a procedure known as the "Strange Situation" (Ainsworth et al. 1978). This is an experiment consisting of eight episodes in which a young child is observed in an unfamiliar environment and is given the opportunity to play with various toys and to interact with an unfamiliar adult, in the presence or absence of its mother. The reunion with the mother has proved to be of particular interest in the study of attachment. Children can be categorized into three groups, depending on how they react to the mother when reunion occurs. Some children greet and touch the mother on her return, others ignore her, and a third group resists or is angry with her. These three styles of reunion behavior are very stable and are related to other behaviors of the child and mother. On the child's side, the reunion relates to factors such as aggression in the home (Main, Kaplan, and Cassidy 1985; Main and Weston 1981), while on the mother's side her emotional expressiveness, sensitivity, psychological availability, and mood influence the child's reunion style. However, it is the long-range effects that are most interesting. Carryover effects from early attachments to later relationships have been proven, and such factors as the mother's perception of her own mother, the quality of the mother's relationship with her mother, and the stability of the mother's family relationships influence her child's behavior (George and Main 1979; Arend, Gove, and Sroufe 1979; Waters, Wippman, and Sroufe 1979; Ricks 1982, 1983).

Things are not always straightforward, however, for the child internalizes both sides of a relationship and may develop two or more models of the attachment figure and of the self (Sroufe and Fleeson 1985). Further, it is not just one's internal models that are important; how one construes these models is crucial (Bretherton 1985, 33). There may be "counteridentification" in which the child actively resists a model (Bretherton 1985, 34), and this may force it to work with a faulty model of reality, leading to inappropriate or pathological behavior (Bretherton 1985, 13). In sum, this research demonstrates the child's emerging ability to attribute subjectivity—internal states—to others (Bretherton 1985, 31), an ability that may become crippled during early development yet remains powerfully influential throughout adult life,[3] provided that basic needs are being met (Erikson 1963). This directly parallels the theory of narcissistic development. The charis-

3. Recent work on event schemata (Mandler 1979, 1983), on active structural networks (Norman and Rumelhart 1975), and on scripts (Schank and Abelson 1977) also demonstrates that internal working models developed in childhood can be very influential in later life. See also Bretherton (1985).

matic personality carries within the self a working model of reality that is in some way defective in its attribution of subjectivity to others —in short, narcissism. This defect inclines such a person to behave toward others in certain ways derived originally from the relationship with a primary caregiver. In later life these behaviors render such a person an attractive focus for charismatic affections by others.

However, to overcome a defect requires that compensations be made. Hence, any talents the child possesses have great survival value when he is attempting to maintain his narcissistic worldview. The followers in this study agreed that certain abilities, especially memory and social insight, were highly developed in their leaders. It is likely that these skills became so well-developed because of their survival value. These abilities are also related to other aspects of charismatic leadership, such as the subtle detachment of prophets and a certain fearlessness they possess. In the developing narcissistic child these traits may form a complex that becomes stimulated to exceptional levels of function. This brings us to the second question posed at the beginning of this chapter: Given the motive to become a prophet, how does one do so? What talents are needed?

In interviews with followers, the most frequently reported gift possessed by their leaders was an acute insight into other people. Some of the examples given seemed to verge on the paranormal—telepathy and omniscience being the most frequent—and were like the tales told of Jesus at the well or of Fritz Perls doing therapy. Excluding supernatural explanations, how can this insight be accounted for?

Kohut insists that charismatic personalities have stunted empathy for others (Kohut 1976, 414), a suggestion that seems to run counter to the extraordinary empathy shown at times by prophets. But Kohut also argues that this stunted empathy may actually sharpen some perceptions (Kohut 1985, 84–87). The leader comprehends his environment "only as an extension of his own narcissistic universe," and he understands others "only insofar—*but here with the keenest empathy!*— as they can serve as tools toward his narcissistic ends, or insofar as they stand in the way of his purposes (Kohut 1976, 417). There are problems with Kohut's usage of the term "empathy" (Oakes 1992, 139–42), but the main point is that the charismatic personality possesses an acute perception of the feelings and behaviors of others. Yet he is unable to truly empathize with them, to feel within himself some resonance with their feelings. He interprets what he observes in terms of concepts that he holds in an intellectual way but not with any genuine opening of the heart. The theories he holds may even be true for him; he may have personally experienced the truth of, for example, the Christian worldview within which he interprets what he sees, but he is unable to suspend this worldview and genuinely empathize with another whom he observes. Lacking empathic responsiveness, he relates his observations to his beliefs rather than to his feelings. Thus it is really a kind of intuitive, intellectual analysis that he is engaged in; he is a "cold" rather than a "hot" system.

To digress briefly in order to describe what this condition might be like, there exist, in the writings of clinicians and some theorists, well-corroborated accounts of extraordinary human perceptiveness. Alfred Binet calculated that the unconscious sensitivity of a hysterical patient is at certain moments fifty times more acute than that of a normal person (Binet, cited Jung 1976). Others have remarked on "the exquisite sensitivity of schizophrenic patients to their social environment" (Dobson 1981) and on the "almost paranoid hypersensitive" awareness of narcissistic people (Balint 1965); Kohut also discusses such phenomena (Kohut 1971, 95). It seems that some deeply disturbed patients are able to sense the unconscious states of others with an almost psychic sensitivity. They can understand others' defense mechanisms even when these are out of the awareness of the person concerned. They probably do this by subliminal perception of body language and paralinguistic cues.

It is likely that in such persons the capacity for communication with another's unconscious has been sharpened in early life, and is maintained longer than is usual. It becomes a kind of subtle emotional radar that makes one a superspecialist in understanding unconscious states, while at the same time limiting one's ability to understand ordinary life. Psychoanalyst Helm Stierlin relates this ability to narcissism. He notes that young children are able to gather and organize data in ways that most adults have lost (Stierlin 1959, 148–49). They can perceive, in a particularly immediate and clear way, feelings and moods in others that are out of the others' awareness. This ability is a carryover from infancy and is similar to certain instincts in animals. Other clinicians have described how, as a result of the crystallization of thought processes in childhood, our way of experiencing the world becomes increasingly stereotyped and zombielike. As adults we no longer experience the immediate, intense, and colorful quality of life radiating toward us from nature. Rather, we experience the world in terms of our already formed and more or less petrified ways of thinking and sensing. Only occasionally may we rediscover something of the lost intense quality of moods and experiences, when the crust of concepts and structures that has increasingly overlaid and denaturalized our consciousness is lifted (Schachtel 1947, 1954). The narcissistic personality is, however, closer to such experience than others, for he has retained much of his infantile mind-set; he sees most clearly when the emperor has no clothes.

Kohut also says that narcissistic leaders are "superempathic" with themselves (Kohut 1976, 414). This may explain why the leader impresses a select few with his divinely inspired insight yet is ignored by others, who dismiss his message as banal or dangerous. For the leader is recognized as charismatic only by those whose needs he addresses and whose values he shares. He epitomizes their concerns. For them he seems to possess the sharpest vision into human affairs. But perhaps his clarity is not into others but only into himself. For others with similar values, complementary needs, or even a similar psychological makeup, his superempathy with his self may appear as an extraordinary insight into the world as they know it. When he talks about others in terms of his understanding of himself, he seems to possess astonishing acumen because these others genuinely are like him.

The group that forms around the leader is at first made up of people who share his vision. His appeal is restricted to them because he does not speak the truths of others. His limited perceptions are less apparent when he deals with his own group, where his clichéd rhetoric and generalized argument are accepted. He relates intensely to them, and develops a heightened sensitivity to their unconscious hopes and fears, for they are like his own. But to those with different values and needs, or whose psychological makeup is very different from his, he will seem to be quite misguided. Hence we have the phenomenon of the charismatic leader who describes the world in terms of, say, the central concepts of the Christian worldview—that is, sin and salvation—concepts that are true for him, and thus he speaks with utter conviction and has tremendous impact on fellow Christians, yet there are others with, say, a secular-humanist worldview, whom he fails utterly to impress. He is unable to understand groups that are different from his, and he fails to understand his own group when it changes.

By viewing the social world as part of his self, the narcissistic prophet lives partly within, yet partly outside, consensual reality; partly in the real world and partly in a fantasy of his own creation. He is sustained by his subjective heroics—he is a legend in his own mind —and he tends to perceive other people as types and clichés rather than as individuals. When they behave differently from how he wills, proving that they are not part of his self, he feels rejected and treats their behavior as a personal affront, a frightening and mysterious disturbance to his solipsistic universe. Thus the prophet suffers when his reality is exposed as fantasy. This may happen often because he is fundamentally out of synchrony with how others view the world. He may take these hurts in his stride because he knows no other existence, but he longs to remold the world into a less jarring place. His sufferings make him acutely sensitive to the sufferings of others. He learns to focus on their hurts, to articulate their hopes, and he urges them to identify their needs with his. In this way he comes to manipulate them, to melt them into his personality, bringing them and their actions under his control as if they were his limbs, his thoughts, and his feelings. The leader does not recognize his limitations; he merely dismisses others whose values are not similar to his own. His inability to comprehend human reactions beyond a certain range may contribute to his ultimate downfall. As his followers change, he may develop a steadily increasing contempt for them, as Hitler became contemptuous of the Germans when they did not completely fall in line with him. This misreading of others is the most common cause of charismatic failure.

Another line of Kohut's theory deals with the social detachment of narcissism. Such individuals are unable to genuinely involve themselves in the affairs of others (Kernberg 1974; Kohut 1971, 1977) because they are psychologically detached from their fellows, a detachment that can be both a strength and a weakness. As Kohut describes it, the profound narcissistic isolation of the disturbed patient precludes any rewarding relationship with others (Kohut 1971, 1977). Less severe manifestations may, however, be another source of the sharp perception of charismatic leaders, who seem not to get caught up in other people's games. In a crisis they can withdraw into themselves, to a more peaceful state, and reflect without fear of intrusion and in a nonjudgmental, amoral way. In this way they are enriched by insights that are not available to others who live more completely within social norms and who align themselves with conventional values (Stonequist 1937). The impression is of a slightly aloof person whose lack of involvement provides him with an overview, a clinical detachment or "strategic vision" (Conger and Kanungo 1988), a free-floating, detached scrutiny that is extremely useful in a crisis and that was well-described in a biography of Fritz Perls (Gaines 1979, 100). Such a person is not overwhelmed by the intensity or closeness of conflict and is able, with a cool head, to accurately diagnose a problem and plan a solution.

Perhaps an analogy will be useful here. Our behavior at the scene of a car crash highlights the difference between the normal worldview and that of the narcissistic leader. When we come upon a fatal crash, we are horrified; we sense our own fears and vulnerabilities in the hurts of those involved. We want to avoid, to drive on, to remain uninvolved and deny our mortality; or we are ghoulishly fascinated by the edge of the abyss: "There but for the grace of God go I." In short, we risk being overwhelmed by our emotions, and have to force ourselves to stop and give help.

The narcissistic leader reacts differently. He is able to comfort the grieving and assist the injured with care and sensitivity because his emotions don't intrude. He does what is required with calm competence because he does not really see these people as like himself. For all his genuine compassion, his feelings are more like those of a kindly vet treating an injured animal than of a human being helping a fellow sufferer. His detachment allows him to respond accurately and efficiently to the situation without experiencing, or at least not to the same degree, the horror and revulsion that normals feel. Of course, as an intelligent person he is consciously aware of the horror of the scene, aware that it could happen to him, but he is driven by an unconscious grandiosity that holds him aloof. Intellectually he knows that it could happen to him, but emotionally he knows that *it won't!*

But there is a paradox here, for it is only by distorting reality that he comes to see it more clearly. That is, by failing to grasp the full significance of external reality, by denying the true otherness of others, the charismatic personality is able to accurately observe their behaviors and deduce their inner states. In time the inner states of others that cannot be explained by his worldview, those parts of reality that contradict or lie beyond his model, may cause problems, but these will be explained away.

Now to memory, for there is something odd about the charismatic leader's use of memory. A lasting impression one retains of any charismatic leader one gets close to is of his singular memory, and of his equally singular lapses. However, memory is not a trait that impresses a researcher in the field doing a short-term investigation, so it tends to be overlooked in studies of charisma. Few scholars mention it, and then just to note in passing that charismatic leaders have excellent memories (Willner 1984, 144–46). But because memory is central to most cognitive functioning, this study sought comments from followers regarding the "central gift" or any "semimagical quality" or "extraordinary gift . . . that seemed utterly striking" possessed by the leaders. All the followers agreed that the leaders had good memories, but several mentioned that they had noticed some oddities. For example, the leaders tended to repeat themselves in a stereotyped manner: "Sometimes he'll say something that he's said a day or so, a week or so, before. He's ma[d]e a point in a particular way and then he repeats it in exactly the same way the second time around. And I'll be sitting there looking in his eyes, thinking, 'Surely you remember telling me this a couple of days back?' But he doesn't seem to, and I've never asked him about it."

From the descriptions received, it was clear that the leaders had developed myths about themselves and the world made from bits of information stored up and practiced over years. These myths were polished and presented as sermons or teachings in which the leaders defined their missions. One follower explained, "If something's happening in [his] life, he gets it up into a story that he tells everyone. He'll repeat that story almost verbatim, but each time he does it, it's like he's telling it for the first time." Another described a "preaching mode" that her leader was in most of the time and in which he went "round and around" without knowing that he did it. Another added, "I'm sometimes uneasy when he does it, because I've heard it before and I know how it's going to go end, but I have to wait for him to run all the way through it before we can carry on."

David Millikan's study of a charismatic prophetess seems to touch on something similar. He described the conversational style of the woman (who was quite elderly when he interviewed her and may have lost her edge) thus: "After several conversations with her it is clear she has a store of stories and insights which, expressed mainly in the form of anecdotes she has repeated many times, have lost spontaneity in the telling and retelling. She is unable to sustain an extended argument" (Millikan 1991, 67).

The effect of this is odd. It is as if the role of prophet—and perhaps even the leader's whole personality—is organized into schemata. The feeling is of watching a pattern of behavior that is consistent but strained, as if the leader's manner of attending and conversing had been set up within a particular role that had been perfected years before and within which he has complete confidence and ease of recall. He has a surety that he can respond to any question with an answer that is already there, somewhere in his head; that has been given on similar occasions; and that he can access easily. Charismatics can range freely over a broad knowledge base, yet much of what they say seems rehearsed and unreal. Sometimes, when taken by surprise, a leader would look momentarily perplexed and quizzical, then go into a kind of intuitive mode, as if he were listening for something within, yet still with the relaxed confidence of one who knows he has all the answers and merely needs a second or two to access them. The seamlessness of these performances was such that one tended to forget that normal human speech and thought are hesitant, uncertain, meandering, and repetitive. The performances were all too persuasive and reassuring to be real. And there sometimes seemed to be an element of play in their delivery. The distinction between the spontaneous and the contrived had vanished, and it became impossible to know how much of what they were saying was genuine and how much was part of some deep personal myth that each had worked out long before. Perhaps most of what they said was genuine, but each lived largely inside a myth of his own creation, and they used their excellent memories to find their ways around within these myths. They tended to repeat themselves in stereotyped ways, to be constantly "in role" or "on stage," yet without any compelling sense of falsity.

These patterns of behavior may be related to a tendency by all the leaders to communicate in clichés—very effectively, but clichés nonetheless. All the leaders, when attempting to explain something, showed a penchant for homely simplifications in the manner of "If-this-beach-ball-were-the-sun-then-our-earth-would-be-a-grain-of-sand-at-the-north-pole" type of metaphors. But clearly they did not think in this way (an analysis of Hitler's personality discussed this trait as "infantilism"; Hiden and Farquharson 1988, 15). It was as if, in needing to have an answer for everything in order to appear omniscient, the leaders had organized much of their personalities into bundles of memorized "response sets" (Chaplin 1968, 426) governed by automatic "if . . . then . . ." heuristics that left them free to work on other problems, and that gave them the reassuring illusion that they had answers. Yet often the knowledge contained within these prepared responses was impressive indeed (see Oakes 1992, 149–150 for a fuller description).

In sum, charismatic personalities have excellent memories that they use in their strategies of impression formation. In doing this they seem to be able to influence the function of memory itself, sometimes improving, yet at other times lessening or distorting, its performance while themselves appearing vaguely unreal.

In explaining this ability we may recall Stierlin's statement that "the undifferentiated child has also capacities for obtaining and organising data that most adults have lost" (Stierlin 1959, 148). This comment links unusual cognitive performances with the undifferentiated state of primary narcissism, and may identify the source of the talents of charismatic leaders. It is as if, in retaining an archaic state of mind, if only partially or subconsciously, charismatic personalities also retain some of the cognitive abilities that go along with it, abilities that lie dormant in most of us. This happens with other unusual talents that are common in children but disappear or diminish with age. Examples include eidetic imagery and map reading. Eidetic imagery, popularly referred to as "photographic memory," has been extensively studied and found to be rare among adults, but about 8 percent of children possess it. The ability seems to peak shortly before puberty and to decline sharply thereafter, making it a trait restricted mostly to young children (Haber and Haber 1964). Map reading is a skill that has a relatively sudden onset at about age three, but, unless it is worked on, seems not to develop much beyond levels achieved fairly early in childhood. If children are given the opportunity to learn map reading, their abilities soon equal or excel those of most adults (Young 1989). The full potentials of these two skills are seldom realized in adults, and there may be many other abilities similarly underutilized. Michael Murphy of the Esalen Institute, who has made a study of such talents, lists twelve psychological functions that he believes have "metanormal" capabilities (Leonard 1992; Murphy 1992).

Hence the reported exceptional behaviors of charismatic leaders may be genuine, and explicable in realistic terms as the development to fantastic levels of otherwise normal abilities. That this is possible is shown by a study in which a student of average intelligence and memory became able, during the course of twenty months of practice, to improve his "memory digit span"—the number of digits he could recall after seeing them briefly—from seven to seventy-nine digits. His ability to remember them after the sessions also improved enormously (Ericsson, Chase, and Faloon 1980). It seems that we all have prodigious latent gifts.

How these talents arise and are developed is not known, but some suggestions have been made. George Klein (Klein 1966) relates memory functions to defense mechanisms, and a study by Ernest Schachtel presents a cornucopia of possibilities. According to Schachtel, an adult's memory is qualitatively different from a child's, and is not fit to preserve children's experiences and enable their recall (Schachtel 1947, 4). During development there occurs a separation of "useful" from "autobiographical" memory, the former becoming increasingly specialized and the latter increasingly subjective. However, split-off parts of a child's memory ability may continue to develop in isolation, becoming highly specialized while retaining their infantile character, and perhaps culminating in fantastic abilities. Chapter 9 will return to this point, but note here the eerie impression that all of this creates. These abilities can easily be mistaken for pathology, giving the impression that the prophet has sprung Rasputin-like with strange powers and dangerous impulses from some hellish realm. Hence the inevitable question arises concerning his mental health: in short, Is he mad?

Although the leader is mostly "normal," there are times when—with a crazed glint in his eye as he talks to God—he seems literally insane. His "glowing unblinking eyes which hold like forceps" (Ellwood 1973, 38), his eccentricities, and his wild countenance, impress others as deranged. Such classic descriptions as "sick-souled" (James 1902) and suffering the "disease of God" (La Barre 1980) catch this flavor of oddness. Conventional psychiatric categories are sometimes used to describe him, but there is much confusion on this. Kohut argues at one point that narcissism is the very opposite of psychopathology, yet elsewhere he asserts that the leader "risks psychosis by his all-or-nothing stance" (Kohut 1976). Charles Lindholm suggests that "the shaman goes out of his mind but is not crazy" (Lindholm 1990). Some charismatic leaders have had psychotic episodes, but the "madness" of most differs from psychiatric illness. It seems to have more to do with the uncanny impression created by the prophet's intense presence, and such odd behaviors as George Fox's bizarre preachings (James 1902), than with any clinical symptoms of paranoia, disorientation, or hallucination (although these latter are present often enough to give one pause).

The prophet's apparent craziness may arise from two sources. First, an extremely narcissistic worldview is likely to strike others as strange at least. This is the oddness in the prophet's sense of reality, of self and others. He sees things differently from others. At times he may be remote, at other moments powerfully present, and later still, just peculiar. Some people find this disturbing and others, inspiring, and the prophet may detect these reactions and accentuate his behaviors to enhance the impression he wishes to make. Second, there may be genuine psychopathology. It seems likely that prophets suffer the same mental aberrations that afflict us all to some degree. Kohut spoke of Hitler as having a "healed-over psychosis" (Kohut 1985), Jim Jones was obviously paranoid, and several Pentecostal leaders have had psychotic episodes (Harrell 1975). Max Weber, who cautioned against the overuse of psychiatric explanation (Weber 1968a, 499), nevertheless sometimes associated madness with charismatic leaders (Robins 1986, 17), while other scholars have developed entire theories of charisma around the so-called "borderline" personality type (Post 1986). The presence of pathology may also account for the altered states and visions reported by some prophet figures as occurring even as young as age three (Harrell 1975, 28).

Charisma may be related to manic depression (Jamison 1993). Now grandiose, then brooding, the prophet may flip-flop through periods of energized positivity and fatalistic negativity, giving to the followers with the one hand but taking away with the other. Joseph Smith and L. Ron Hubbard were exemplars of this pattern.[4] Manic depression, which is also thought to be related to creativity, has been found to have a significant genetic component. In addition, at least some personality traits are heritable, allowing for the possibility that the entire narcissism-charisma complex may be genetically related to manic depression (Horizon 1989; Hodgkinson et al. 1987; Loehlin 1982; Jamison 1993).

It is hard to say how abnormal behaviors develop in charismatic

---

4. Miller 1987; Foster 1992. Foster argues that Joseph Smith suffered from manic depression, and his theory is supported by research that correlates manic depression with creativity in the lives of artists and scientists, as well as by studies of heredity that support a genetic basis for the disorder.

personalities. Whatever role they may play in the life of a particular prophet, and whatever is the balance of environmental versus biological influences, can only be inferred retrospectively and will vary in each case. But regardless of genetic factors, the prophet's behaviors are primarily—though not solely—the result of his social context, for even major psychotic disorders require the right environmental conditions to emerge. He is neither inherently mad nor purely the mouthpiece of God, nor even especially mentally healthy. Rather, his behaviors arise from the interaction of his nature and his social milieu, and his mental aberrations may form an intrinsic part of his message. He is not insane, but he is highly creative, and this may better explain his eccentricities.

The vast literature on creativity will only be touched on here. Donald MacKinnon's classic study of successful architects is probably the best place to begin because he sought the conditions of childhood that facilitated creative expression. He found that parents of creative individuals gave their children greater freedom and independence, and expressed greater confidence in their children's abilities, than did other parents. Their children grew up with greater than usual self-acceptance, and this allowed them to explore all manner of things that others might feel threatened by. Such children also were able to speak about themselves in unusual ways, were more open to their feelings, and were intuitive and perceptive rather than intellectual. They grew up to be extremely skeptical of social institutions. However, there were ambiguities in their identification patterns with their parents, and they seemed to be both saner and crazier than normals (MacKinnon, 1962).

According to Carl Jung and others, creative persons are lopsided individuals (Jung 1954) who retain "the courage to experience the opposites in their nature and to attempt a reconciliation of them" (Whiteside 1981; MacKinnon, 1962a, 1962b). Creative women are often "masculinized" with traits of aggressiveness and independence, whereas creative men tend to be "feminized" by the traits of tenderness and sensitivity. Such individuals identify closely with all creation and tend to regard all forms of life with reverence. Their courage appears as a sense of destiny, of having been chosen to reveal some facet of the life force. It enables them to scale the barriers between conscious and unconscious thinking, and to risk madness and the loss of personal identity in the pursuit of an ultimate truth (Whiteside 1981).

The courage to perceive and experience the opposites of one's nature, and the commitment to work at reconciling them, stem from certain paradoxical mental skills that seem closely related to both narcissism and charisma. These skills combine elements of infantile oneness—a sense of play, euphoria, openness to experience, and fearlessness—with adult traits such as discipline, endurance, and focused problem-solving, in such a way that each set of elements complements rather than cancels out the other. Some examples may illustrate this. The element of *detached involvement* is central to both charisma and creativity. This is the stance of the creator—a cool head directing passion, emotions at a distance, "reason in the state of ecstasy" (May 1975)—in which two opposing tendencies fuse. Similarly, *mindless perception* involves a Tao-like openness to stimuli coupled with intellect and knowledge. This is the unconscious (mindless awareness) breaking into consciousness (mindful understanding) to create an awareness of the limits of knowledge and a mood that seeks to go beyond them (May 1975).

Another example of opposing tendencies coming together is *delayed closure,* in which the creative person delays closing his mind on problems yet works very hard to try to solve them. There is a feeling of driven play in his handling of problems. *Converging divergence* is a further example, wherein lateral thinking (De Bono 1970) is combined with ordinary logic, the interplay between these two thinking styles leading to novel solutions to problems.

But perhaps the most important ingredient is *constructive discontent* —the emotion-based need to oppose and improve. Faultfinders who challenge norms are often met, but this factor refers to a constructive yet radical and active response to tensions and conflicts, sometimes described in literature on child psychology as "creative destruction." In addition to these, a degree of selfishness, a quietly confident humility, relaxed attentiveness, and flexible persistence are aspects of creativity (Maslow 1968; McMullen 1976). These behaviors clearly parallel the fearlessness, perceptiveness, detachment, and confidence that characterize charisma.

The creative processes of charismatics have been studied, and the results are consistent with the descriptions above. In her doctoral research into charisma, Laura Hall (Hall 1983) administered tests measuring creativity to charismatic community leaders. She verified that they were highly creative people—the highest subscale score in her tests was for originality (recall Weber's remark that in its pure form, charisma "may be said to exist only in the process of originating"; Weber 1964, 364). Alexander Labak, in a similar effort with charismatic university professors, verified traits such as flexibility and openness. His subjects also showed less than normal development of conscience and high self-actualization (Labak 1972). The studies in the volume by Jay Conger and Rabindra Kanungo also offer insights into the creative processes of charismatic individuals (Conger and Kanungo 1988). In sum, although these studies are too few to develop a comprehensive understanding of the charismatic's creative processes, they nevertheless permit us to conclude, first, that charismatics are indeed highly creative individuals, and second, that the mental skills involved in creativity seem to be very closely associated with the complex, narcissistic mental states characteristic of charisma, and hence they may share a common origin. Perhaps the fundamental dilemma of narcissistic individuals—What is my relation to the world? (Little 1985, 6)—also provides the tension that drives creativity.

In discussing creativity, Kohut has argued that each person attempts, throughout his life, to follow an agenda laid down in the self during infancy. This is not a detailed life plan. Rather, it is felt more as a set of emotional pushes and pulls, inner tensions, patterns and cycles, that influence the decisions made at key turning points in life. This agenda is the inner context for one's lifework, the basic creative drive of one's life (Kohut 1977). For most people it is expressed in conventional ways of work and love, but for prophets it becomes a passionate striving that consumes all their energies. In the words of Wilhelm Reich (Sharaf 1983), it is a "life-affirming flame" that may even be perceived as another identity, a muse that drives one mad if not obeyed.

What might the agenda of an extremely narcissistic person such as a prophet be like? It should, in crucial ways, repeat the basic dynamic of the early fusion of mother and infant, either symbolically or substantively. Later, as the child grows, the agenda becomes obscured by learned concepts, values, and roles; it gets overlaid with culture, education, and tradition, and it is channeled and transformed by socializing influences to such a degree that when it finally emerges in adulthood, it may do so as a utopian ideology—a mission or a calling or a prophetic career—but at base the psychological meaning of paradise is mother love.

The transition from childish hopes to utopian vision occurs during incubation, when the youth translates infantile experiences into mature concepts and feelings. In so doing he creatively rearranges his mental world. The developing prophet-child's creativity is spurred to extreme achievements by the tension between his egocentrism and the world's indifference. Deep down he *knows* that things should be other than they are, and his fertile mind translates his early narcissism into a "memory or vision of paradise" (Heinberg 1991). The emerging prophetic vision, because it stems from an insoluble conflict between the prophet's narcissism and the world (neither of which can be easily changed), exists as an immutable force that drives him forward to reinterpret social events and to claim special status for himself. If the prophet can get a handle on the world and make it reflect his egocentrism, he can be reassured. If he can share this reordered social reality with others, he may serve their needs and they, his. Hence he is inclined toward mastering the skills of social and personal manipulation, both by his own needs and by the needs of others. By influencing others in the way he once influenced his mother or primary caregiver, he realizes his, and their, hopes for salvation.

Now, to summarize what might be known of the earliest life experiences of prophets, clearly there has to be a base of extraordinary natural talent or intelligence to begin with; the ancients were right—the hero really is exceptionally endowed. However, there must also be a special relationship with a primary caregiver, commonly but not necessarily the mother, so that the growing child develops two conflicting unconscious fantasies, one of omnipotence and the other of vulnerability. These may be characterized as "Mommy and I are one" and "Mommy will not love me unless I am God." The effect of the first is to permanently retain some connection with the narcissistic phase of development and all that is associated with it, including powerful aspects of infantile memory and empathy. The effect of the second message is to drive the child ambitiously, and angrily, to re-create the mood of the first, stimulating to exceptional levels whatever talents and narcissistic traits the child possesses. Two faculties that are most likely to be stimulated to exceptional levels—because of their potential survival value—are memory and empathy; a modest increase in each may greatly enhance social mastery. In addition, narcissistic people seem to be naturally creative, perhaps because of some overlap between these traits. However, while the overall effect of all this may strike some observers as strange or even pathological, it is not a mental disease in any usual sense. Narcissistic development may be quite natural, given its context. With ongoing differentiation of the personality—creative fragmentation—the narcissistic stream becomes crystallized and refined, then transformed by socialization and matured until in time, if the child does not suffer a breakdown, he may outwardly appear little different from others. But beneath the surface there is a world of difference, for such a person experiences the self and the world in a fundamentally different way from others. This difference leads to an important discovery, that there is a "something wrong" with the world that he and only he can and *must* fix. This leads to the next stage—incubation.

This period of early narcissism is postulated as the first stage in the development of prophets. Because of the difficulty in obtaining data about it, it is also the most theoretically problematic of the life stages. The approach taken here has been to extend Heinz Kohut's theory of narcissism to explain the genesis of adult charismatics. This is inevitably a speculative exercise, but an explanation of the motivation of the prophet is crucial. Why he does what he does determines his meaning for us. If it were shown that he was merely mad, or that he really was inspired by God, we would think of him differently. In suggesting that he may indeed be a little mad, and may also be inspired by his sense of God, but that his main impetus is his creative attempt to solve his own life problems, we embark on a creative and speculative enterprise ourselves.

The theory advanced here locates the need to lead and the buoyant confidence to do so in an early relationship with a primary caregiver. The source of the prophet's unusual talents, especially his social insight and exceptional memory abilities, must also be explained. The theory proposes that these may be integral components of infantile narcissism, or likely developments from it. Early narcissism influences the whole of development in a systemic way, so that a developmental line is set in process that results in the emergence of a charismatic personality (given favorable conditions).

It is the nature of this inquiry that there is little direct evidence about all of this. Yet despite the theory's lack of supporting data, it does not merely hang in a vacuum. Four lines of argument can be made for it. First, it is based on a prior and closely related theory that has gained considerable respect among social scientists (Kohut 1971, 1976, 1977). Second, it is consistent; that is, it contains no contradictions and does not conflict with any other body of psychological knowledge. It leads in a logical manner to a credible theory of charisma. Third, where the theory can be matched with observations, it fits; adult charismatics are extremely confident, are often hostile, possess powerful memories and acute social insight, and so on. Something like what the theory describes seems to have occurred in the early lives of prophets such as Werner Erhard, Bhagwan Shree Rajneesh, and Swami Vivekananda. Last, it parallels other recent theories in social science, particularly Bowlby's work on the attachment system, that credibly explain how such developmental processes might work. Of course, such theorizing will inevitably be wrong in some details. And there are great variations from case to case. There may also be other powerful influences not discussed herein, for example, biology (Horizon 1989; Jamison 1993). But generally the theory fits, and it leads logically to the next phase of development, incubation.

4

Stage Two | Incubation

Extremely narcissistic persons are often almost forced to become famous, since otherwise they might become depressed and insane. But it takes much talent — and appropriate opportunities — to influence others to such a degree that their applause validates those narcissistic dreams. Even when such people succeed they are driven to seek further success, since for them failure carries the danger of collapse. Popular success is, as it were, their self-therapy against depression and madness. In fighting for their aims they are really fighting for their sanity.

—Erich Fromm
The Anatomy of Human Destructiveness

The narcissistic personality emerges from childhood into adolescence with an orientation to the world that bestows certain strengths but is fundamentally at odds with reality. Hence he can never be completely at peace, despite whatever triumphs come his way. By seeing others as extensions of himself, he gains a fearlessness and perceptiveness they lack, but as a consequence he can never fully identify with any group and is always an outsider. Further, his very fearlessness and perceptiveness may be seen by others as threatening, his detachment may be viewed as coldness or indifference, his autonomy may lead to conflicts with authorities, and so on; for every plus there may be a minus. Unless he is raised in an environment sensitive to his needs and providing appropriate roles for his special abilities—for example, India or shamanistic societies—his development is likely to be difficult. Perhaps some potential prophets are broken by this process and become suicidal or permanently injured. However, the leaders in this study appeared to have negotiated this period with varying degrees of success. Several patterns emerged.

Incubation seems to be basically a prolonged crisis. If he has emerged from childhood with a powerful sense of self-esteem, the narcissistic personality may dream unattainable dreams but find himself unable to fulfill them. He may then be left feeling bewildered by his failure and forced to search himself for answers. Or, if he has emerged from childhood with a wounded self-esteem, he may find the entire world a frightening, unpredictable place. Such a person faces, in addition to the predictable developmental stresses of this period and whatever emotional conflicts he retains from childhood, the additional problems caused by his narcissistic view of the world. There are few valid generalizations to make about all of this; the stunning variety of human resourcefulness and the complicating factor of the situation, as well as the lack of any common focus in the lives of the leaders, renders this stage difficult to describe. Information about it is reconstructed in a somewhat piecemeal fashion from the leaders' and followers' recollections, and is therefore only suggestive. Yet the incubation period must be postulated in order to span the transition from early narcissism to later stages.

Some of the leaders studied herein developed powerful visionary dreams in this time, even to the point of living in self-constructed fantasy worlds for prolonged periods. Most seemed to need some kind of refuge. Paul Clavell spent most of this phase in the priesthood—a role in some ways analogous to the prophet—and reached the next stage only after the painful discovery that "all that I believed in, my life, the church, and God, was bullshit." For others a selflessly supportive partner was clearly a great help; Harry Huntington's marriage was described by one follower as "That's not a marriage, it's a Bible class."

There are possibly subphases involved in this stage. Periods of confusion, loss of direction, searching, overcompensation, and denial may alternate with times of highly energized work toward a goal in which the charismatic personality throws himself into a project such as a career or the church in an attempt to solve his problems by sheer willpower and hard work. The goal may not be of long-term importance to his life, but the pursuit of it brings some relief from conflicts by narrowing the range of problems faced. All of the leaders studied seemed to have had one or more such projects in their young adulthood, and to have alternated between periods of intense work and easy living. The project may fail, or the developing narcissist may achieve much only to abandon it; most of the leaders in this study had abandoned major projects at some time in their lives to strike out in new directions, most frequently in this stage.

But what seemed to be common to all the leaders was that this period was one of continual change—none settled into a stable career —as they sought some higher purpose to their lives. It was also a time of difficulties, of prolonged struggle to answer what were really adolescent questions of identity; not for nothing did Adolf Hitler title his autobiography *Mein Kampf* (My Struggle). Fred Thomson seemed to breeze through this time, making all the appropriate responses to problems encountered, and in discussions he tended to romanticize this period of his life in the manner of a *Boys Own* all-conquering hero, but his ex-wife could remember two occasions when he faced emotional difficulties that suggested something more severe than normal adjustment difficulties. What seems to have been most needed by the leaders in this phase was some sort of refuge—the priesthood or a similar career, a supportive marriage, or some project—in which they could live out their grandiosity on a small scale, or perhaps symbolically, while preparing themselves for greater things.

Six themes recurred in discussions with the leaders about this stage: (1) a sense of not belonging to any group, (2) construction of a personal "myth of calling," (3) splitting of the personality, (4) radical autonomy, (5) conflicts with authorities, and (6) the acquisition of practical skills appropriate to a later prophetic career.

The Sense of Not Belonging to Any Group

The clearest indication of the sense of not belonging was the growing awareness by the leaders during the incubation stage that they were somehow different. This discovery came largely as a response to their perceived failure to fit in with others, to clearly define themselves by reference to a particular group. Bro John wistfully recalled that "I was never one of the boys," and Paul Clavell remembered how even at the age of eleven he was asking himself, "Is this all there is?" Arnold Harper said:

> When it came to the spiritual side of things, I was looking for somebody whom I could go to and sit at their feet and learn; I was looking for older people that I could go and learn these things from. And I couldn't find them. And that was a heartache to me. So here I was, I had to set sail and pioneer. Well, that's what pioneers are about, I suppose. Pioneers haven't got other people to learn off. . . . and so I had to depend on God.

This sense of not belonging to any group is not merely alienation with its associated sense of loss. Rather, it means a sense of detachment and absence of commitment, of not identifying with—not deriving one's values from, nor having any allegiance or obligation to—any reference group, class, social stratum or whatever. Joshua Einstein expressed this well:

> I remember about the age of twenty, I used to smoke dope a bit. And whenever I did, there'd be this gulf between me and others. It happened time and time again. It never became a problem, but I always knew in my heart that whatever I was involved in, whatever I had going at that time, girlfriends, it was gonna be temporary. It troubled me a little. It got me wondering about myself. I'd see people putting down their roots and I'd think maybe I should, too. Is there something wrong with me that I don't? But the way they were doing it was not right. It wasn't gonna work. I knew that, and I wondered why they couldn't see it. It made me think a lot about myself. My father and sister always used to say I was different, but I never realized where it was gonna take me.

Construction of a Personal "Myth of Calling"

Perhaps the single feature of this stage that stands out most clearly is the construction of a personal "myth of calling" by each of the leaders. Information on this emerged when they were asked, "When did you first realize you were different from others?" Answers tended to be of the style "I've always known I was different . . ." or "I've always felt close to God in my heart," yet there were additional statements that implied there had been times when the leaders had been less sure of their callings. Recognition of their specialness seemed to begin only in their teens, but it developed quickly.

The function of the "myth of calling" is to interpret the differences the prophet discovers between the way he sees the world and the way others see it—that is, to reconcile the way the world is with his narcissistic orientation—in a positive manner. The prophet develops a distinct sense of his own calling, of being "chosen" or at least of having some extraordinary gift, in order to account for why his worldview is so different from that of others—why he doesn't fit or belong. He could, of course, interpret these differences negatively as some failing on his part, but this would be unlikely because of his underlying grandiosity; it also wouldn't be functional. Arnold Harper again:

If I look back now, I could look back and I would say, . . . I would feel, ah, that God was preparing me then by the things that happened, but I didn't know then. I didn't know, I didn't have any understanding or consciousness of anything like that happening. But when I look back on my life now and I see that there were things happening in my life, and the way I was inside, in my own heart, my father always used to say I was different to the others.

Similarly, Fred Thomson:

I recognize this as a pretty big difference, that I had never had that sort of fear. While I've felt embarrassed in some situations, and I've felt nervous about going into some places, there was never the feeling that I might be totally destroyed, totally whatever. I know that nobody would ever do that to me. And I realized that this was really the thing that Rajneesh was offering. This was the thing. It wasn't that he knew what was happening in these groups and he went on these astral travels and he did all these other so-called miraculous things. That was all bullshit. That's all part of it. The fact was that somewhere—and he dates it back to the time when he was twenty-one—. . . he'd had the same feeling, . . . he'd had no doubts. And this, regardless of what he talked about, regardless of what his image was, or regardless of how he behaved, people were picking up this underlying message that here was a man with no doubt. Here was a man who really knew. And he knew very deeply inside himself that he was okay and that the great universe was okay, and that the whole situation was okay. And I recognized that I had this same feeling.

One way of understanding this myth is to invoke Daniel Levinson's notion of a guiding "dream" or vision for life developed by the young man (Levinson 1978). The dream of the prophet becomes a calling or "vocation" (literally, a voice), dimly heard at first and probably competing with other dreams and voices, but eventually it emerges as the best way to reconcile his narcissism with the reality of the world around him. This is implied in the above extracts but not stated explicitly. What is heard are hints, tentative suspicions that something odd may be occurring, vague intuitions of something extraordinary at one's shoulder, but seldom bold black-and-white statements. Incubation is a period of hesitancy and trial. The leaders in this study were pragmatic and explored many possibilities, arriving at a surety of their calling only after years of trial and error. They did not opt for a prophetic career early and then spend the rest of their lives living out a detailed agenda laid down in their twenties. Yet for all their slow and cautious development, once they settled upon their myth, it seemed to become fixed in their minds. Of course not all narcissistic personalities interpret the differences between them and others, and between their view of the world and the way the world really is, in this way. Heinz Kohut dealt with many dysfunctional narcissistic patients, some of whom seemed to have found the strains imposed by their condition too much.

A frequent way by which the myth of calling is developed is through recourse to the Bible. Whatever happens to one, there is a parallel somewhere in the Bible that interprets the event as in some way related to God's will. The Christian leaders in this study used the Bible as an oracle to provide meaning to their personal struggles, interpreting the events of their lives as evidence of God's guidance and seeming to retain, perhaps as a residue from childhood, a "magical" worldview.

The myth of calling as described here is similar to the personal myth discussed by Ernst Kris. As Kris outlines it, the personal myth is "particularly firmly-knit and embraces all periods of [life] from childhood on" (Kris 1956, 654). The solidity and cohesion of this myth were clear during interviews with the leaders. Despite several intimate revelations by them, there was a feeling that one never really got through to them. Their absence of self-doubt was striking, and they never shed their certitude about themselves and their callings, even as they poured their hearts out on occasions. Kris's description of this precisely parallels my experience of "a special type of resistance to explorations of their personal history. The certainty that things could not have been different, that their recollection was both complete and reliable, was, though not explicitly verbalised, omnipresent, whenever the past was first approached" (Kris 1956, 654–55).

Kris also suggests that the personal myth derives from the "family romance," a "fantasy of one's origin born out of the pressure of the day" (Kris 1956, 679). He argues that the myth derives from "a relatively undisturbed pre-oedipal development . . . followed by traumatic experiences during the oedipal phase" (Kris 1956, 674). This fits closely with Kohut's theory, and significantly, Kris also emphasizes the function of memory in all of this (Kris 1956, 678–79). Last, Kris notices a similarity between the way the personal myth was developed among his patients and the way many artists reenact an "image of the artist" in their own lives, borrowing parts of their autobiography from cultural traditions (Kris 1952; 1956, 680). This suggests that the leaders in this study may have behaved in similar ways, perhaps unconsciously constructing their personal "myths of calling" along the lines of cultural images of prophet figures.[1] Charlie Tantra described how this was for him.

> I went through a period, . . . years actually, of reading mainly biography. I know now that I was searching to try and find out who I was, looking for parallels with my own experience. I'd read these books and wonder if the same things were going to happen to me, if my life would be the same. I visited a medium once to try and get some answers . . . she was surprisingly accurate, as it turned out. I was, like, waiting for something to happen, looking for signs. Eventually it did, but . . . I didn't recognize it then, did I!

Splitting of the Personality

Kohut speaks in several places of "splitting" of the psyche, both horizontally and vertically.[2] This suggests a rejection of parts of oneself, typically through repression (horizontal splitting) or dissociation (vertical splitting). This process may be adaptive, allowing the child to mature socially by repressing antisocial impulses. Or it may help in the development of extraordinary abilities (through the vertical splitting off of a talent and the cultivation of it). Kohut argues that Sigmund Freud's inability to appreciate modern art and music resulted from his neglect of certain portions of his self: "I believe that in Freud's work, as is the case with all great achievement, the intensity and profundity of insight in one area had to be paid for by a comparative flatness in

1. Erik Erikson has analyzed Hitler's (1939) construction of his "myth of calling" in *Mein Kampf:* "The syntax promises a fairy tale, a myth . . . not that his story had no basis in fact . . . nor that its fiction was mere fake and nonsense; myths never are. A myth blends fact and fiction in such a way that it "rings true" to an area or an era, causing pious wonderment and burning ambition. The people affected will not ask about truth and logic; the few among them who cannot help asking will find their reason paralysed" (Erikson 1942, 475).

2. See especially Kohut 1971, 176–99. This idea originated with Freud and was developed by Melanie Klein.

another" (Kohut 1977, 297). Elsewhere Kohut speaks of heroes who "gave over their total selves to [their] ideals" (Kohut 1980, 494), thereby transcending themselves and their past (temporal splitting; Marcus 1961) and of others who "abandon . . . the core of the self" (Kohut 1977, 117). He also reports that several of his narcissistic patients felt threatened by "fragmentation" (Kohut 1971, 1977).

Something of the sort appears to have taken place within the leaders of this study. Each seemed, to varying degrees, to have split off parts of himself in order to give the remainder over to his calling. At the extreme, Arnold Harper totally gave himself over to God, abandoning the person he had been and most normal human appetites and desires. When he was asked about the personal satisfaction he derived from his role (as distinct from the satisfaction of doing God's work), the following exchange occurred:

HARPER: This is something you people find hard to understand—that people aren't doing something for the self-satisfaction and the pride that's in it and the reward of accomplishment . . . cause that's the general thing that happens in society. But to me I've got a job to do, and I know it's my job to do it, and I would have a fear of failing to do that job . . . it's a tremendous responsibility. There are all these people, their lives, where they're going, and their children, that's the thing that's before you all the time, it's the thing before me now, night and day. Now you say "Apart from God's glory and all the rest of it." Well I can't think any other way.

QUESTION: But surely you must look around sometimes at what you've achieved, with all the other people, sure; for God, sure; but I bet you must walk around and chuckle sometimes at what an adventure it's been.

HARPER: Umm. No, most probably I've never allowed myself to think like that. When I gave my life over to Christ when I was twenty-one, I knew then that I was gonna have to suffer a lot of things, I was gonna have to sacrifice things, and I didn't do it for some gain. I did it out of appreciation. I was so thankful to God. I was thankful for what God had done now in my heart, and in my life, the peace of mind and soul he'd given me, and the answers he'd given me. I was just so thankful that I wanted to do anything that would please him, no matter what it was. And that was my pleasure. But I look back and I'm thankful, I'm very thankful in the real sense of the word for what has happened. I can see these children here and I'm thankful. These children can come up to me and they say, "Arnold, if you hadn't come here, we wouldn't have been born, and we really owe our lives to you, the fact that we're even born," because the children wouldn't have even been born that have been born here. And I know I'm thankful, my wife and I are thankful about that. And we'd say yes, it's been worth it, because it's produced something. But I'm not, I don't find it in my heart that I have much time to sit down and start thinking, say, "Well now, isn't that great, look at what we've done." I just see that there's so much that we haven't done and there's so little life left. . . . Have we done what we should do? My fear has always been that I'd fail. And I wouldn't want to fail God. I'd rather die first.

A less extreme split had occurred in Paul Clavell. His vision of salvation was meant to be achieved through personal growth, but he had a profound "blind spot" about some of his own behaviors. A follower said:

There's a very definite desire on his part to serve God. I think, I believe, that it's from his innermost soul . . . [but] he has a need to be on the top of the heap. . . . He comes into the room and he looks miffed if people don't notice he comes into the room. . . . He'll go into a restaurant and he'll immediately project out and everyone knows he's there . . . "I'm here." He exudes confidence all over the floor, and yet somehow that's not really Paul. Maybe it's the double messages I don't get. In fact, when I dream about [him], it's almost like I dream about two different people. . . . I've tried and I've tried to explain it, to show it to him, his arrogance, and he'll listen or seem to listen and even understand, and then he'll go right ahead and do the same thing again.

Paul admitted that he encountered frequent bitter misunderstandings from other people, yet added that the reason was a complete mystery to him. When asked, "If you were asked to pass on your accumulated wisdom in the form of a statement that others might use as a sort of guiding insight to help them live their lives, what would you say?" he responded instantly with "If you can't listen, you're nothing."

This kind of two-sidedness was shown by every leader. Each had, totally or partially, given himself over to a dream, ideal, or God. The result was either a person like Arnold Harper, who lived every waking minute of his life in driven service to his God, or someone like Paul Clavell, for whom this splitting was less complete. All of the leaders seemed to be divided into two utterly contrasting parts: the visionary and the "shadow," to use Jung's term (Samuels, Shorter, and Plant 1986, 138–39). What accompanied the shadow was an almost total blindness to its nature and a denial of any portion of it that crept into awareness.

Perhaps the best example of this was Fred Thomson. Fred claimed he was God and behaved in a grandiose manner most of the time. Yet three dissonant traits stood out: his inability to have close friends; his need to control others and to define reality in his terms, so as to always be right; and his refusal to compromise or accept criticisms or appear vulnerable. Probably these traits indicate a deep disturbance that is fundamental to charismatic personalities. For example, L. Ron Hubbard admitted he could not have friends (Miller 1987, 218), and Rajneesh, Jim Jones, and Chuck Dederich displayed similar behaviors (Milne 1986; Gordon 1987; Reiterman and Jacobs 1982; W. F. Olin 1980). Similarly, some of Kohut's narcissistic patients could not admit a mistake or ask for help, so great was their need to feel omnipotent and self-sufficient (Kohut 1971, 1977). But Fred's splitting seemed to have a pathetic side. It was as if he had abandoned the core of his self (in Kohut's words; Kohut 1977, 117), and this gave him an eerie "hollow" quality in times of extreme stress. A follower described this:

> I recently watched him go from topic to topic, selecting only those bits of information he was prepared to let in. If we were talking about X, he'd be right in there; if we were talking about Y, he'd be right in there; but he didn't seem to have some central part of himself constantly balancing things out and harmonizing them. It was as if he'd flip from subject to subject and in each one he'd be totally absorbed while he was in it, then he'd put that down and go on to the next. If I challenged him on something, he'd find some neat way of sidestepping it or taking it out of the picture, showing it to be irrelevant. . . . And I realized that that's what makes him so good with the ladies, or as a leader: when he's there, he's all there, really there; he has this unique quality of attention that he puts all of himself into. But there's no real center to anything. He has this full-on attention thing because he holds nothing of himself back, he has no center [to hold back].

Heinz Kohut has described how one may give oneself over to a vision or ideal so totally that one loses or abandons his "soul," so to speak. Fritz Perls has described doing this in therapy (Lankton 1980,

191), and Joshua Einstein seemed to take a perverse pride in having achieved the state:

> I am a function. I just live my function. . . . See, at this point there's only the function, there's only function, there's only who I am expressing. . . . In the past I was looking for acknowledgment or trying to get something. Now to me that all is a joke. See, to me, whether you like me or dislike me, who gives a shit? If you're alive, that's great; if you're not. . . .

In sum, despite their brilliance, all the leaders except Arnold Harper showed dramatic blind spots about their own shadow behaviors—the split-off portions of their selves that were obvious to everyone who knew them yet were massively defended against by the leaders. In contrast, Arnold seemed to have given himself over to God so totally as to have wiped his slate clean of discordant behaviors. Yet it is likely that he was merely a little further down the same road that the others had taken.

Radical Autonomy

Despite being group-oriented, the leaders studied were extremely individualistic. Their independence and rugged determination to follow their own paths were best described by Paul Clavell.

> All the good things I've ever done in life, all the really exciting things, have been me swimming upstream. Nearly everything I've done has been, as I've perceived it, . . . so much on the cutting edge of life, that the status quo organizations, the people with the power, say "No," they're not going to support. . . . after I initiate a program or something and do it, and then leave it, then the mob come in and they want to do it. And that's the story of my life. I always seem to be ahead of the mob.

At some point in their lives the leaders had decided (or perhaps they really had no choice) to live according to their own feelings and intuitions, their personal vision or relationship with God, rather than by deferring to reference groups, social conventions, or cultural norms. Although they conformed in their daily lives, they were nevertheless utterly committed, in the long term, to their own visions of reality. They seemed to have decided to run the risk of temporary disapproval from others—quite harsh disapproval in some instances—in the trust or on the gamble that if they followed their vision and succeeded, eventually their critics would be won over. They expected to have to go it alone from time to time, usually in the face of fierce opposition. They were not merely autonomous in any moderate way—people who "knew their own minds" and "stuck to their guns"—they were grandly autonomous in the pursuit of their visions at every turn.

This radical autonomy, and the splitting of the personality that accompanies it, is probably necessary for great achievement. It seems to have begun in earnest in the incubation stage (although no doubt the roots lay much further back). During childhood, narcissism may not lead to major conflicts with society. Childhood is, after all, a time of play, of creativity, of indulgence of unusual behaviors as childish or playful—"He'll grow out of it" is the maxim, indicating that the child's behavior is not to be taken too seriously. But this changes in adolescence, and the young adult's behavior begins to be taken very seriously indeed. He must work for his place in the world rather than receive it gratis. Conflicts have ramifications rather than being merely part of yesterday. Hence the developing narcissist begins reflecting on his behavior, developing theories about himself and testing them out in the real world. It may be a painful time, but if he has exceptional intelligence and imagination in addition to his narcissistically derived traits of detachment, confidence, and so on, he is likely to interpret any conflicts between himself and the world as indicating his specialness. And, if he is patient and persistent, he may come to prevail in such conflicts.

Several of the leaders told stories that demonstrated their autonomous behavior and foreshadowed their later charismatic styles. Arnold Harper told of his resignation from the church rather than compromise the Christian truth as he knew it. Fred Thomson spoke of his dramatic walkout from an Esalen encounter group. Joshua Einstein recalled being expelled from an est group when he refused to go along with the est philosophy. In each case the group was abandoned without regret when it had served its purpose. These "walkouts" were viewed by the leaders as significant turning points in their lives, marking crucial decisions to throw out the old and begin anew. Yet probably none had ever really given the groups their full commitment in the first place. Rather, they had used the groups to develop themselves and, having got what they could from them, moved on. In later years

these dramatic walkout stories became symbols of the leaders' specialness and proof of their callings.

Conflicts with Authorities

Conflict with authorities is virtually a truism of charisma, but it didn't
show up strongly until early adulthood. None of the leaders in this
study was a troublesome child or wildly rebellious adolescent. Only
when they reached their early or mid-twenties did they consistently
find themselves in trouble with the authorities. Several spent time in
jail, and even those in professions or the church struggled against
officialdom. This pattern continued over the rest of their lives. Examples include Leo Haley's "hustling" lifestyle; Paul Clavell's many
struggles against the church hierarchy; Arnold Harper's refusal to accept help from hypocritical Christians when he was in need; Fred
Thomson's mockery of the air force after he nearly crashed and severely damaged a plane in flight training; Joshua Einstein's early career manufacturing LSD in South Africa; and so many other examples
as to make conflict with authorities virtually one of the defining characteristics of charisma.

It is easy to see how these five themes may be closely related. A
highly autonomous individual may have no sense of belonging to a
group. To justify his condition, he may develop a flattering personal
myth. To adapt himself to this myth, he may repress or split off aspects
of his self. Sooner or later he may run foul of the authorities because
he has little commitment to them. Yet for all this, the leaders in this
study had not been merely dissolute in this phase of their lives. Rather,
they had worked hard for their various goals, as if hoping to conquer
the unkind world they found themselves in. If they were not yet ready
to part company with convention, neither were they prepared to bow
to it. Instead, they set out to master it. To do this, they had to develop
various skills, some of which would prove useful in their prophetic
careers.

Acquisition of Appropriate Career Skills

If one is to gain a following, it is important to be seen as successful. Of
the twenty leaders studied, eleven had operated their own business
during the incubation stage of their lives. These ranged in size from

small craft workshops or farms to large-scale businesses employing dozens of workers. All had been successful, but their enterprises were relatively short-lived (average about six years). Six other leaders spent most of these years either in the church or in ashrams. Of the remaining three, one migrated halfway around the world—a task that probably absorbed most of his energies; one was a poorly educated female with few career opportunities; and there is insufficient data about the last. Hence virtually all of these leaders were, prior to their careers as prophets, successful—or at least secure—financially. A few had been fairly wealthy before, but most had only been supervisors of small businesses. One was propelled into the prophetic role by financial collapse. For several it was important to be seen to have had much and to have given up everything for the cause, even financing it from their own pockets.

Max Weber has argued that charisma is opposed to all forms of rational economic activity (Weber 1964, 362). However, the communal groups studied herein provided for the well-being of their members through various enterprises (modest as these sometimes were), as did several of the noncommunal groups. It seems that rather than being indifferent to rational economic activity, the charismatic leader accommodates himself to it. Early in his career the prophet recognizes the importance of financial expertise, and during the incubation stage he sets out to acquire it. Wealth—or its abandonment—may become a qualification for the prophet (as poverty may be incorporated into a myth of otherworldliness), but the followers and their leader still have to eat. Prosperity is never seen as an end in itself, but the canny mastery of at least some life skills was important for every leader.

Along with conventional career skills the leaders cultivated a particular set of abilities that primed them for later leadership roles. For example, Fred Thomson, in pursuing a sales career, became involved with an American confidence-building and sales-training organization from which he later launched a second career as a psychotherapist. For some of the other leaders, running their own small businesses—or even, in the case of Leo Haley, living as a street hustler and constantly making deals—gave them the financial and managerial skills that later enabled them to organize their followings.

A key component to this is the "giving" orientation, an interpersonal style described by Laura Hall as constituting "the capacity to give of self and resources [that] is an essential element in getting others to give" (Hall 1983, 98–99). The leaders were invariably described by followers as generous with their time and energies, and as constantly supportive and available. They seemed to have discovered that giving to get is in the long term a far more successful strategy than merely taking, as the literature on self-disclosure and reciprocity demonstrates (Jourard 1971; Jones and Gordon 1972; Savicki 1972; Derlega, Harris, and Chaikin 1973). Another skill developed in this period and refined to unusual levels is communication ability. Five occupations, each involving the communication arts, were overly represented in the leaders' lives. The first of these was teaching; four of the leaders were experienced schoolteachers, and Swami Divyananda had been an associate professor at an American university. The second occupation was that of clergyman; six of the leaders had worked in the church as monks, ministers, or lay preachers. In addition, Swami Joe and Swami Divyananda had spent many years in ashrams in India. The third career was selling; four leaders had successful sales careers behind them, as did Leo Haley, albeit in a different way. Counseling and alternative healing comprised the fourth career path; nine of the leaders were counselors or alternative healers with many years' experience. Last, there were the entertainers; Charlie Tantra had been a successful filmmaker, Leo Haley had led a rock band, and Paul Clavell had a background as a broadcaster and an accomplished amateur musician. In addition, Swami Joe, Bro John, and Suzie Shiva had been involved in many amateur musical or dramatic productions. Several of the leaders had had multiple careers in the communication arts prior to adopting their prophetic roles—they included Charlie Tantra and Fred Thomson. Only Kit van Voon had no previous history as a professional communicator, but it was clear that he, too, was a "raver" (his self-description) who possessed the gift of gab. Kit was the leader who immigrated from Europe, an exercise that probably absorbed much of his energy for many years (his first language was Dutch). This may have led to his atypical developmental path.

In Chapter 3 the cluster of creative motivations and behaviors called the "life-affirming flame" (after Wilhelm Reich) was described. This originates in the agenda laid down in the self of an infant. Because it is largely subconscious, the "flame" may be experienced as a separate personality in the psyche of the leader, as a muse or God. Or it may be felt only as a passionate inclination toward this or that interest or activity, but always tending toward a sense of oneness with the parent or "great other" in some form. For the prophet it becomes the unique form of creativity, and it involves the gradual development of a visionary theory and a manipulative practice. The theory justifies the leader's narcissism by interpreting it as a sign of special calling. It reinstates the feeling of infantile oneness with the mother by articulating a salvation gospel with the leader as God's messenger. Practice involves the mastery of the skills of social influence necessary for a charismatic career. Sometimes the practice is deliberately aimed at becoming a prophet. For example, Leo Haley was raised in Jamaica and became a Rastafarian almost as a normal part of growing up. He never envisaged himself as a leader until after his arrival in a country where he met fellow blacks eager to hear the Rasta message. He interpreted this as a calling from God, and then he consciously set about acquiring the skills of leadership. More often, however, the acquisition of manipulative skills occurs semiaccidentally, perhaps as part of training for a career (all the occupations listed above have significant social-influence components to them), or under the guise of personal growth or religious training. Either way, the effort is total; few ordinary folk set out so deliberately and with such persistence to master manipulative skills, virtually remaking themselves in the process.

The narcissist is an excellent student of manipulation because of his detachment and keen perception. Also, because he has such a fundamental conflict with the world, such a precarious grip on reality, he must be ever alert to gain whatever leverage he can. A little success in this pursuit leads to continued application, more success, and inevitably a career path as a student of manipulative strategies. This becomes a major focus that continues in one form or another for the rest of his life. It may be experienced merely as an abiding passion or as a preferred career choice that happens to open up new opportunities, but for those leaders in this study who had the largest followings, it seemed to be part of a deliberate effort to recruit others into a charismatic relationship.

A common manipulative strategy used by the leaders in this study was an argumentive style that was calculated to subtly shift the ground of any discussion from whatever matter was being talked about toward some area of an opponent's personal insecurity. In this technique, the leader observed the process of an opponent's conversation and identified some point of hesitancy or uncertainty. This was not always a flaw of logic or an error of fact; the conversation may have been on some topic about which the leader knew little and would have been unable to detect such a mistake. Rather, it was more likely to be some personal unsureness on the part of the opponent that the leader's exquisite social perception targeted. In some way, often by metacommenting, the meaning of whatever the insecurity involved was exposed. Typically, what was said was an observation that the opponent seemed "a bit steamed-up about this" or was "finding it hard to say what all this is about." In this way the opponent was invited, sympathetically and seductively, to expand upon the very point of weakness. Or the leader claimed not to understand what was meant at a particular point, perhaps even saying that the opponent was not making sense. This usually led to a further exposure, and then another, until the opponent stumbled over his words and began to look uncomfortable. At this point a well-timed dismissive glance from the leader was all that was needed to intimidate, the other person being glad to have the subject changed to how he might redeem his soul or whatever.

A stunning example occurred during this study when Free-Love Farley demolished a building inspector who had visited unexpectedly and demanded to examine some recent construction. It was clear that Farley did not know the various fine points of the regulations that governed such inspections, and also that he had something to hide, but by drawing the inspector out and by focusing on his paralinguistic performances, he soon had the man on the defensive. Eventually Farley persuaded the official to return to his office to recheck some detail, assuring him that when this had been done, the inspection could proceed. Presumably by then the issue in question would have been taken care of.

The use of other manipulative techniques varies from leader to leader and may be specific to the milieu in which each works. Christian prophets may become adept at preaching, glossolalia, and pastoral care. Human Potential leaders master sensitivity training, group dynamics, the use of self, and the "action methods" of psychotherapy. For the Western gurus of Eastern religions there are other practices to master, such as meditation, "magical" abilities, and the cultivation of an inscrutable, paradoxical wisdom. Basically, what is involved is learning to speak the inner language of one's followers better than they can articulate it themselves, and to use it to influence them. What the leader seeks is some handle on people's emotions that allows him to appear extraordinary and to project a prophetic image, to speak in language clearer than the truth.

Mastery of the communication arts provides a solid base for later inspirational leadership. The leaders in this study initially learned their repertoire of manipulative strategies in the occupations listed above, but they did not do so solely within them. Fred Thomson, while a young man, became interested in hypnotism, which he tested experimentally on his children. Joshua Einstein traveled the world, attending personal growth workshops run by famous Human Potential gurus. All the leaders had, in their younger days, been eager "seekers" attending courses and seminars. Besides these techniques of social manipulation, at least three other adjuncts to leadership were cultivated: appropriate qualifications, appropriate knowledge, and lifestyle image.

In some quarters a total lack of qualifications is the best qualification, but most of the leaders in this study had some kind of qualification—formal or informal—relevant to their charismatic status. These qualifications were not merely formal credentials, although sometimes they were just that; each suited a specific niche. That is, they were important adjuncts to the credibility of the leader to perform his prophetic role. For example, Reverend William Hart, who headed a "last days" Christian group with a survivalist orientation, had formal qualifications as a natural healer. Charlie Tantra and Fred Thomson, both Human Potential leaders, had liberal arts degrees. Suzie Shiva, Free-Love Farley, and Bro John, each of whom had founded a commune, had lived in other communes prior to starting their own. In short, all of the leaders had qualifications of one sort or another that carried considerable weight within the group they headed but might have been irrelevant in other groups.

These qualifications may not seem especially important until they are lost or invalidated. Frank Jansen, a Pentecostal pastor, was told by a superior in his first church, "In difficult times anyone who has a stable marriage, happy kids, and a successful career will attract a following." He did just that, but he lost all credibility with his flock after he and his wife divorced. Another leader, when accused by police and ex-members of child abuse, lost sufficient of his following to throw his movement into a crisis from which it has not recovered—not because the charges had been made but because of his attempt to lie to his followers after earlier having established a reputation as one who fearlessly told the truth. In sum, the qualifications are specific, objective achievements or signs of calling that have special significance within the particular worldview of each movement. The leader may seldom refer to his qualifications, yet all the followers are aware of them and this awareness becomes part of how they define him.

Just as important is appropriate knowledge. If the prophet is a Christian, he must master the Bible. If he is a commune leader, then there is a literature on communalism and alternative farming methods to be mastered. If he is a therapist or healer, again there is a relevant body of knowledge to be learned. This knowledge may really be little more than a prop; one leader described psychotherapists by saying, "Every therapist needs a theory to believe in, but it's the belief that cures, not the theory." Yet this knowledge may carry the day in confrontations with opponents or dissenters.

An even more important adjunct to the charismatic role is lifestyle image. Ruth Willner has drawn attention to the exploitation of mythic images by charismatic political leaders (Willner 1984). Such leaders cultivate, in the minds of their followers, parallels between themselves and sacred cultural images—for example, Hitler as a Teutonic knight, and Ayatollah Khomeini as "the once and future Imam." By cloaking themselves in a sacred mantle from the past, these leaders were able to imply and project a divine status for themselves. In a similar manner the leaders in this study were aware of the impact their personal styles had on their followers, and they deliberately cultivated their images. A common icon was "Jesus—the man of the people"; not the mystical Christ, nor God incarnate, but the inspired carpenter was the most frequently invoked image.

The leaders were earthy types, "jacks of all trades," who had been variously an auto-body repairer, a pest exterminator, a farmer, a mill worker, an orchardist, and a gold miner. They felt it important to be seen as simple folk. They mostly married and had children, struggled as small businessmen, and had small town backgrounds. They did not elevate themselves above their followers, nor did they develop any regal bearing or style. Instead, they relied upon their natural strengths to advance their programs, and where they did project an image of themselves beyond their immediate following, it was one of "extraordinary ordinariness."

Another icon invoked was the rugged individualist in conflict with authority, the "Man Alone" of John Mulgan's novel (Mulgan 1972). Kit van Voon, Bro John, and Free-Love Farley developed this image of themselves. Conflict with authorities has already been discussed, but it may be significant that in these conflicts the leaders were either alone (as in their younger years) or they headed a band of "marginals"

(Stonequist 1937) lacking political clout. The character of their opposition was always individualistic, usually with them firmly in command. They never really functioned as part of a team, let alone a protest group or an activist lobby. They developed an "outsider" status for themselves, and the rural agricultural character of some of their communal efforts fostered a back-to-the-land image (though this was more apparent than real in most instances). Although they headed large groups, in some ways these groups merely reinforced the burden of aloneness of the leaders by adding to their responsibilities while being clearly subordinate to them. The leaders may have created the groups, but they never belonged to their creations. Other examples include Swami Divyananda and Swami Joe, who consciously wore the mantle of the Indian guru Swami Muktenanda; Fred Thomson, who modeled himself on therapist Fritz Perls; and Arnold Harper, who saw himself as an Old Testament prophet; The other leaders variously claimed to be a reincarnation of Jesus, to be in contact with the Great White Brotherhood of Theosophy, or whatever.

There are certain traits that equip one for leadership. For example, a habit of continuing education may become important when a leader applies himself to mastery of, say, a technical manual or some piece of town-planning law. All the leaders had inquiring minds and were widely read, but at some time they had—probably consciously— adapted their knowledge to extend their personal influence. This was clearest among the Christian leaders, who could cite chapter and verse of the Bible to justify their actions, but it was also the case for the others, whether they cited a history of communalism, pacifism, psychotherapy, or whatever. Knowledge is power, and at some point the leaders had set out to increase their power through the acquisition of knowledge.

So also with lifestyle image. It is likely that the leaders were selected by their followers for devotion and surrender because they projected appealing images (Little 1980, 1985), and to this degree the leaders were not completely in control of their fates. Nevertheless, they were too astute not to be aware of this process and to help it along by emphasizing whatever mannerisms worked best, and by sloganeering.

Last, there is a particular "last resort" manipulative strategy that most charismatic figures seem to develop. It has been described in psychotherapy literature as "crisis induction" and "escalation." Basically, what it involves is the solving of a problem by the production of a much greater one. In the context of the lesser problem the followers may be alienated from the leader, but in the context of the larger problem they cling to him. Of course, only the prophet is able to solve the larger problem. An example of this among historical prophets occurred when Muhammad turned a domestic conflict about his wives' jealousy over a slave girl he desired into an all-or-nothing choice as to whether they wanted him to remain as their husband. Leaving them with a revelation containing the words "It may be, if he divorce you, the Lord will give him wives in your stead who are better than you . . .," he retired alone to a tiny, bare room; he spoke to nobody, seldom journeyed out, and played the part of the wounded innocent. When faced with such a dreadful choice and the stigma of divorce, the wives soon fell into line and accepted Muhammad's dalliance with the slave girl (Lings 1986, 277–78). A similar manipulation occurred when one of the leaders in this study was challenged by his followers over his financial dealings. He turned the issue into a choice over whether he would remain living with them. Their intention had merely been to call him to account, not to drive him away, but by raising the stakes he cowed them into docility and they agreed to accept his misdeeds. This is a high-risk strategy—"crash through or crash"—but one fitting to the all-or-nothing streak of prophets who are able to keep cool heads in crises.

• • •

None of this is meant to imply that charismatic prophets are merely cynical exploiters of humanity. Rather, they are realists who enjoy adapting and learning new skills, and are as attracted to power as any comparable person, say a bureaucrat or an intellectual. Their narcissistic detachment and acute perception of the motives of others make them superb students of human behavior. But their desire for dominance is related more to their need to construct a narcissistic world for themselves to live in rather than to any perverse lust for power. In their younger years most did not see themselves as deliberately preparing for a prophetic role. They enjoyed learning manipulation for its own sake and for the opportunities it opened up to them. Perhaps, if they could have seen where such expertise would one day lead them, they might have reacted with apprehension. There was no previously thought-out master plan for control. Rather, effective manipulators dream of a better world, and some go on to become prophets.

The incubation stage is perhaps the most interesting in the sequence. Early narcissism is forced on the child by external circumstances, but in the incubation period the basis of the future prophetic role is laid down. Incubation is a difficult time; whereas most people would be incapacitated by the relentless and illusory claims of a narcissistic personality, the ego of the gifted person may be pushed to its utmost capacity by such pressure and embark on objectively outstanding achievements (Kakar 1981, 177). How some people survive, and even manage to thrive, in adversity has been studied. It is now known that there is a range of strategies and defenses that help.[3] Several studies have verified the existence of an incubation stage—a period of "incipient charisma"[4]—in the lives of charismatic leaders. Examples, especially of the creation of the personal myths of calling by prophets, occur in the biographies of J. H. Noyes, L. Ron Hubbard, and Kathryn Kuhlman (Thomas 1977; Miller 1987; Buckingham 1976). The social influence tactics of prophets have been discussed in several biographies (Bord 1975; Johnson 1979), and have been attested to by others who have been close to them (Davis and Davis 1984).

Scholars have also identified elements of practice in the leaders' lives, including their "legitimacy claims" of appropriate qualifications, appropriate knowledge, and lifestyle image.[5] But incubation is, above, all, a time of experimentation when the roles provided by society are tried and found wanting. The developing narcissist or "incipient" prophet may channel his best efforts into these roles, but his failure to fit in, as well as the failure of the roles to satisfy, leads to conflict. For Bro John and Harry Huntington this involved spells in prison. For Paul Clavell and Charlie Tantra it concerned their failures to fulfill the

3. A review of relevant research on "invulnerable" children has been published by Cohler 1987.
4. Tucker 1968. Similarly, Friedland has written that "While charismatics are continually being generated, their 'charisma' can frequently be unrecognised or indeed be considered peculiar, deviant, or perhaps insane" (Friedland 1964).
5. The acquisition of fake degrees has been a feature of the lives of several contemporary prophets (Enroth 1983, 175). The usefulness of these false claims to legitimacy may be gauged from the wonderful gesture of L. Ron Hubbard, who publicly resigned his degrees to protest "the bombs of psychiatrics treatment" (sic; see Miller 1987, 256). Hubbard gained considerable publicity from this stunt, and of course never mentioned that the degrees were fraudulent. The roots of such legitimacy claims may go back to the story of Jesus' conversations with the teachers in the temple (Luke 2:41–50).

roles assigned to them by their families, and their decisions to strike out alone for their visions. In struggling with their conflicts, these leaders devised unusual adaptive strategies that resulted in the acquisition of manipulative skills that later inclined them toward leadership roles. These skills built upon the narcissistic orientation to the world and the exceptional talents of the first stage. The prophets of this study were well-placed, by virtue of their detachment, exceptional cognitive abilities, and their need to survive with their narcissism intact, to become excellent students of human behavior. They emerged from this time with powerful manipulative skills, a sense of personal specialness, and exceptional talents, and were driven by unconscious needs to reenact in their daily lives and relationships their early relationships with their primary carer(s) and an accompanying hostility toward those who opposed or refused to be part of these reenactments.

What the developing narcissistic personality really does during incubation is to stay open—in an adolescent sense—for much longer than others. In the same way that teenagers are open, exploring, experimental, hypersensitive, and creative in their approach to life, so charismatic leaders do not emotionally close down in their mid-twenties. For many people, if one meets them at twenty-five, one can predict what they will be like at fifty-five. But prophets stay open and searching; their role experimentation continues; life retains its vividness, its ardor, and its mythic qualities, its passion and its frontier mentality, its paradoxical sense of pregnant pursuit. This may be a failure or a triumph, but if one does this, one may discover new resources in later life. At the very least the prophet develops a show-biz personality and a taste for the underworld. Provided he can cope with the problems that the rigid adoption of the adult role usually solves, he may find that with time his thoughts clarify, his energy increases, his moods stabilize, his mastery of the social environment matures, and his philosophy crystallizes. If spirituality is his craft, he now discovers that he has learned as much about it as anyone he meets, and may feel called upon to teach others. Experimental openness is the key. The American leader Da Free John (Avadhoota), while a young man, spent sixteen years experimenting to "find out what works" and develop his following. A follower explained:

What he did was, as he said, he consented to become like the people who came to him, to show them to themselves. And he went and entered into this whole . . . where he submitted himself to every conceivable excess and in the midst of it called the people with him to penetrate that moment, and he'd ask them the questions: Is this God realization? Is this happiness? Does this serve happiness? Does this serve God realization? And so he always drew people back to what he called the great matter, whereas we are always tending to be distracted by the experience itself. And so he did that for sixteen years, and on the basis of that created this extraordinary teaching, and basically a new culture of spiritual realization.

To summarize the incubation period, the narcissistic adult discovers he is different from others—does not belong—and develops a "myth of calling" to explain this difference in an ego-flattering way. In order to realize his calling, he splits his psyche, repressing some parts of himself while developing others, throwing himself totally into his calling and going all out for his vision, ignoring or defeating critics. This leads inevitably to conflict with authorities, through which, by trial and error, the leader develops himself to become an extraordinary being, or burns out in the attempt. A great deal of conscious effort, and much sheer good luck, is needed during this time. The task is immense; it involves the development of conventional career skills, financial and managerial skills, the "giving" orientation, extraordinary communication ability, sophisticated manipulative skills, effective argumentation styles and strategies, appropriate qualifications, knowledge, and lifestyle images, a habit of continuing education, and the kind of ruthless nerve required to carry out the last-ditch "crash-through-or-crash" manipulative strategies that prophets use. If, despite all of this, the world ignores the prophet's narcissistic claims, he becomes extremely frustrated, but he typically responds by pushing himself to new heights of development and achievement. The underlying sense of this period is "I am nothing and I should be everything." A relative of one leader said, "In some way he always felt famous, but the world didn't understand." It is a knife-edge time that determines whether or not the prophet's talents are viable. It may result in transcendent striving or impotent hatred. If the prophet is able to wring some concessions from the world, some acknowledgment of his specialness, he may go on to a prophetic career, the next step of which is awakening.

5

Stage Three | Awakening

I was on that journey and nearly at Damascus when about midday a bright
light from heaven suddenly shone round me. I fell to the ground and heard
a voice saying, "Saul, Saul, why are you persecuting me?" I answered,
"Who are you, Lord?" And he said to me, "I am Jesus the Nazarene and
you are persecuting me." The people with me saw the light but did not
hear his voice as he spoke to me. I said, "What am I to do Lord?" The Lord
answered, "Stand up and go into Damascus, and there you will be told
what you have been appointed to do."

—Acts 22:6–10

Of the twenty leaders studied, thirteen had experienced mystical or
quasi-mystical awakenings prior to adopting their prophetic roles. Of
the remaining seven, there is insufficient evidence for the three deceased leaders; Gary Melsop and Golden Tara are excluded from con-
sideration because they were not interviewed personally (although
the latter claims to be enlightened); and the other two had had odd
experiences that could arguably be considered religious. The nature of
these experiences varied greatly. Not all were felt to be pleasant, and
only about half could really be described as blissful or ecstatic in the
manner of many traditional and popular accounts of mysticism. In
only six instances did God speak to the leader, and even of these only
three contained any kind of revelation. The messages were mostly calls
to action or words of reassurance; the theological details and other
components of what are usually regarded as revelation were worked
out later by the prophets themselves. Many experiences had clear paranormal implications, typically leading to information that the prophets
reported they could not have discovered otherwise or, in one instance,
to finding a large amount of money that was desperately needed.
When retelling their experiences, the leaders recalled feeling ambiva-

lent about them when they occurred. If there was some call to action by God, the most common response was incredulity. If there was also euphoria, mood swings, or paranormal phenomena, the prophet's most likely response was fear that he or she was going mad. The most profound effects concerned how the prophets reordered their lives as a result.

Generally what seemed to happen was that at crucial times in their lives the leaders experienced significant events that gave them new understandings of the nature of ultimate reality and of their destinies. This led them to abandon old roles and behaviors, and adopt new ones. The experiences ranged from the utterly prosaic, in which the prophet reported only that he experienced a profound insight into life or that certain thoughts played on his mind (perhaps as the result of some great coincidence), through fairly modest reports of feeling led by a divine power, to full-blown ecstatic encounters with a deity, complete with hallucinations, divine revelation, and paranormal phenomena. If there was a series of such experiences (which was most common), they tended to build in importance from "pennies dropping" through to transcendent revelations of the nature of reality. The experiences also were consistent with each leader's beliefs about the world; overtly religious leaders typically heard a voice from God, while the less spiritually inclined reported more mundane occurrences that nevertheless provoked them to deep thought.

Much has been written about the religious experience, and this literature will be mentioned only selectively here. The classic study is William James's *Varieties of Religious Experience*, but more relevant here is Anthony Wallace's study of what he called "revitalization movements." Wallace found that almost all of the prophets he studied had received their callings or their visionary insights from mystical experiences (Wallace 1956). Another pioneer, Weston La Barre, argued that many of these mystical experiences had in fact been produced by hallucinogenic drugs (La Barre 1980). It seems that the moral bases of many cultures, perhaps even Christian culture, are derived from shamanic or mystical experiences.

Research by Ralph Hood, based on the work of the philosopher W. T. Stace (Hood 1970, 1975, 1977a, 1977b, 1978; Rosegrant 1976; Hood and Morris 1981; Stace 1960), has verified eight core components of the mystical experience. These are (1) ego loss—in the mystical experience consciousness is retained but one's sense of self is lost, an experience that may be felt as absorption into something greater than one's self, a sense that "I am God"; (2) a unifying quality—all things are experienced as being in some way united, everything is perceived as "the One"; (3) an inner subjective quality—the experience of all things as being aware, alive, conscious at some level; (4) timelessness and spacelessness—the concepts of time and space seem to become meaningless, time seems to stop, and the mystic joins with the universe eternal; (5) a noetic quality—one is convinced that the experience contains valid knowledge, *Ultimate Truth!*, that one knows *the All*—not every little thing, but the great Truth beyond; (6) ineffability—the conviction that words cannot convey the nature of the experience, which is in some way beyond language; (7) ecstasy—the experience is intense and usually pleasurable, although some reports are ambiguous and a few express agony, such as "I felt as if I were being torn apart" and "I could not stand it anymore"; and (8) sacredness—the experience is sensed as inherently sacred, and feelings of mystery, awe, and reverence overcome the mystic.

Hood has since shown that these core components reduce to two main factors. The first is an intense experience, not essentially religious and not necessarily ecstatic; this is the pure physical and emotional sensation. The second factor is that of interpretation, and it is influenced by one's life history and expectations. The mystic may have a profound, intense experience, which he then interprets as true, sacred, ecstatic, a gift from God, and so forth. Without this act of interpretation the religious experience might be viewed as something quite different, even frightening. The factor of interpretation is crucial, for agnostics and atheists also have extraordinary experiences but do not interpret them as religious. Stace discusses these as "borderline cases" (Stace 1960), sociologist Peter Berger has written of them (Berger 1969), and Bertrand Russell recalls one in his autobiography (Russell 1967–69, 148–49). Friedrich Nietzsche has left a good account:

If one had the slightest trace of superstition left in one it would hardly be possible to set aside the idea that one is the incarnation, mouthpiece, and medium of almighty powers. The idea of revelation, in the sense that something suddenly and with unspeakable certainty and purity becomes visible, audible, something that profoundly convulses and upsets one, simply describes the fact. One hears—one does not seek; one takes—one does not ask who gives; a thought suddenly flashes up like lightning, it comes of necessity and unfalteringly formed—I have never had a choice in the matter. One is seized by an ecstasy, whose fearful tension is sometimes relieved in a storm of tears, while one's steps now involuntarily rush along, now involuntarily lag. . . . Everything is in the highest degree involuntary but takes place as if in a tempest of freedom, of absoluteness, of power and divinity. (Nietzsche 1961, 19–20).

These unusual reports alert us to be cautious when studying awakening. For there is a "standard model" of mysticism that is assumed by many authors (Bucke 1901; Underhill 1930) and is typified by the story of St. Paul (quoted above), but that may in fact be quite rare. In this model, awakening is a seen as a sudden, unprecedented, once-in-a-lifetime, total, and permanent transformation of the person wrought by supernatural means. But the accounts in this study differed from the standard model on at least a dozen points. Arnold Harper's conversion to Christianity is an example.

At twenty-one, Arnold's life centered on parties, booze, and sport, but he began to change after his brother was killed. His brother had been living the same kind of "sinful" life he was, and had even said one night, "Arnold, I'm going to change, I'm going to give this all up." Arnold had set a standard for himself that, for all his sinfulness, he hadn't broken, but he feared that his brother had. He had had to rescue his brother from trouble recently, and afterward his brother had written a poem that predicted his death. Arnold thought very deeply about that, but he kept on living the same way.

Arnold now found himself getting depressed. He was bored with going to dances every night of the week, and he began brooding about his life. He noticed how his friends' families, who seemed to be so happy on the outside, often argued and fought, although they tried to hide their quarrels. There seemed to be no happy families. He wondered, "What's my life going to be like? If I get married, we'll have some happiness, we'll have some sorrows, we'll have some children, some will live and some will die, they'll get married, they'll go away, they'll leave me and my wife will die and leave me, or I'll die and leave her, and after we've worked all our life for a home or something, we're gonna die and leave it. If this is life, there's got to be more to it than that." He felt that most people's lives were a sham of unhappiness and dishonesty, but he also felt unable or unwilling to change his own life. He described his feelings in the words of the Paul Robeson song "Old Man River"

—*tired of living and scared of dying*—but added, "*If you'd seen me, you'd have thought I was enjoying life to the very full.*"

One night as he lay in bed, suddenly, like something booming inside him there came a voice: "*I want you to be my minister!*" He was astonished and confused. He asked, "*Who's that? Who? What?*" The only idea he had of a minister was of a preacher. When he pictured himself like that, he felt ridiculous, but the voice seemed to demand an answer. Arnold had always felt he was fairly level-headed. Now he thought, "*I'm going silly. I'm hearing voices. I must never tell anybody, because if I do, they'll think I'm mad.*" So he kept it to himself, but he couldn't forget how the voice seemed to demand a response. He was afraid to say "*No!*" because it seemed too important, but he also was afraid to say "*Yes.*" Soon his secret began to wear him down, and his friends noticed something happening to him. He had been a bright and happy person, but now he lost weight and became afraid to meet others, and was reluctant to talk.

Next he had a heated argument with a coworker and resigned his job. At the very moment they were arguing, a stranger entered their workshop and asked if they knew of anyone prepared to start up a business in the country. Arnold instantly replied, "*Yes, me.*" So he went to work in a small country town. At first business boomed, but then it slackened. To save money, he asked an aunt who lived in the town, and who had previously offered to board him cheaply, if her offer still stood. He had not accepted it at first because this woman and her family were practicing Christians. "*Do you still want to board me at a pound a week?*" he asked her. "*Arnold,*" she replied, "*I'll board you for nothing.*" Nobody had ever done anything like that for him before. He had always had to battle, but this woman took him into her home, fed him, and even made excuses to her husband for Arnold's lapses when he came home drunk. She told him that she felt that God's hand was on him, and that she had put her faith in him.

This family read Scriptures aloud. One night Arnold overheard them reading about Israel becoming a nation, of how Jerusalem would be given back to Israel, and how the last days would follow soon after. The next week Ben Gurion declared Israel a nation at Tel Aviv, and soon after, Israel was recognized by the United Nations. Arnold was rocked. He began to feel that he was living in the last days. Now he wondered: Perhaps if the Bible was true on those things, it was true on other things, too. He began to worry about how he would be judged.

Then he nearly killed himself playing rugby football. During a hard game he suffered a heart attack and ended up in hospital. Lying in bed, he felt that *his life was falling to pieces. He still had not given the voice his answer, but it had continued to play on his mind. Now he began to believe in God and judgment, to believe that he would have to face up to God, and that because of the kind of person he was, he would be cast out. He was afraid he would die and be damned for eternity.*

One night, while recovering at home, he became delirious. He thought the end had come, that Christ had come back and had taken everyone away. The family he was staying with could not get him back to bed, so they asked him to come to a church meeting with them. He was still very sick, so at the meeting the charge nurse sat on one side and his aunt on the other. Again something happened inside of him. He began to shake so violently that the pews shook. He felt a tearing inside, as if one part of him was saying, "This is what you've been looking for all these years," while another part said, "Don't; you'll lose all your friends and everything will be against you." In the middle of the meeting he collapsed in a heap on the floor. As he lay there, sweating and crying, he made his decision to let everything go for God, to give his whole life for Jesus, and to hold nothing of himself back.

Prior to this, Arnold had been one of the boys, but within a week he was out on the street corners preaching. His drinking mates couldn't accept it, and privately they ridiculed him. But from that moment on, he was at peace with himself. He found a love for spiritual things growing within him. It was not an effort; he didn't have to stop himself from wanting other things, they simply didn't mean anything to him anymore. Within twelve months he was leading a congregation. He found a knowledge and an understanding of life that he never had before. He could give answers to questions about life and God that he had never thought about. This became his new life. He went on from there and never looked back.

It is possible that when scholars analyze reports of religious experiences, they are misled by the sheer drama of the stories and they consider too brief a time span. This is, after all, how these experiences are usually recalled by those who have them, and it results in dramatic, condensed accounts. However some of the leaders in this study had had several such experiences and were able to look back on them over a period of twenty or more years. From their vantage points much of the novelty had faded, and the experiences had become for them merely steps on the road each had traveled. Arnold's story suggests that the "standard model" of mysticism may be refined in the following ways.

1. Awakening is most often a series of interconnected events. Rather than being a single transformative experience, it may really be a sequence of related events, any of which may be powerfully significant to the person, that in fact form an unfolding agenda, no portion of which could really be said to be more important than another. In Arnold's case there were six main events: the death of his brother, God's voice, the meaningful series of coincidences that led him to live in a strange town with Christian relatives, the establishment of Israel, a health crisis, and his final conversion at a church meeting. Arnold saw God's hand in all these events, and around them he wove a fabric of interpretations that led to his prophetic career.

2. Awakening is extended in time. It may not be a discontinuous interruption of the flow of life, nor is it always the neat four-stage process modeled by some theorists with a clear-cut precipitating crisis, a discrete act of surrender, a religious experience, and finally "new life" (Batson and Ventis 1982). Rather, it may be the result of deep struggles that stretch back over years, and of a willed effort to solve personal problems. Arnold's process took over two years to complete. The roots of the mystic experience may lie far back in childhood, and its fruits in the distant future.

3. Awakening readjusts most of one's life concerns. Rather than being solely of a religious nature, awakening encompasses and rearranges all aspects of one's life. It may not even be primarily a religious phenomenon. Arnold's experience took in most of his life concerns—sport, work, health, religion, family relationships, and world events—and one could argue that it was as much about his fears for his health, or his relations with his family, or just his time of life, as it was about his soul. The process may be felt as religious, but it embraces all of one's life—personality, relationships, values, and lifestyle.

4. There are specific triggers for awakening. Ralph Hood found that certain triggers led to mystical experiences. These usually involved sensory deprivation, typically time spent in an isolation tank or alone in the woods or the desert, and a certain style of religious thinking. In addition, stress may be a factor. In one of Hood's experiments, subjects who anticipated great stress but who in fact experienced only mild stress, or who anticipated mild stress but who subsequently experienced great stress, reported experiences similar to mystical states. In this study, four of the leaders reported that their awakenings were

precipitated by the unexpected deaths of people close to them (as in Arnold's story). Others were clearly experiencing a period of crisis following some other major life transition. Four were precipitated by meeting another prophet. There also may be genetic factors that incline some people toward mysticism; Ramakrishna, Ramana Maharshi, and Krishnamurti seem to have had literally dozens of such experiences (Bharati 1976).

5. Rules and practice do not produce awakening. From Arnold's story it is clear that meditation, special diets, ritual practices, and so on are not necessary for awakening. Yet many religions claim a methodology for attaining the state. Daniel Batson has shown that these generally involve drugs, meditation, and reading or chanting sacred texts (Batson and Ventis 1982). Agehananda Bharati has identified the four components of most mystical regimes as withdrawal from society, spiritual work in the form of physical discipline and theological study, celibacy, and a special diet. He has also discussed whether such factors as education, ideology, moral excellence, and so on may lead to awakening. His conclusion is that possibly yoga, psychotherapy, and asceticism *may* lead to it, but that what is most needed is "a certain psychosomatic readiness" involving physique, nutrition, an open-minded experimental attitude, and, for some, such triggers as drugs and ritual copulation (Bharati 1976, 113, 139). None of this guarantees that one will experience awakening, but the mystical experience may come to those who try very hard over a very long period of time (Bharati 1976, 53). The common thread in all of this is an attitude of playful open-mindedness. (It must be noted in passing that while mystics are often affronted when their awakenings are likened to drug experiences, sometimes accounts of drug experiences are more interesting and meaningful to others than accounts of mystical states; Rogo 1984).

6. Awakening is willed. In considering the leaders' awakening experiences within the contexts of their entire lives, it is difficult to avoid concluding that these experiences were in some way fated or willed. Arnold Harper was transformed by an extraordinary series of events that were mostly beyond his conscious control, yet the consistency with which he sought religious interpretations for these events, and the depth of his emotional involvement in them—even leading to suicidal thoughts—is striking. Another person might have been merely puzzled by a series of apparently unrelated and mostly quite

prosaic occurrences, but not Arnold. We all lose loved ones, suffer health crises, witness odd coincidences, and have spiritual insights, yet few of us are driven to become prophets. Although Arnold reacted pragmatically to events as they occurred, and was reluctant to accept them at face value, he also worked painfully and slowly toward the particular interpretation and outcome that transpired.[1] He had to struggle with himself toward a spiritual rebirth. Perhaps, therefore, given the intensity of the struggle and the consistency of his later life, the outcome may have been preordained from the beginning. In short, he became a prophet because he willed himself to. Quite why he willed himself to is another question—perhaps involving a stage of early narcissism, assuming this could be shown to have occurred—but the sheer tenacity of his creative effort shines through.

The possibility that religious awakening may somehow be willed has been discussed by Batson and is consistent with the yogic view that enlightenment may be worked at (Batson and Ventis 1982; Bharati 1976). Heinz Kohut's theory about the "healthy" delusions of heroes, who may be sustained through a crisis by a vision of God, also assumes that some purposive working-through process underlies the hallucinations experienced (Kohut 1985). For Arnold and the other leaders in this study, it is likely that a mind-set of religious theorizing and personal questing had been established a long time prior to awakening. If the specific triggers that overwhelmed Arnold with spiritual significance and precipitated his awakening had not occurred, others probably would have. He was a mystic waiting to happen.

7. Awakening has no ontological significance. Perhaps the biggest mistake we can make about the mystical experience is to take it too seriously. Mystics emerge from their awakenings with insights that they usually believe to be the literal truth. Typically the mystic believes that he alone has the truth, or that the "God" who spoke with him is the only true God, or that his is the only path to salvation. But this cannot be so. Mystics invariably contradict each other, and clearly not all can be right. One seer meets Jesus, another meets Krishna, another meets the Great White Brotherhood or the Void or whatever, each of which is "God" or "the Highest." These beliefs are mere self-serving fancies, and the degree to which the prophet uncritically accepts his vision is a

---

1. Arnold Harper once told me, "When a man talks to God, it's called prayer, but when God talks back, it's called schizophrenia."

measure of his limitations. The danger of the mystical experience is that one may be led into the kind of nonsense attributed to the fourth-century theologian Arian Aetius, who claimed, "I know God as well as He knows Himself" (Otto 1958, 179).

Batson divides religious experiences into creative and noncreative types. The difference between these depends on one's response. A creative awakening results in the mystic's becoming more tentative about his beliefs, more self-critical, and more willing to do the hard work required to grapple with complex moral issues (rather than re-treating to absolute categories of sin and salvation). A noncreative awakening results in the mystic's becoming more rigid and fanatical, less reflective and self-critical, and embracing simplistic answers to complex moral issues (Batson and Ventis 1982; Allport 1950). Hence, awakening has no ontological significance in itself; it is merely a meta-phor of the prophet's mind and a vehicle for personal salvation. (Adolf Hitler had a mystical awakening at Pasewalk Hospital in 1918, follow-ing the defeat of Germany; it led to his decision to enter politics.) Yet it is tempting to think that mystical utterances reveal some great truth if only we could interpret them correctly. Perhaps they do, but only about the mystic who has them; it has been estimated that over fifty million Americans have had some kind of "born again" experience (Robbins 1988, 4).

8. Awakening is not related to morality. In his very influential book *Cosmic Consciousness*, R. M. Bucke argued that the mystical state is an evolutionary development linked to moral progress. According to Bucke, awakening happens only to healthy, moral, intelligent people (mostly men) at the peak of their powers (average age thirty-five). This theory is the secular version of the approach of many religions, which view awakening as signaling some special grace or virtue on the part of the mystic.

This is unlikely to be the case among the leaders studied herein. Several had been involved in various unethical acts, and during the time of the study three were convicted of sexual improprieties. It seems, therefore, that awakening is unrelated to morality. On this Bhar-ati says, "The mystic who was a stinker before he had [the mystical experience] remains a stinker, socially speaking, after the experience" (Bharati 1976, 53); awakening may be experienced by anyone, "high-caste, low-caste, dog eaters, nay, even women as the Bhagavadgita charmingly puts it" (Bharati 1976, 20, 65). Bharati scorns mystics who would be world leaders and reformers, pointing out that their reports are often antisocial, self-indulgent, artificial, and paranoid (Bharati 1976, 87–88). Most good people don't have mystical experiences, and many who do have them are not especially good people. It also is hard to see how morality is involved for those prophets who, if they can be believed, experience some kind of awakening as young as age three (Harrell 1975, 28).

When prophets claim that they experienced mystical awakenings in childhood, they usually imply that this indicates some special calling and, hence, some moral excellence. While this may be possible, it seems unlikely. Of all the leaders in this study, only one claimed to have had an awakening experience in childhood, and he had for many years been thoroughly immersed in Hinduism, where these claims are part of spiritual lore; in India no self-respecting guru would fail to have had what Eliza Butler has called "signs and portents at birth" (Butler 1948). When the leaders were asked questions such as "When did you first realize that you were different from others?" and "What have been the main turning points of your life?" only this one leader spontaneously mentioned such events during childhood. In fact, many people can recall uncanny occurrences during childhood when their minds were much more open, fluid, and suggestible than in adulthood, but childhood memory is very unreliable. To selectively recall these events and then to retrospectively interpret them as having religious significance may serve the needs of the moment, but it distorts the truth. This notion of being marked from birth for a future shamanistic or mystical career sits well within a supernaturalistic worldview, but it may be more mythic than factual.

9. Awakening solves some problems yet causes others. Arnold Harper was at first reluctant to become a minister because he could see the life it meant for him. Not only would he have to change his lifestyle in ways he would have preferred not to, but he would also have to live without the comforts and security of the good life. Perhaps even that would have been worth the price if it had brought some relief from the problems besetting him. But he would also have to carry out an awesome task—to do God's work—and to be responsible to Him alone. It is no wonder that he hesitated. Like the Old Testament prophets, he cried out, "Why me, Lord?" when called to do His bidding. Arnold struggled with this dilemma for more than two years.

This suggests that the problem-solving perspective on mysticism held by Batson and others may overlook some of the consequences of mystical experiences. While awakening solved some of Arnold's problems, it led to others even more difficult. Kohut suggests that after the struggle of awakening, the mystic goes about his work with a new calm, and it is this calm that allows us to distinguish between the creative response of the mystic and the mania of the psychotic. Perhaps the mystic exchanges an inner turmoil for an outer one, but even this may provide only a short respite from struggle. That awakening may be problematic is implicit in accounts of the lives of many prophets. For example, it seems that L. Ron Hubbard received awakening when he wrote *Excalibur* in 1938, but his failure to find a publisher for this work that, he believed, "would have a greater impact upon people than the Bible" precipitated a long and painful reevaluation of himself. Sometime later he wrote to his wife of "strange forces" he felt stirring within that made him feel aloof and invincible, and of the struggle he faced trying to answer the question "Who am I?" (Miller 1987, 80–81).

10. Awakening is not permanent. In Eastern thought, awakening results in a permanent change such that from then on, the enlightened one dwells in God consciousness. This seems unlikely. Although two of the leaders did claim to be in a permanently enlightened state, they were vague about what they meant by this and hedged their claims so as to excuse some obvious lapses from divinity. One claimed to be able to "contact God at any moment," but added that he chose not to at certain times in order to learn something important, even if this meant making a costly mistake. The other claimed to be "permanently high on truth" but asked, "What is truth?" Other leaders frankly admitted that their awakenings had receded, and some were even puzzled at the suggestion that it should be any other way. They never felt that this lessened their credibility; it was just the way things were. One explained that nobody could remain in that state for long—it was too arduous—and he scoffed at tales of mystics living in the state for weeks or months at a time. For some, awakening had occurred several times in their lives, and they were able to make comparisons. Some awakenings had been more personally meaningful than others, and some had felt incomplete in some way. But it was clear that none of the leaders was in any kind of permanently altered state.

11. There is no hierarchy of awakened states. Implicit in much of the literature about mysticism is the belief that there is a ladder of progressively more lofty and elevated states of awakening; that there

is an "upward path" wherein certain "levels" are "higher" than others. While some of the leaders assumed this, they were unable to be very precise on the subject and it was impossible to discern any elevation or progression in any of the descriptions given; they seemed to be equally real and rooted firmly in the circumstances and being of the leaders concerned. In fact, the more elevated the claim, the less credible it seemed; Arnold's frank account rings true, whereas those of some others do not.

Of well-known modern mystics, Maharishi Mahesh Yogi has listed seven ascending stages of consciousness through which disciples are supposed to pass. Similarly, Avadhoota has spoken of having "gone beyond" the consciousness of "only God" into an even more cosmic realm. However, John Wren-Lewis, a scientist who has devoted much of his life to investigating mysticism and who is fortunate in that he has experienced altered states himself, interprets these utterances differently (Wren-Lewis 1991). To him there is no ascending path, merely the same phenomenon viewed differently from different per-spectives and at different times in one's life. There is, of course, much to be gained by a leader who one-ups his competition in the spiritual marketplace by claiming to be more enlightened than they. Criticism may be dismissed by saying that the critics don't know what they are talking about because they haven't "gotten that far" yet. But it is likely that those who claim to have experienced ever more advanced mystical states do so in order to recruit and bamboozle followers rather than to aid spiritual understanding.

12. Awakening is less important than is usually thought. Because of the points listed above, it seems likely that awakening is much less important in the lives of prophets than is often assumed. It is mysteri-ous and exciting, but it is solely a psychological phenomenon. Even in religious terms it was not seen by the prophets in this study as the only —or even the best—spiritual reference point. They tended to regard awakening as remarkable but incidental to their development. Further, given the life histories of these leaders, their experiences were probably of fairly minor psychological importance to them. Arnold reported that God had spoken to him only three times, and two of these times had been unrelated to his unfolding prophetic career, although in one of them God led him to his future wife. Yet the thrust of Arnold's life was toward service to God, and the main source of his inspiration, after his initial awakening, was Bible study and service to others. He

relied on God for opportunities and a favorable climate for success rather than for explicit instructions or revelations. In short, Arnold was exactly the kind of person to have religious experiences—if he hadn't had them, it would have been surprising—but they were not the source of his energy or vision.

• • •

Critical biographies of prophets (as distinct from hagiographies) suggest that awakening is a willed creative effort that results as much in the beginning of a new and problematic stage of development as in the resolution of what has gone before. Many prophets suffer major reversals of fortune after their initial religious experiences; adaptation to their new visions involves long periods of readjustment to the world (see for examples the studies of J. H. Noyes and Kathryn Kuhlman: Thomas 1977; Buckingham 1976). Like most human behaviors, awakening is fraught with error. In the spiritual quest there may be many false starts, aborted attempts, and quite mundane experiences that teach one more than any hallucinatory ecstasy ever could.

Daniel Batson likens mysticism to creative insight in which a cognitive "gestalt switch" occurs in the way the person views the world (Batson and Ventis 1982). Hence the mystical experience is a special kind of creative act with four stages. In the first—preparation—some life problem that the mystic has been unable to solve leads to a deep personal crisis that is seen as basically of a religious nature. In the second stage—surrender—the exhausted mystic gives up and relaxes his conscious problem-solving efforts. This allows the unconscious mind to grapple with the problem. Now a different kind of "thinking" (if it can still be called that) comes into play. It is symbolic, involving strange images, rhythms, emotions, and body tones, mostly occurring out of awareness. This "primary process" thought now grapples with the problem. In the third stage—illumination—these unconscious images, feelings, and symbols suddenly spring into consciousness, perhaps as a hallucination in which the mystic hears the voice of God telling him what to do. Or the answer may be less direct—a striking dream, perhaps, or a profound moment of self-transcendence, insight, and ecstasy. In this way a resolution of the problem appears. In the final stage—verification—the solution is tested in real life. Hence the fourth stage is a time of sorting the false from the true.

Like Batson, Kohut sees the mystical experience as a creative self-transformation resulting from a courageous act of will—enacted at depth—in which symbols of omnipotence are used to sustain one through an exhausting, fearful creative effort (Kohut 1985, 5–50). Kohut studied lone German resisters to the Nazis during World War II and found that many of these sanest and bravest of men and women had hallucinatory experiences of God that sustained them through their ordeals. Kohut concluded that the ability to have these "pathological" states should be seen as one of the accomplishments of healthy functioning, rather than as neurotic or regressive.

Hence it is likely that the awakening of the prophet represents the culmination of a long struggle to solve deep personal conflicts, seen in religious terms as a quest for God realization. Following the original flame—the agenda of the infantile self—through its many and varied recastings and transformations in childhood, adolescence, and adulthood, the archaic inspiration emerges at last triumphant and transcendent. The mystic now rediscovers his self in a special way—as one of the leaders told me, "No one else can know me as God knows me"—and from this discovery taps a tremendous reservoir of energy and confidence.

The leaders' creative achievements, and the energy spent gaining them, probably added to their later appeal. They were intelligent, pragmatic men and women, natural questioners, and the insights they reached were their own, discovered through intense struggles. Having experienced the truth of their discoveries, they gave themselves over completely to them in what Batson has called "New Life" (Batson and Ventis 1982). Unable to accept conventional values, they worked hard to find other truths. Having found them, they now had far more certitude than do those who have not personally experienced the reality of their values, who have accepted uncritically the conventional beliefs of society. The leaders' deeper knowing, the confidence that was gained as a result of their successful quests for truth, shone out to others as a beacon and became the base for their subsequent charismatic appeal.

In addition to the energy released and the confidence and certitude gained, a new coherence of the personality and focus of attention emerge as a result of awakening. Previously isolated aspects of one's self become integrated around the central organizing principle—the adoption of the prophetic role—and disconnected bits of knowledge now become organized into a systematic view of the world. This new consciousness is grafted onto what remains of the old self and worldview, and the whole is streamlined into an efficient unit and suffused by the energy released. Perhaps a close parallel lies in the difference between the self-taught person and the formally trained scholar. The autodidact's knowledge may be just facts, whereas the scholar's knowledge is a tool. The self-taught person may know more, yet be unable to apply that knowledge systematically. After awakening, the prophet sees into the heart of things with a clearer eye than before, although he may remain limited intellectually. And what is seen most clearly is the path ahead, his mission.

6

Stage Four | Mission

The hidden purpose of the charismatic group is not to "succeed" but to experience itself.

—Charles Lindholm
Charisma

A charismatic prophet at the height of his power is an awesome figure whom anyone may follow if the conditions are right. At this time the prophet heads an organization committed to the dissemination of his or her teaching, and is acknowledged by the followers as the source of their ultimate good. The leader is able to demonstrate on a daily basis his extraordinary abilities, which he has developed as a result of the stages that have gone before. This "mission" stage is most commonly described as charismatic leadership.

Much has been written about this part of the prophet's life. There are tales of miraculous deeds and wisdom teaching as seen through the eyes of the followers. But what is seldom understood is that these stories are often modeled on the events of the life of Jesus. As Eliza Butler has pointed out (Butler 1948), the myth of the magus is the basis for many prophetic legends, and Jesus has been the prototypical magus in the Western world. Further, despite the value of the many excellent insider accounts of cultic life, the Gospels remain among the best descriptions of what daily life in a cult is really like. What the Gospels show is that one of the main functions of the charismatic prophet is to change the lives of his followers. He does this by teaching and by personal example. The daily experience of the followers is of a continuous moral and religious challenge as new teachings are propounded that overturn the old ways.

It is useful to think of charismatic leadership as comprising two

114

components (Hall 1983). The first—charismatic being—includes those aspects of personality that inspire compliance with the leader's will, especially his personal integrity, awareness of others, style of thinking, energy and alertness, lack of inner conflicts, physical appearance, and certain beliefs and attitudes such as his sense of calling (Hall 1983, 63–85). The second component—charismatic action—includes leadership strategies that compel compliance (Hall 1983, 86–100). These include good communication skills, future vision, acting as change agents (risk-taking), and what was described above as the "giving" orientation, an interpersonal style of generosity, warmth, optimism, and inclusiveness.

These attributes support what may be described as the "charismatic claim" and what Christine Olden has described as the "fascinating effect of the narcissistic personality" (Olden 1941). This is the claim, made in every action and aspect of the leader's being, to be the sole source of ultimate good for others. Olden studied an ugly, old, dirty, toothless, vulgar, and uneducated faith healer who was the darling of hundreds of elderly women in Berlin before World War II. Although this man was utterly without finesse or skill of any kind, and had been arrested by the police several times and imprisoned, his charisma attracted the most desperate and vulnerable section of the population through the force of his self-confidence, exhibitionism, and grandiosity. He received huge donations and built communities and churches. Calling himself "Jesus Christ Incarnate" and "Maestro of the Cottage Cheese" (his cure-all for all ailments), he had an appeal that seemed to lie primarily in his evocation in the minds of his followers of their own narcissism, which they had sacrificed as children in order to fit in with the world, to become "realistic." Perhaps deep down we all long for that lost early fusion with the mother (Silverman, Lachman, and Milich 1982). When we see someone still behaving in this childlike way, we may become mesmerized and think, "Such was I, before the world got to me." Along with the vision of a better life that such leaders promise, we seek the magic key to childhood that they seem to hold—in all, Paradise (Heinberg 1991).

The leader's charismatic claim comes from a certainty that he or she possesses a special connection to a transcendent power and that others must obey this power. In this study, the sheer audacity of the leaders' claims was striking. It was mostly conveyed by body language, tone of voice, and other paralinguistic cues that cannot be easily described, but some anecdotes may carry the flavor. For example, one of the questions asked sought the leaders' responses to their "shadow" or "false self." But no leader acknowledged that he had such an aspect to his personality. Most of the leaders also claimed to *really know* who they were in a special way quite different from how others know themselves. One leader fixed the interviewer with his eye, then leaned back and gloated, "Look. No fear. Whenever you look in anyone else's eyes, you'll see fear. But not me." Another asserted, "See, the trip is, everyone knows who they are but very few people claim it. . . . I know who I am." When a third was asked, "What is your deepest fear?" he answered, "My deepest fear is that people [don't] listen [to me] . . . it means that they become a total failure. . . . 'Cause I'm safe. I'm safe because what I do, I do for the good of them."

This stark totalism of the prophets' claims, what Heinz Kohut has called their all-or-nothing streak (Kohut 1976, 404), often involved a confrontational either/or choice presented to the followers. One leader, after recruiting a following for a communal lifestyle, blithely announced one day:

> You're all forgetting one thing. . . . None of you would be here if it wasn't for me. If any of you leave, the rest of us can still carry on. But without me this place will collapse. So I'm going to have the final say.

Another gave a slightly less bald account.

> I was determined that I was going to lead . . . I was determined that I was going to handle the finance . . . I was determined that I was going to have authority. . . . I said to the brethren, "I'm going to confront this. I'm gonna handle it, and if you can't trust me with that, you can't trust me with your souls. That's the way it's going to be."

Although some followers abandoned their leaders after these claims were made, others became even more devoted and inspired. The fascinating effect of these total claims—implicitly claims to be the sole source of ultimate good for others—while based in part on successful past leadership, also seemed to be related to enduring themes of faith, hope, and love in the followers' hearts.

Faith was aroused when the followers began to wonder "Can this be true?" "Just how far can this person carry this?" "Can he really produce the goods?" "What will happen if he fails?" There were two aspects to this: the sheer, audience appeal of watching someone on the knife edge (Will he? Won't he?) and the inner confusion experienced when encountering a charismatic claim, especially the concern that "If I accept this claim, what are the implications for the rest of my life?"

Hope was aroused in wishes and thoughts such as "Please God, let this be true" and "Dare I believe?" Hope has been mentioned by some philosophers and theologians as the underpinning of the utopian impulse, and perhaps also of religion itself (Bloch 1986; Kung 1974). Hope constitutes the core of our restlessness, a yearning for the better life. As Augustine put it, "The heart will never rest until it rests in thee." Anyone may sense this latent hopefulness among his own responses when encountering a charismatic prophet with values akin to his own.

Love arose with reflective wonder and awe in the face of the charismatic claim, and it led to what Kurt Wolff has called "cognitive love," the suspension of all prior beliefs in a moment of surrender (Wolff 1976). This is a complicated state of light and dark. There is pain and a sense of loss, of "This nearly was mine" and "Such was I before the world got to me," of sadness and perhaps even envy and resentment. But there is joy also, for in the extreme narcissism of the leader we find we can reconnect with our own long-abandoned narcissism. We meet one who defines his self in his own terms, who lives by his own rules, as we ourselves once did, at least to a far greater degree than we do now. Childlike wonder is rekindled, wonder at what might have been. In that instant the golden gate of childhood swings momentarily ajar, and we sense that the prophet is one who is still, in some fundamental sense, at play in paradise, as we ourselves once were.

After affirming the charismatic claim, the followers' feelings about the leader are never again straightforward. A mixture of love and hate, envy and fear, trust and suspicion is never far from the surface. Every meeting may become a test of the leader's claim. If the leader makes a mistake, there is outrage and glee, a sense of loss as well as a defense that "I always knew he wasn't for real." The fascinating effect of the charismatic prophet at the height of his powers is complex and deep, touching on primal fears and desires. The religious impulse is colored by psychological impulses. Of course, many people who meet a prophet remain unmoved or are repelled. Yet others respond by giving up all they have in order to follow. Each follower is reacting to his own unique combination of narcissistic yearning and the natural, legitimate human response to enduring transcendent values. But there are also good reasons why potential followers may reject the charismatic claim. They may have different values, and thus the leader's message may seem so alien that they reject it. Or their life situations may prevent them from getting involved. Some may fail to be fascinated, aroused to hope, or moved to reflective wonder because of some limitation in their selves. As Marlow in Joseph Conrad's *Heart of Darkness* puts it, "A fool is always safe," meaning that the allure of charismatic enthusiasm cannot tempt the person too blind or too stupid to recognize what it awakens within him—that is, one who is unaware of his own depths (Coles 1989, 59).

Once the claim is made and the fascinating effect occurs, the prophet recruits a following and reaches the apex of his development—prophetic leadership. Most of the leaders in this study had experienced leadership before, but prophetic leadership is different; it is "transformational" rather than merely "transactional" (House, Woycke, and Fodor 1988). That is, it is based on duty to the highest good rather than on personal gain. Some of the techniques of social manipulation that the leaders developed in their earlier years may be useful in the short term, but converting these into an enduring leadership style is not easy. The literature on charismatic movements abounds with examples of powerful, inspirational prophetic figures who were unable to sustain their initial momentum and whose movements collapsed due to failures of leadership (Melton 1987).

For some of the leaders in this study the mission phase did not start clearly. They made several false starts, mostly because of external factors such as opposition from secular authorities that resulted in the abandoning of some plans and the redirection of their movements. One group was forced to wait for seven years before it could live communally on its property because of town-planning opposition. This necessitated a compromise by the leader. Hence, making the charismatic claim is one thing, getting a mission up and running is another, and maintaining it over many years of hardship and adversity calls for a special set of skills. Sometimes it may be best to abandon one mission and begin again elsewhere.

Also, the concerns of leadership change as the followers increase in number. In the small groups of this study the leaders focused on the mundane issues of domestic life and work. Like Jesus of the Gospels, a meal or a fireside chat, tending the sick or helping with the children became an opportunity to demonstrate their teachings in a practical, intimate way. These occasions also provided material for subsequent sermonizing. But in the large, wealthy, international religious and commercial empires, the leaders had more impersonal relationships with their followers. They communicated mostly on the level of dogma and through books and tapes. The popular association of esoteric teachings with cult leaders probably derives from these famous figures, whereas the leaders in this study engaged in more mundane activities.[1] It may have been the interviewer's presence that led them to focus as often as they did on intellectual, theoretical, or theological issues in attempting to explain themselves. Mostly their conversations were simple and geared toward practical matters, and it was the leaders' sense of mission, personal warmth, and qualities of being that were the main inspiration for the followers.

At this stage of the movement the leader's focus is on the individual followers and their welfare. A common strategy used by many of the leaders to manage this phase was described by Arnold Harper:

> I'll tell you the secret of running a community: keep the women happy. If a man is unhappy or resentful about something, he'll go quiet and wait for something to change. If it's work, then he'll get his satisfactions from home; if it's home, then he'll lose himself in his work. And you can pick it out and go and ask him, "Well, what's wrong?" But if a woman is unhappy, she'll criticize and undermine and pick away at things, and by the time you've worked out that there's something she's not happy about, she's spread it around and there's another half a dozen involved and her husband's up in arms and the place isn't working—and goodness knows, it may be only a little thing. With the men you can sort it out as it happens, but with women you've got to give them what they want before they ask for it. If the women are happy, the men will be happy, . . . if they aren't, the whole place starts to fall apart.

Some variant of this philosophy was practiced by most of the leaders. It need not be interpreted as thoughtless chauvinism. Rather, it seems to have been a deliberate strategy for the management of a charismatic community. The leaders placed great store on traditional

1. Actually, Reverend William Hart did use religious ritual and flamboyant style. Unfortunately, the data are insufficient to explain quite how or why he did so (although his theological justifications are many).

feminine concerns, that is, children, relationships, health, and the home. By seeing that daily life was secure and pleasant, and by valuing highest the virtues of family life and work, the prophets ensured their leadership among the majority of their followers.

To achieve this, the leader has to do several things. First, he has to be constantly watchful. Every action of the followers must be observed and assessed, and its meaning in the total scheme of things understood. This is hard work, and there is little time for relaxation or complacency. Second, the prophet has to oversee everything. If the leader is male, then he must understand the woman's world of children and domestic life as well as being able to direct the men. He must constantly project an image of boundlessness and unlimited possibility. He must meet all on their home territory. (Female leaders usually appoint a male lieutenant to this role in order to avoid power struggles with men.) Third, the leader must arrange the group's priorities so as to point to enduring transcendent values. This means—effectively— women and children first. Last, the leader must, in all things, communicate love. The followers scrutinize the prophet's every move, and although some do this blindly, enough do it critically to spot any pretenses or duplicity. When the leader gives way to anger or intemperance, he may be judged severely. In time a legend of what the prophet is "really" like develops among the long-term followers, some of whom come to see him in fairly realistic terms. The leader is allowed to be human—but not *too* human—only so long as he successfully guides the group, and this means that he must communicate love in everything he does.

In the mission stage the leader is driven by a purpose that is no longer personal but interpersonal and organizational. In all the preceding stages only his own salvation has been at stake. Now he must take responsibility for the welfare of others in the midst of large-scale social forces mostly beyond his control. If he succeeds, it is by focusing on the enduring realities of the followers' lives—their relationships, children, work, and practical concerns—and by a kind of pragmatic opportunism with regard to management and the accumulation of wealth. Rather than constantly inspiring the followers with a transcendent vision—which the leader nevertheless frequently does—his main effectiveness comes from getting people's lives working for them in a practical manner. The followers' loyalties are gained from the practical effects the prophet has on their lives. Contrary to popular stereotypes of cult leaders as aloof fanatics, it was the practicality of the prophets in this study that was most striking. They were warm, down-to-earth, pragmatic, and above all, caring leaders. One met his death in a car crash on his way to seek a home for a young person who needed a refuge. They had the ability to encourage their followers to grow in areas that the followers had not known they were capable of. One woman told me, "He never lets you believe you can't do it."

Yet although the prophet's leadership rests mostly on love and practical guidance, he cannot avoid power struggles and petty politics. He must become as Machiavellian as any other successful leader. The public face of such leadership is of fanaticism and manipulativeness, whereas the followers see mostly love, but the reality may be an endless, lonely struggle. For this the leader pays a price, as Leo Haley confided:

Leaders are people who suffer a great deal. Whether you be the leader of a group, of a corporation, or you be the prime minister . . . they suffer a lot and they got to be strong . . . they got to be vibrant, they got to be tolerant . . . and they got to be in control all the time of themselves. . . . Leaders are frustrated people . . . and when the time comes and you are frustrated and you've got to go and make a decision and do things, that is when you've got to call upon that strength to make you deal with things. You can't sort of give way to weakness . . . [and] that strength can only come from one person, from one source, and that is God . . . if you don't have God, then you're not a leader. . . . People are gonna hate your guts, especially when you speak the truth. . . . You need strength, but the single most important thing is you have to be positive and you can't make mistakes. . . . If you make major mistakes, you're gonna just lose everything. . . . At all times it's gotta be right . . . you don't move until you are 100 percent sure that this is right. . . . And people tend to look at the things that're bad rather than the things that are good. . . . There's always someone in the group who . . . becomes jealous. Now what he's gonna do is try, if possible, to organize a group around him, and it becomes a faction. Now there's something that I've always feared, probably because I've seen it every day, and I have to deal with it every day. . . . It's always a problem . . . you always find people who are gonna disrupt and try and prevent progress. And that is something I fear.

The prophet draws his strength from God or, in Kohut's terminology, images of omnipotence (Kohut 1985). Despite this, he is under constant pressure from his followers and he risks becoming preoccupied with issues of power. He may be tempted to bend his teaching to self-serving ends, subordinating his vision to his need for control. The prophet is accused of being power-mad, but this is not quite so. Rather, power is necessary to realize his divine vision, which may be narcissistic at base, but in itself power holds little interest for him.

This description of the mission stage has focused on charismatic being and charismatic action. But the quotation from Charles Lindholm that heads this chapter points to something much more dramatic, that is, to a particular experience peculiar to the charismatic group that is more important to the members than their declared aims. Lindholm suggests that the success or failure of the group is not what is most important; success and failure are secondary to the intensity of the collective experience (Lindholm 1990, 110). Victor Turner, Emile Durkheim, and Max Weber have also spoken of the extraordinary feeling of communion that charismatic groups generate (Turner 1969, 1974; Durkheim 1915; Weber 1968b; Schmalenbach 1961). This occurs during "charismatic rituals" that they discuss. Lindholm speaks of the "charismatic moment" (Lindholm 1990, 189) when discussing the special experiences that the rituals evoke. Hence the prophet leads a double life, shepherding his followers within a viable and secure organization, and creating within this organization the charismatic rituals that constitute the essence of the group. However, before we can discuss the charismatic moment and charismatic rituals, we must understand something of the followers: who they are and what motivates them. This is the subject of the next chapter.

7

The Followers and Their Quest

Virtually everyone leaves Utopia after a time. The quick and hearty do not necessarily defect early, nor is it always the witless who linger on. One leaves when he has gained what he came for, when his commitment is exhausted, when it is no longer necessary to sort through the breviary of questions that concern his freedom.

—Tom Patton
"Foreword" to W. F. Olin's *Escape from Utopia*

Who are the followers and why do they follow? In Chapter 2 Max Weber's view—that the followers are seeking salvation—and Heinz Kohut's—that they are seeking support for a creative effort—were presented. These claims are compatible if we accept that salvation involves creativity. Neither approach rules out the possibility of other factors influencing the followers' behaviors. Weber also said that the followers are drawn to the leader because of their extraordinary needs, but he is silent on quite what these extraordinary needs are (Camic 1980, 9). This chapter will describe the followers and explore their motives.

Charismatic groups have often been seen as movements of the oppressed, or at least of individuals in crisis who have been shaken loose from traditional values by rapid social change (Cohn 1970; Melton and Moore 1982). This view tends to see the followers as needy, "permanently emotionally scarred," or "incomplete unto themselves" (Post 1986, 684; Hummel 1975, 768). Young people who join cults often do so in order to solve personal problems, what one psychiatrist has called a "desperate detour to growing up" (Levine 1984). Thus joining a charismatic movement is a kind of therapy (and indeed, some studies do show improved mental health among followers; Richardson 1995; Kilbourne and Richardson 1980). But terms like "oppressed" can be hard to define (Jarvie 1964, 162–69; Firth 1965). In fact, the largest survey of communal groups shows, as one of its strongest findings, that people join such groups for a wide variety of reasons, and that they come from all levels of society and comprise pretty much all types of people (Zablocki 1980). Members of cults tend to come from the ranks of the haves rather than the have-nots. They are mostly white, educated, and middle-class. Usually they join when young (ages eighteen to twenty-eight), single, and at some turning point in their lives that society deems proper for making crucial decisions about career, marriage, and religion (Melton and Moore 1982, 29; Berger 1981, 378). In fact, many scholars have dismissed the notion that followers are driven by need, arguing instead that they are motivated by love (Tucker 1968, 735), hope, freedom (Camic 1980, 9–11), and ultimate concerns (Barnes 1978, 2). Others have explained that "the purpose of charisma is to examine the law" (Sennett 1975, 180).

By far the best study of the conversion process is Eileen Barker's *The Making of a Moonie* (Barker 1984). Barker spent years interviewing hundreds of followers of the Reverend Sun Myung Moon and found that apart from a range of small differences in values (mostly in favor of the Moonies), there were no really significant differences between members of the group and nonmembers. Yet even this research focused mostly on negative issues; it queried whether or not the Moonies brainwashed their converts. The underlying assumption of such work is that there may be something wrong with anyone who would join a cult (Barker began by asking, "Why should—*how could*—anyone become a Moonie?" [her emphasis]).

But what if members join for mostly positive reasons? Perhaps—as one scholar has suggested—joiners may be more flexible and adaptable than average (Lifton 1961). In Benjamin Zablocki's study of American communes there were far fewer people from broken homes in communes than in the normal population (Zablocki 1980). And the educational level of the followers of Rajneesh was far greater than most of the rest of the population (Latkin et al. 1987). Although it can be shown that each group attracts subtly different kinds of people (Wuthnow 1976), and that no single generalization applies to them all, many followers may be brave idealists. Those joining a stigmatized group know that their family will probably disapprove, their friends may reject them, and public opinion and the media will ridicule them. Perhaps it takes courage to be a Moonie. And, contrary to the stereotype of cult members as closed-minded fanatics, they are at least open-minded enough to consider joining; most people's minds are utterly—fearfully—closed to the possibility.

As part of this study, the Adjective Checklist (Gough and Heilbrun 1983) was administered to a sample of thirty-one followers chosen to represent ten different charismatic movements. In a related effort, the Adjective Checklist was also administered to over seventy members of a single charismatic group twice, with a year between measures. In both of these studies the followers emerged as so "normal" that the composite profiles appeared quite bland; the subscale scores all fell within two standard deviations from the mean (Oakes 1992). Hence the followers studied herein appear to be fairly representative of the general population, at least as measured by the Adjective Checklist. This parallels other research, which has shown that members of new religious movements are not significantly different from the normal population (Richardson 1995). There are a few studies that reach different conclusions (Galanter 1979, 1980), but this is to be expected. Conversion to a charismatic group is not a universal process (Barker 1984). People join for reasons that differ from person to person, from place to place, and change over time. Sometimes quite normal people behave in unfortunate ways, especially when in a group with a charismatic leader. Nevertheless, despite the inclusion of a few damaged and disturbed members, the negative image of charismatic groups really stems from concerns about the group process and misplaced idealism, rather than from fear of deviates.

Max Weber felt that while charismatic groups may be useful vehicles for change and upward mobility, they may also stifle personal responsibility and create dependency. Some studies seem to support this, although invariably the authors urge caution when interpreting their results (Richardson, Stewart, and Simmonds 1979). It is true that some followers are needy and dependent (as are many nonmembers in ordinary society), but we need to consider the entire life histories of such people. It is not unusual to find followers who have insight into their dependency needs, and who can discuss these if approached sensitively. Such followers are likely to have a goal that they are aiming for, and following a charismatic leader is their strategy for achieving this goal. They may accept their shortcomings in the same way that most of us accept that we are of only average looks and intelligence. They persist in doing the best they can, trying to balance their strengths and weaknesses in pursuit of their goals. Far from responding with blind faith and unquestioning obedience to the leader (Willner 1968, 6–7; Weber 1946), they are quite capable of deserting the leader should their long-term best interests be threatened (Tucker 1968, 736; Balch 1980). Most new religious movements lose their converts almost as fast as they gain them.

In sum, charismatic appeal is too widespread and varied a phenomenon to be reduced to a simple explanation such as that people follow charismatic leaders because of economic distress or personal deficiencies. Rather, joiners may be "yearning for some moral absolute" (Jones and Anservitz 1975, 1104), and in following such a leader "they do not follow him out of fear or monetary inducement, but out of love, passionate devotion, [and] enthusiasm" (Tucker 1968, 735),[1] Charismatic followers join the leader *for* something. The stated aims of the leader and the beliefs of the group are important, but the membership also performs a function for the follower. There is likely to be a deeper agenda for the followers, which may be different in each individual case. Certainly charismatic groups attract some short-term, transient members whose need for the group is brief and who move on fairly soon. But for longer-term members, deeper hopes are likely to be present.

Discussing anyone's deeper motivations is bound to be a speculative exercise, especially when a phenomenon such as charisma is involved. But in this study two questions seemed, time and again, to tap into the followers' deeper agendas: What has been your major change or achievement in your time here [with the leader]? If something happened that forced you to leave the group and [the leader], and you could never return, what would be your most enduring memory? It requires only the modest assumption that what these long-term followers currently have—their lifestyle, security, peace of mind, friendly relations, and so on—is more or less what they joined to get several years before, to show that many of the answers to these two questions were more accurate explanations for their followership than were their automatic recitations of their group's rhetoric. When asked why they joined, members usually say that they joined their group because of some ideal such as salvation, enlightenment, or whatever; they may

1. For a summary of research into the personalities of cult members, see Richardson 1995.

pad this explanation with complex philosophy or psychotheology. The explanation may be true in many, many ways; but when asked what joining had allowed them to achieve, or what leaving the group would mean to them, quite different themes emerged. When followers in this study were asked these questions, their responses revealed agendas that may be characterized as the "great work" each had joined their leader in order to perform. These great works were not consciously expressed as such, and probably did not involve set agendas with timetables and specific goals. Rather, a member's great work is a hope held for future possibilities for a transformation of one's self. It can be deduced retrospectively from the changes that the follower makes in his life after joining the group.

Recall that according to Heinz Kohut, Freud's relationship with Fliess involved (on Freud's part) an opportunistic, dependent, and somewhat ruthless need for a strong figure on whom to lean while engaging in a difficult creative effort. Similarly, many followers, before joining the charismatic group, actively searched for a vehicle for their great work. Some explained that they were searching for people with values similar to their own, to join with in a safe, stable, utopian environment in order to marry and raise children. For others, more clearly therapeutic goals were sought. For a few, nothing less than a complete change in their life course was desired. Either way, some aspect of what Kohut has described as the playing out of the agenda laid down in the infant's nuclear self seems to have been involved (as nearly as can be ascertained; Kohut 1971, 1977). Hence the process of recruitment does not involve the followers being spontaneously swept off their feet by a leader, nor does a group of followers "construct" a leader; leader and followers find each other for their own purposes (Little 1980, 1985).

The great work is discussed in detail in Chapter 8. It occurs at depth and must be distinguished from a simple description of the cultic life of the follower. This latter involves the follower in three relationships: with the leader, with the group, and with the self. The remainder of this chapter will discuss the first two, but it is the followers' relationships with their selves, especially in the pursuit of their great work, that constitutes the core of charismatic involvement.

There seem to be four key themes in the process of the followers' attachment to the leader. Each is characterized by a particular sensibility on the part of the follower, and they form a (somewhat) ordered sequence. The first theme is faith. Faith has been described as the orientation upon which the religious traditions of the world are based (Smith 1962). It is the underlying state that guides the followers' search for a vehicle to express their great work—that is, faith that such a vehicle exists and that the great work is possible (Smith 1979). Many informants spoke of seeking a vague "something" before meeting their leader, a something that would represent to them, or bring them closer to, their ultimate concerns. As one said, "I needed him to tell me what it was I was seeking." This "seekership" culminates in the seekers finding a leader whose values coincide with their own, and who can serve as a vehicle for their great work. The faith that such a leader exists and that one's great work is viable is implied in a positive view of life as a whole.

The second theme is trust. As the seekers get to know the leader, their impression is of someone they feel they can really trust—for the first time in their lives—with everything! The leader is the first person the seekers have ever met whom they feel this way about. Believing that he truly lives for his cause and is someone to whom they can confide their secret thoughts and their deepest fears and hopes, with whom they need never pretend, the followers trust the leader in a way quite unlike the trust one places in friends or family. The followers' first impressions of the leader may be negative or superficial—mistrust of the leader's rhetoric or interest in his sex appeal—but over time it is the leader's integrity that the followers respond to, sensing someone, they believe, who has taken a stand from which he will never—perhaps can never—withdraw.

Courage is the third theme. In time the followers conclude that the leader is someone who lives completely in accord with their ultimate concerns. The prophet is living proof that the divine life is attainable; he makes living one's convictions seem simple and natural. This gives the followers the courage and inspiration to attempt their great works, to live in accordance with their own ultimate concerns. These concerns, since they are similar to the prophet's, presumably are attainable by emulating the prophet's behavior and following his injunctions. The followers yearn to receive instruction (and the leader yearns to instruct), but most of all the followers take heart that what is sought is attainable through effort and courage.

The last of the recurring themes in the attachment process is projection. In continuing contact the followers come to see the prophet as the embodiment of their ultimate concerns, that is, as the exemplar of a sacred lifestyle, the fount of divine truth, or, as Christians put it, God incarnate. A study of the Rajneesh movement has it that "there was a tendency to see him [Rajneesh] as the origin of the love they [the followers] felt rising in themselves" (Gordon 1987, 59). But, as Feuerbach argued, "God" is an illusory reality that represents to people the qualities they regard as ideal (Hinnells 1984, 258). The disciple merely locates these ideal qualities in the person of the prophet through a process that is active and deliberate, albeit mostly out of awareness. Hence follower and leader use each other, each for his own ends. A relationship of symbiosis or codependence, perhaps even of mutual exploitation, is set up. This does not mean that each party is equally responsible for everything the other party does, but it suggests that there is a far greater degree of reciprocity and mutuality involved in the leader-follower relationship than is commonly thought.

To summarize thus far, the followers have great works that they hope to achieve, agendas laid down in their infantile nuclear selves that they hope to express. They actively seek a vehicle for this expression, in faith that such expression is possible. They meet and come to trust the prophet as a suitable vehicle for the expression of their great work. From the leader is drawn the courage needed for a difficult task. Like the analysand who creates a transference neurosis with the analyst, the followers project their ultimate concerns onto the prophet. The prophet is thus little more than a catalyst or a symbol for the followers, who are really having a relationship with their own selves, or with their ultimate concerns, rather than with another person. Of course the leader has an independent existence, which may confound and surprise at times, but the followers are unlikely to think too much about this.

A striking thing about the followers is how little they seek to know about the leader's background. Few ever ask searching questions and critically evaluate the answers. They prefer to let the leader's daily example serve as the testimony of his truth, and hence as a vehicle for their great work. To question too closely would be to disrupt the pleasant flow of here-and-now fusion. The followers are attempting to live their ultimate concerns, to enter into an active, personal relationship with these concerns in daily life. For myriad reasons, life has led them to a point where they need to measure their self against a present God in all His immediacy, not an abstraction or mere routinized charisma.

For the passionate seeker, nothing short of a personal encounter with a great truth seems to satisfy.

This conclusion seems to run counter to the observation that many members of communes and alternative movements join in a time of crisis in their lives, apparently seeking a refuge and a helping hand. Such crises may, however, be the result of a long-standing frustration of the joiner's great work. Yet most people experience crises in their lives without joining cults or communes. Research by family therapist David Kantor into the "critical identity image" may go some way toward resolving this apparent conflict. According to Kantor, the critical identity images one has of oneself are derived from past experience and underlie one's sense of identity. He says that people have only two or three key images for each major dimension of their lives, that is, for their emotional relationships, for their power relations, and for their spiritual-ideological relations (Kantor 1980, 150). He believes that "We are especially open to the formation of new critical identity images during the transition periods that mark development throughout the individual lifecycle" (Kantor 1980, 150). This fits with the facts of conversion to alternative movements in which most joiners convert at transition points in their lives (Melton 1987). What seems to happen is that a transition crisis occurs that demands a reappraisal of the meaning and direction of one's life. Initially there is a narrowing of focus due to stress (Bord 1975, 489), but later there may be an openness to the formation of new critical identity images.[2] For some individuals this openness to new possibilities leads them to join social or religious movements in order to realize the program laid down in infancy in their nuclear self (Kohut 1971, 1977).

Personal and social crises have odd, unpredictable effects. Sometimes people discover strengths they never knew they had. Groups facing threat may generate powerful levels of cohesion that were totally lacking before. Far from individuals becoming less effective during crises, they may improve their performance dramatically. Crises are opportunities, and the really fundamental shifts in our lives take place at major transition points in our development, the "predictable crises of adult life" (Sheehy 1974). Rather than falling into a trap when needy, the converts may be rising to an opportunity they were pre-

---

2. For example, during the incubation stage of the creative process; see Batson and Ventis 1982, 78.

viously unaware of (Singer 1961, 194–95; Wallace 1956, 264–81; Lasswell 1960, 198–99; Redl 1942). Thus the apparent conflict between the notions that (a) the followers join in crisis, seeking refuge, and that (b) the followers join in order to pursue a great work of personal recreation, may disappear if we understand the joiners' lives and motives in all their subtlety and complexity.

The social rewards of belonging to a charismatic group are important. These involve not merely an enlarged social circle and support network, but also fraternity in the spiritual sense. Victor Hugo's epigram "To love another person is to see the face of God" conveys the flavor of this. In a charismatic movement the followers become psychically transparent to each other. An extraordinary demystifying of human behavior occurs. Life is lived quite literally by learning new things each day: about one's friends, one's self, and one's God. Given this learning process, and the need to achieve a great work, it becomes possible to speak of a natural history of the follower's relationship with the group. Six progressive stages of charismatic involvement can be identified. These vary in duration, and not all followers pass through every stage. This is because while every stage is a solution to a problem posed by the previous stage, it also raises new problems. One option is always to abandon involvement with the group (although even this carries a price that may grow greater the more stages the follower has gone through). The stages are discussed below.

The "Arrival" Persona

Having committed himself to the group, the follower embarks upon what amounts to the exploration of another planet. The space, people, politics, customs, timetables, and organization of the group must be understood, and there are many surprises in store. This process is one of enthusiasm, arousal, excitement, and adventure. There is a feeling of "presque-vu," of being almost on the edge of a great discovery. The follower celebrates his arrival, yet is apprehensive of the people he will meet. His mood is positive and accompanies declarations of commitment and euphoria. And for a short while he is the leader's favorite.

In this adventure the protocols of meeting and greeting go much deeper than elsewhere. Probing questions from others seek out the intimate details of the new joiner's family background and spiritual journey—the chain of events that led up to his or her arrival. The superficial chitchat of introductions soon gives way to a much deeper contact, and it is not unusual for newcomers to find themselves the center of a circle of half a dozen members who quietly listen and ask questions about their life history. Problems of mental and physical health, family conflicts, sexual peccadilloes, and other personal failings are spoken of frankly and are seen as necessary stepping-stones on the path to full inclusion in the group. In this the newcomer is measured against the standard of God's forgiveness or equivalent notions, rather than against the norms of the greater society. This early self-disclosure bonds the newcomer to the group (all of whom have been through a similar process) and leads to greater openness and self-disclosure from others.

However, beneath this deeper-than-usual self-disclosure the joiner remains watchful. Secrets that may be judged harshly by the group (despite their ideals) or that may compromise the joiner too much (despite his enthusiasm) are held back. Some thoughts, feelings, and behaviors that the joiner does not wish to disclose are suppressed. These may include sexual desires, laziness, and doubts about the nature of the group or the leader. In sum, there is a joiner role that allows great freedom yet still has some rules, and that both joiners and members enact with their guards half down.

Skills and talents, an appealing personality, sexual attractiveness, or a relationship with another member may be used to ease one's way into the group. However, each of these carries a burden. Engaging personalities risk being revealed as pretenders; the sexually adventurous may find their role empty. The skilled or talented may come to be seen as only their skills or talents. Sooner or later the arrival role must be abandoned and some substance shown. The great work is in part a task of self-confrontation. This factor is a constant in all charismatic groups; the longer one remains, the more deeply one becomes known by others. This is scary, and many followers leave rather than face the prospect. It may be several years before the real person is revealed and allows others to know him or her as he or she knows their own selves. The arrival persona obscures problematic behaviors and eases entry into this process. It displays some depths and points to others. For a very few joiners, what you see is what you get. But for most the arrival persona enables them to retain some comfort in old ways while bonding with the new. The reasons why joiners adopt such personae are the same as for people everywhere—they fear rejection. Only when more realistic relations develop, often through conflict and testing, does one's inner nature show. But for now the new member is on a honeymoon with "God's people."

Popular accounts of the behaviors of new members sometimes paint a very negative picture. Two common stereotypes are of the glazed-eyed, maniacal fanatic, and the cold, aloof, robot. When such behaviors do occur, they are more likely to be the result of personal conflicts—which may have little to do with having joined a new religious movement—than with any brainwashing or traumatizing process (Melton and Moore 1982).

Niche Work

Once the euphoria of membership subsides—usually within about three months—serious work must be done to find one's place in the group. Three niches must be found. The first is the work niche. The charismatic group has mechanisms for fitting new arrivals to undemanding work. Even the talented joiner goes through an initial period of gardening or licking stamps as a kind of ritual humiliation to show that all enter as equals. Some joiners are fit only for menial work, while others have to be either rejected or tried in a variety of jobs until some use is found for them, often doing domestic chores. The new job may raise old conflicts. One may find oneself working alongside people whom one would prefer to have nothing at all to do with, but these are God's people—the chosen few. Also, because the joiner now works for an authoritarian cult, he must accept different standards in work performance, perhaps an unreal perfectionism or a complete contempt for quality. The hardest to accept is the arbitrariness that seeps down from above; a particular piece of work that the follower has labored over becomes—by fiat from above—unnecessary and is abandoned. Members may be routinely switched from one job to another in order to avoid the establishment of little empires and to reinforce that no one is irreplaceable. Somewhere in the middle of all this there is a balance where one is respected for one's skills and contributions, but the path to finding it may be arduous.

Then there is the social niche. Typically, new members join a solidarity group made up of other recent arrivals and some low-status long-term members. They may adopt (or be adopted by) mentors or parent figures, who then serve as guides and protectors. These "young lambs" may go through a phase of fanaticism, seeing the world in terms of black and white. Or they may be irreverent, thumbing their noses at a status they have not yet earned. New members usually begin on the edge of the group and slowly work their way toward the center. In some of the groups studied, however, some joiners had gravitated quickly to the center of the group, usually as a favorite of the leader, spent about a year there, and then left. Quite what was going on for these people is uncertain, but they were extremely socially adroit and impulsive.

The excitement of getting to know a large number of strangers is stressful and leads to inevitable conflicts. Old patterns of behavior reemerge unchanged and affect the new relationships in odd ways. There are some whom the joiner never gets close to, and other friendships may be very short-lived. Some members seem to have values that are the very opposite of what the group is about—Jesus needs his Judas. Others seem coldly judgmental and distant. But it is the sheer loss of power over one's social life that most distresses. The follower realizes that his inner life is no longer his private preserve but is monitored by others according to a standard he doesn't quite understand. He has made considerable sacrifices to join "God's people," who now stand revealed as having all the quirks and failings of the people he left behind.

Last there is a "self" niche. It seems paradoxical that in a group that values honesty, the members spend a lot of their time developing roles, but most do this. No one can live in the moment or be totally open and holy all the time, so a new persona must be developed. In order to fit in, joiners accentuate some aspects of their personalities and suppress others, thus developing a "cult persona." This is a recurring topic in anticult writings (Hassan 1988), and the charges that cults cause personality change have some basis in fact (Richardson 1980). But it is still the follower's personality that is being reshaped, not something alien that is grafted on. One of the joys of leaving the group is that one feels that "at last I can be myself again," by which is meant one's noncult self.

An important reason for developing a cult persona is to manage the dissonance between one's hopes and the reality of life in the cult. During this phase the new recruit sometimes wonders what he has come to, why he does the things he does, and may suspect that beneath his best efforts he is actually behaving in the same ways that he behaved before joining. These behaviors did not produce happiness then; will they now? Sometimes he sees through the personae of others—senior members—and finds that they are not totally happy or enlightened either. Doubts about the long-term agenda of the group may surface. The new member questions some appearances and glimpses a lie, or he may come to be skeptical of the stories he hears, or even finds himself telling stories that are untrue. The new member is not brainwashed, but he or she develops a personality that combines aspects of the former self with the group's expectations, and that manages the tensions of membership. A few followers remain on the edge and never really fit in, either leaving the group after a time or being accepted by others as social isolates whose hearts are in the right place. There are always some old-timers who never make it to the center or who cannot maintain a close relationship with another person. These members gravitate to the newcomers for comfort.

Letdown

After having settled oneself into the group and made all the initial adjustments to membership (this takes at most a year), a period of disillusionment occurs. No longer can times of unhappiness be dismissed as part of the fitting-in process. The follower is now well accepted by others, but old problems remain and salvation or enlightenment seems as elusive as ever. Personal transformation has not occurred. The social life of the group may not satisfy; some members are knaves or fools, and others betray the ideals of the group. The organization itself has grave flaws; members are expected to be honest with each other but dishonest to the outside world (and in time the follower learns that there is not complete honesty within the group either). The leader appears less and less like God's messenger and more like an ordinary human being. But perhaps it is the loss of freedom that most irks, along with the loss of one's prior friends, family, and standard of living; the many compromises and sacrifices that have to be made daily; and the loss of control of one's personal destiny. This is a time when second thoughts dominate. The follower may also engage in a power struggle with the leader. Eventually, if the new member is to remain, it is on the understanding that he is play-ing a part in someone else's game but can bend the play to his own advantage.

Goal Work

At some point the recent arrival makes a decision either to leave the group because his destiny lies elsewhere, or to continue despite his disappointment. If the latter happens, the follower decides that al-though his earlier belief in the leader's perfection and the group's specialness was naive, there nevertheless remains sufficient truth and love adhering to the leader and the group to justify continued member-ship. The follower may explain this by saying something like "Jesus was human, too," or "the leader's failings make him more real to me." The follower believes that in his time of disillusionment, he saw the dark side of the group, but that nevertheless he may still realize his great work there.

The follower now adjusts his cult persona to this new reality. There are as many ways of doing this as there are followers, but what usually happens is that doubts become denied, criticisms are suppressed, and the leader is perceived selectively in order to bolster the image of him that the follower needs. Handy rationalizations are devised to rebut critics, but what the follower is really defending is his own great work and all that goes with it, rather than the integrity of the leader. Devo-teeism and dependence arise as a result of needing the leader for one's great work; by fulfilling the leader's agenda, the follower hopes to fulfil his own. One of L. Ron Hubbard's followers reported that "part of his brilliance was that he motivated you to do extraordinary things" (Miller 1987, 287), and a follower of Chuck Dederich noted that the one unforgivable sin at Synanon was "refusal to change" (W. F. Olin 1980, 210). Hence the followers have much to gain from their coopera-tive efforts with the leader, as does the leader—it has been suggested that Laxmi, a prominent devotee of Rajneesh, was primarily responsi-ble for Rajneesh's success (Milne 1986, 15).

But there is a risk, for the leader may be unworthy of the follower's trust. The follower may compromise himself with the authorities or with loved ones for the leader. This compromise may require greater commitment to justify, with increasingly extreme proclamations of love and the benefits of membership (Kanter 1972). Eventually he may follow the leader so far down a corrupt path that he feels he cannot get off. Now he trusts because he must. This may be what happens in some cult catastrophes; the followers become so compromised by the leader that they have no choice but to do as he says, even down to deceiving themselves.

Outsiders often criticize the extreme commitment of group members. But what is really happening is that leader and followers are conspiring to realize a vision that is falsified daily. For the cult is not paradise, and the leader is not God. Hence the follower is embattled; to squarely confront the many failings of the leader and the group is to call into question one's own great work. Only by daily recommitting himself can the follower continue to work toward his ultimate goal. Each follower works out a secret compromise, acknowledging some things while denying or distorting others. Clearly this is a high-risk strategy that may go awry. In discussions with followers one often senses that in some corner of their hearts they keep a critical eye on the many inconsistencies of the group. Most can reflect on their extremes, such as being led into antisocial behaviors because of their dependence. Sometimes they feel bad about this. Later they might wonder "How could I be so gullible? All the warning signs were there, so why did I ignore them?" Outsiders wonder this, too. What is overlooked is the deeper agenda that the follower joined for, and that required the leader's support to perform. Perhaps, paraphrasing Ernst Kris, we might describe followership as surrender in the service of the ego (Kris 1952); that is, an act that appears to be regressive but is freely willed and somewhat controlled, and that constitutes a temporary strategy in the pursuit of a higher goal.[3]

Success or Failure

When the young woman who joined the cult with an agenda to marry and have children in a loving spiritual environment finally has her husband and child, or when the tired and divorced middle-aged man who joined the group to rediscover his youth remarries, or when the

3. The case for therapeutic regression has been put by Balint (1965) and Winnicott (1960). Wolff (1978) and Gordon (1984) provide supportive perspectives on this interpretation of involvement in alternative movements. Camic (1980, 19) describes the followers' behavior as "altruistic surrender."

teenager who joined her Christian friends to work for God points to actual accomplishments she has achieved, they have succeeded in their great works. Others may achieve the same goals without joining charismatic movements, but this was their way, and now that they have succeeded, they may enjoy the fruits of their efforts. Such psychological rebirthing is one of the main functions of the cult. The key to success is the discovery of one's own strengths, values, and integrity. It involves not so much total transformation or enlightenment—although there may be episodes of both—as hard work in some area of ultimate concern to the follower. By the time the follower achieves success, he will also have gained a prominent place in the group.

But sometimes there is failure; the young woman's husband becomes unloving, or the middle-aged man is unable to maintain the new relationship, or the teenager becomes burned out by her long hours of hard work. Sometimes the failure is not one's own, or deep-seated personal problems may obstruct one's path, or the demands of membership may be too many and severe. There are many reasons for failure—not everyone starts from the same place in life—but often the cause arises from a fear of one's self, for it is one's faith and being that are being tested (see Chapter 8). Group involvement forces the follower to confront unpleasant aspects of his self that he might prefer to deny. At the moment of self-confrontation he may lose his nerve, or deceive himself about who he really is. Trust can be terrifying, especially when it forces the abandonment of cherished self-images; better to distrust and stay safe. In giving up his previous persona, the follower may feel that he is losing his soul. He may prefer to retain the comforting image he had of himself before he joined the group, and to see the prophet as false. This at least lessens the pain, but what has been lost is seldom understood. The hope that one could have it is gone, but life will bring other opportunities.

If there is failure, the follower becomes polarized. He may stay and make another try, but there is likely to be, in the immediate term at least, a sense that not even God can help him. Some who fail become embittered against the leader, blaming him for their loss. Others become even more dependent. They may fall apart emotionally and withdraw to the fringe of the group. Typically such followers seek out the leader on a daily or hourly basis to try to reestablish some sense of their self. Their involvement in the group is now recast in more fluid terms—living in the here and now, taking one day at a time, trusting God and eschewing all aspirations, and whatever will be, will be—for failure ought not to occur in heaven. A fine man in one of the groups studied was divorced twice by women he married there. Each rejection involved a rival and split apart his fledgling family. It seemed as if his great work was doomed; some aspect of him was inherently unfulfilling to women even in this ideal environment. Symbolically, he was unacceptable to the angels in heaven. At his lowest points he returned to his leader for support. The mental gymnastics he put himself through to retain his hope and self-esteem were pathetic, but he clung on rather than forsake his great work. Eventually, after many years of effort, he succeeded.

The deepest dynamics of how individuals mature and grow spiritually are mysterious. Each of us has our black hole, our suicidal thoughts, our mad moments, as well as those times of surrender so mild that we fool even our own inner censor. We mostly live out our raptures and convulsions in silence, for the struggles we speak of are not our real struggles. But charismatic involvement provides a confrontation with one's ultimate concerns. To fail therein leaves one damaged at one's core. Or perhaps it merely reveals an earlier damage of which one was previously unaware, a damage we all share. Perhaps there can be healing there, too.

Leaving

Each of the groups studied had lost far more members than it had retained. And most of their original members had left. On average, less than 20 percent of those who joined, stayed on for more than five years, and fewer still stayed for ten or more years. Ex-members who still felt warmly about the leader were those who had succeeded in their great work. They had used the group for their purposes and moved on at the right time. Success gave them a new appreciation of the leader, gratitude for his help, and also pragmatism about his faults. They no longer needed to believe in him so intensely. Usually by the time they were successful, they had witnessed some of the leader's less savory attributes—his mistakes and excesses. They held few illusions about his nature but retained a fondness. After success they felt restricted by the group and needed new challenges. The commonest pattern was to remain until the next group crisis (charismatic groups have lots of crises) and then move on. Probably they never again joined a charismatic movement.

Embittered ex-members tended to be those who had in some way failed at their great work. They felt conned, that they had been tricked into believing the unbelievable—and indeed some had, although most had contributed to their own miseries. But there is a special pain felt by one who has deliberately chosen to abandon reason to follow another—in deep trust and love—into an unknown darkness, only to fall flat on his face. Typically, when such a follower confronts the leader over this hurt, the leader refuses to bear any responsibility for it, even mocking and rejecting the follower. Perhaps the follower did something unethical for the leader, and in the throes of guilt needs the leader to share the burden. When the leader laughingly admonishes, "Well, you did it, not me," and dresses the tragedy up as a spiritual lesson, the follower feels betrayed—"burned to the bone," as one described it—trust evaporates, and the great work is no longer possible in that situation. Now, rather than seeing the journey as the goal, the follower chooses to leave, blaming the leader when he finds out that the impossible ideal is, after all, impossible. The failed follower leaves when it suits him, sometimes with open hostility toward the group. However, there are shades of success and failure, and even in the most rigid groups there are degrees of membership. Some leave to join another charismatic group. Some leave, then rejoin and go through the previous stages again, and continue on to later stages. Some make several attempts to join a group, several attempts at a goal, each time achieving partial success; and so they come and go, remaining, ambiguously, a part of the group.

Each stage may become a trap. Members may get stuck in one stage and lose themselves. If they don't move on, they become vulnerable to the excesses of the group. If one doesn't find oneself in such a group, then someone else—usually the leader—will possess one. Charismatic groups usually have some members who are stuck at various stages. Leavers are sometimes those who have become stuck and withdraw rather than continue to go round and round. Lacking their old sense of purpose, they may forge a new one by opposing the leader and his group, becoming "career apostates" (Foster 1984b). These are disillusioned ex-followers who battle against their former group, often at great personal cost, by attempting to publicly expose every scandal associated with the group. Fortunately for them, charismatic groups usually have a lot of skeletons in their closets and dirt under their carpets, so the "mission" of the career apostate can become a full-time vocation.

After having spoken with several of these people, none of whom was necessarily "wrong" in his opposition—there genuinely were falsehoods and crimes that needed to be aired—I nevertheless gained the impression that they were driven by some need for absolution. A common refrain ran something like "I . . . was so hoodwinked while in the group that I, too, condoned or took part in these misdeeds." Hence it seems likely that career apostates are trying to make amends and assuage their own guilt through their actions. But that is not all, for there is a particular discovery that people make about themselves in charismatic groups that many find especially hard to accept. It concerns how easily one can sell one's soul, how shallow one's sense of ultimate concerns really is, and how readily one can perform the unspeakable. One ex-member described this:

> I was married, I had four children, my wife and I were relatively happy, so to speak. Then I fell in love with this other woman, a member, and she was also married with kids. It was fantastic sex, I was in a constant lather. Fortunately, she was not available; she had her feet on the ground and there was no way that she was going to leave her family. But what I have to live with is the knowledge that I could have. Everything I'd worked for—my kids, my life—there is a small and shitty part of me that could have swapped it all for sex. I don't like that part of myself at all. . . . I can just see my kids crying, "Daddy, please come home." How close I came. . . .

It is not pleasant to contemplate one's moral frailty. Better to deny it and avoid charisma. The more self-esteem one can place between moral frailty and one's self-image, the safer one feels. Against a background of overall success and achievement, such unpalatable facts may be reduced to insignificance; but if they are associated with some deep failure, they can be especially hard to bear. In waging war against cults and charismatic leaders, career apostates may actually be waging war against themselves.

There is great trauma associated with leaving, even for the successful follower. He has invested his deepest hopes in the leader, and leaving is like another leaving of home. The leaver may never be so close to—so trusted and accepted by—others again, so it is important that he leave with someone with whom he can share his knowledge and experience of the cult. There is a tremendous culture shock of reentry to the outside world, and many leavers enter therapy. Not even wealth and renewed contact with one's family of origin can insulate against this. And most of all, that sense of purpose—the sense of being engaged in something vital and important—is gone. A new direction will appear, but it takes much longer than is comfortable.

Leaving is the natural culmination of joining, though this is less true of messianic groups where successful members often choose to stay. Such groups value truth as the highest ideal, and once they have found the truth, they do not want to stray from it. In contrast, charismatic groups have love as their highest ethic, and because the followers carry that within them, they may be more inclined to leave. Truth is usually felt to be external, embodied in the leader and the group, and to move away from the truth is to move into error. Love is internal. To move away from the group, especially if one takes one's spouse and children, is merely to move away from a particular place and group of people, who may remain as friends.

During involvement the follower experiences a range of extraordinary emotions, some of which are relatively minor but others may be of shattering intensity. He also receives powerful insights into his self and the nature of reality. These are often associated with the many rituals and extraordinary events that punctuate the life of the group, or they may occur through some interaction with the leader, or as part of the follower's great work. The events take place in the context of inspirational leadership, without which they would not occur. For it is the leader who is the main focus of the group, who orchestrates its actions and moods, who carries the burden of responsibility for its success or failure, and it is his direction that largely—though not entirely—permits such moments to occur. Hence the follower's relationship with the leader influences the manner of his departure. For it is the leader who ultimately is left behind, used and abandoned, outgrown. He may protest followers' departures; curse them and predict disaster; attack their relationships, their mental health, their sex lives, their children, and their hopes. The wisest of the followers will accept this stoically, for they never know when they may need him again, but with the success of their great work, he becomes irrelevant. The followers leave him for the same reason they came to him—they have many more lives to live (Thoreau 1983). Few prophets accept this with grace. It was beautifully expressed by a woman ex-member:

I gave him my inner child and every secret thing. I held back nothing.

Life became a quest to reveal every part of myself to him. I said I loved him, but I always knew that there was something missing . . . I blamed myself for that and thought that if I tried really hard, then whatever it was that was missing would fall into place. And slowly I saw that it never would, that this was it, that it would never feel right . . . because he . . . was stuck on being the guru. And that made me realize why I had never really been able to love him. You have to have some return for that to happen, and he never did. That was what was missing, what kept us apart despite all our talk about love. . . . He was a great teacher but a lousy human being. . . . Eventually I got to the point where I could predict what he'd say and do. . . . Still, it was a great game. I learned a lot, I owe him more than he'll ever know—he sure cut the ground away from underneath churchy religion—but as I matured, I left him behind. It took me a while to see that was what was happening. And in a way I'm still a devotee, not of him but of what he stood for. I carry a little Fred inside me to this day. I still ask myself at times, "What would Fred say about this?" It's Fred at his best, and that's how I like to remember him.

8

The Charismatic Moment

It came to pass that Jesus came to a village where a woman named Martha
welcomed him to her home. Her sister Mary sat at the Lord's feet to hear
his word. But Martha was worried about the serving and said to him,
"Lord, don't you care that my sister has left me alone to do all the work?
Tell her then to come and help me." "Martha, Martha," the Lord answered
her, "you are troubled and anxious about many things. But one thing is
needful. Mary has found it and it will not be taken away from her."

—Luke 10:38–42

Whenever we have eye contact with another, we make decisions: to move closer or to keep our distance, to open our heart or to remain closed, to trust or to mistrust, to reveal our true self or to remain in role, to signal "Yes" or to signal "No" to ambiguous possibilities. We make these choices out of awareness and usually forget we have made them. What might it be like to choose "Yes" with such force that one lays open one's entire being, holding back nothing, trusting as one has not trusted since infancy, to another with all his darkness and mystery? Such is the charismatic moment, which Charles Lindholm has described as an ecstatic transcendent experience opposed to the alienation and isolation of the mundane world. He adds:

The paradigm established by Weber and Durkheim, and restated by psychological theory, claims, in fact, that society is based upon a deeply evocative communion of self and other, a communion that offers not reason, but lived vitality. Without this electrifying blurring of boundaries, life no longer has its savour, action is no longer potent, the world becomes colourless and drab. (Lindholm 1990, 189)

The charismatic moment is just such an "electrifying blurring of boundaries." It is basically an experience of love that cleanses and

144

reenergizes. Similar moments may occur naturally at other times throughout life, at transition points such as birth, death, and coming-of-age, during romantic love and creative work. Many societies have devised rituals that echo the shamanic rite and produce such moments. These ceremonies may be as trivial as football matches (Cole 1973) or as profound as the Catholic Mass. Their function is to restate the group's core values and reintegrate the members into a communal bond. In charismatic groups there is also a range of ritualistic practices intended to evoke deep communion, and they, too, range from the shallow to the deep. They make use of natural transitions, especially the transition to membership, and they create an ambience that consistently signals such moments through symbolism associated with clothing, diet, customs, and other aspects of the group's life. They reaffirm the passionate "Yes" that members make on joining. What is distinctive about rituals in charismatic groups, however, is that they are focused upon a single individual—the leader—who is always near the center of the action. Rituals in a charismatic community may be much more intense than elsewhere because the leader's aim is to realize a new revelation rather than merely to restate earlier revelations.

In Humanitas, one of the groups in this study, a central ritual concerned the births of children. Whenever a mother entered labor, all the members of the group gathered together in the main meeting room of the commune to support her and to help the birthing team deliver her baby. The leader presided over the team, which included the medical personnel (doctor, midwife, and assistant), the mother's family (including nonmembers of the commune), and other members of the community with close relationships with the mother or father. Thus the entire commune and some outsiders—up to three hundred persons —participated in most births (the exceptions being births that were problematic in some way). This practice resulted in an increased sense of solidarity, bonding, group cohesion, commitment, and identity among the members. The practice was perceived by visitors and members alike as something special by which the group defined and reaffirmed its central values. One visitor likened the births to "Masai warriors proving their manhood by killing a lion with a spear."

When discussing their particular visions for themselves and their group, the members often referred to these births as demonstrating the essential nature of their ultimate concerns. Other practices, such as regular encounter groups, drug experiences, and even the promiscuity that characterized the group, similarly served to generate charismatic moments of transcendence that members identified as the raison d'être for their joining together. Further, these practices were seen as lying along a continuum of spiritual growth such that certain actions and experiences were seen as "good for your growth," that is, as challenges leading toward spiritual advancement. Members who undertook these challenges were "growthful" and were especially dedicated to the leader, whereas those who avoided such experiences drew the group's disapproval and their ultimate sanction—the label "avoider." In time all of this came to be so personalized to the leader that growthful members were defined as those who did everything the leader said. To be an avoider meant that one was "in a fight" with the leader and, by definition, the group.

Charismatic rituals are the prophet's main creative achievement. At one and the same time the ritual satisfies the leader's narcissistic needs and transforms the followers; the former, by re-creating a world within which the leader is omnipotent, and the latter, by emotionally revitalizing all who participate in it. The rituals lay an emotional and spiritual base for the community. Hence an important task, perhaps the *most* important task, for the prophet during this time is the construction of charismatic rituals. They are his or her framework for the exploration of love and truth. Each is a set of guidelines that allows people to come together and celebrate the mystery that lies between them.

Frank Jansen, the ex-leader of a Pentecostal church in this study, has given a glimpse of the rituals used in his group. He explained how he performed them, the effects, what his motives were, and the underlying psychological dynamics of such practices.

A Pentecostal minister works in two worlds. On the one hand, he's trying to get to the top of the corporate ladder. But on the other hand, the real challenge for him personally, covert and unacknowledged even to himself, is how he is seen by his congregation. He would rather be remembered by history as a great clairvoyant, although that's not a word he'd use, than as chairman of the board. But he can't admit it, to himself even, because his belief system doesn't allow him to acknowledge it. Don't forget that the great man of the church is not the president or accountant, it is the man who bears gifts . . . those who are weak on gifts tend to be good administrators.

Their challenge is always to themselves. In the gifting the personal question is always "Will it work tonight?" And then the question comes . . . "Why did it work tonight when last week, when I staged it with music and so on, . . . it didn't work? . . . For the Pentecostal minister the unction of the Holy Spirit takes him out of himself; it is not he who is speaking, he is "channeling," to use a spiritualist term. In this he can behave aberrantly but define this as sanctioned by God. . . . The divine sanction is required only for situations that are abnormal. There's no question of self-doubt because it's not the self that's speaking.

When I was in a trance, and that's not the right word for a Pentecostal preacher, there was a definite shifting aside of the self. Yet Scripture says that the prophecy is always subject to the prophet. You had a confidence to say things that you didn't really know you were going to say next. In a natural frame of mind I wouldn't have said it. I would have been riddled with self-doubt. . . . We would have moments of this, but we wanted more; they were never enough. But we're asked or expected to be in that state all of the time. Some people believed that had I been in the right spiritual state, I could turn it on at will. But I couldn't.

Revivals stir sexual energies. Where there is a heightened revival, there is a heightened sexuality. . . . [Take] tent evangelists . . . there is a long tradition of parodying the leading charismatic figures as highly sexual people. . . . Almost every Pentecostal minister of note I can think of has had some kind of sexual aberration, mild perhaps, but odd nevertheless. What isn't known is far more interesting and widespread than people realize. It doesn't seem to happen where they have staid and stoic people. . . . [Take] Aimee Semple McPherson: she used sex, preached of the Song of Solomon with seminude blacks and diaphanously clad girls. . . . They use sex, there is a sexual component to their practices and teaching.

Pentecostal ministers are as much performers as preachers. It's nothing to hear of a bunch of them getting together after a meeting to let their hair down at the local motel. And they do all sorts of things, from leaving one of their number without his clothes in the motel pool — harmless stuff like that — to calling up demons and talking to them and things like that. It's a situation of very high energy. But at the time I never felt sexual, although I could easily transform it. I did once . . . at the point of orgasm I've become prophetic. I gave Ann [not her real name] a reading of what it was like to be in her womb. Poor Ann wondered what the hell was happening. There is a prophetic mode. It's the shift of the ego or self. The ego stands aside and the channeling of the message that comes through is free to come through. I had an explicit feeling of being in the womb. I gave a free, spontaneous flow of words, couched in King James English, about her womb. It was like rebirthing but it wasn't. It was just a very detailed description of her womb.

When you are in this mode, your voice changes, all sorts of modulations and so on affect others. Hyperventilation. It affects others and they go into it, too. There's a distinct physiological component to the response. And people then go to churches to get this kind of experience and it becomes meeting dependency.

This account of blurred sexuality and mysticism is similar to one given by David "Moses" Berg, founder of the Children of God (Davis and Davis 1984, 89), albeit with greater self-awareness on Jansen's part. But what is most revealing is that this account shows that the power of the leader is not reliably under his control. There is an unpredictable, experimental element that keeps both the leader and the followers uncertain as to whether or not the spirit will move tonight. Perhaps it is their combined yearning—sincere and hopeful—that produces the charismatic moment. Also, the hint of sexuality in Frank's account reminds us of Max Weber's mention of orgies (Weber 1968b, 273). It is likely that many charismatic groups have a secret inner teaching that includes orgiastic rites at one extreme of the continuum of their rituals. Of course some groups will not feel the need to go all the way, and the members of those who do, are unlikely to speak freely about these practices. In this study most members were extremely open when discussing their personal lives, but at times they showed an almost rehearsed and coordinated avoidance of some aspects of their group's life. There are, however, two sources for such material. One is apostate accounts, and the other is nearby communes or rival groups that follow a given group's progress keenly and often can be counted upon to gossip freely.

The glimpse of a secret, inner doctrine occurs in many religions. For example, the prophet Muhammad, in speaking of the several "degrees" of enlightenment, reserved some of his teachings for the select few who would understand. One of his oldest followers, Abu Hurayrah, once told a junior follower, "I have treasured in my memory two stores of knowledge which I had from the Messenger of God. One of them I have divulged, but if I divulged the other you would cut my throat" (Lings 1986, 327). What could Abu Hurayrah have meant? It is likely that what was involved was some kind of fusion with God. Muhammad spoke of two paradises, the greater of which—Ridwan, or "good pleasure" (Lings 1986, 95)—involved the soul drawing nearer and nearer to God's love until God becomes "the hearing with which he heareth and the sight with which he seeth and the hand with which he graspeth and the foot on which he walketh" (Lings 1986, 328). This is the ultimate state of the soul, but it hardly justifies a cut throat.

Similarly the Mormon prophet Joseph Smith, in a sermon a few months before his death, spoke of his inability and refusal to convey his deepest message to his closest followers: "You never knew my heart; no man knows my history. I cannot tell it. I shall never undertake it; if I had not experienced what I have I should not have known it myself" (Foster 1983, 98). The leaders in this study were asked what they thought of this strange passage. The best answer came from a Rastafarian leader: "I know what that man means. He is a man of God and he is telling his people that they cannot know his heart like God knows it." This poignant response is no doubt partly true, but it still does not resolve the problem: What is so distressing about that which cannot or must not be revealed?

It is likely that what is being referred to here is some secret teaching about the amoral nature of the charismatic experience. "To the pure all things are pure" Paul proclaimed (Titus 1:15), to which Augustine added, "Love and do what you will" (*Oxford Dictionary of Quotations* 1979, 21). Rajneesh said, "Authenticity *is* morality." Overlooking for the moment the fact that such teachings are sometimes used to justify unethical behaviors, the sense is nevertheless of some truth so great, some ecstasy so powerful, that it takes the group beyond normal morality and into a supradivine realm. This is most likely to occur during charismatic rituals that sharpen the otherworldly focus (Durkheim 1915, 381). According to Emile Durkheim, the rituals are awesome and "cause men to lose sight of the distinction separating the licit from the illicit ... [making] it almost necessary to violate the rules which are ordinarily most respected" (Durkheim 1915, 383). He also says:

> The passions released are of such an impetuosity that they can be restrained by nothing. They are so far removed from their ordinary conditions of life, and they are so thoroughly conscious of it, that they feel that they must set themselves outside of and above ordinary morals. ...
> The sexes unite contrarily to the rules governing sexual relations. Men exchange wives with each other. Sometimes even incestuous unions, which in normal times are thought abominable and are severely punished, are ... contracted openly and with impunity. (Durkheim 1965, 247)

Nothing disturbs in this state where "one thing needful" (Luke 10:42; Psalm 23) dispels even the fear of death—not just one's own personal death but also the death of those things that give our lives meaning and that we are prepared to die for, the death of our loved ones and our ultimate concerns, the "death of meaning," in Ernest Becker's sense (Becker 1962). "One thing I ask of the Lord, this is what I seek; that I may dwell in the house of the Lord all the days of my life, to gaze upon the beauty of the Lord, and to seek Him in his temple" (Psalms 27:4).

Therein the lowliest triumph equally with the highest, beyond where good and evil lose their meanings, where the life impulse itself —what Weber calls "pure charisma" and that exists only in originating (Weber 1964, 34)—reconciles all to all. According to Weber, such rituals are rare and usually occur only in the early periods of emergent social movements. Then, the charismatic community is characterized by a belief in the special talents of the leader and the emotional bonding of the followers to him, and an estrangement from the world as a whole. Such pure charisma is based on face-to-face contact, and its nature is inherently creative, revolutionary, and world-rejecting (Schweitzer 1984, 18, 33, 327; Weber 1968a, 1002, 1121, 1123).

In sum, charismatic groups, like all societies, devise rituals that enable their members to experience their depths and restate their central values. These rituals are presided over by the leader. They range from the mild to the profound and are usually more intense than others performed elsewhere. If the stated purpose of the ritual is to worship God or to celebrate some event, its function is to disinhibit the followers and to bind them to the group (Weber 1968b, 273). The most powerful rites may be secretive and orgiastic, may mobilize sexual energies and transport the participants to an amoral realm that violates customary ethical codes and banishes not only the fear of physical death but also fear of the death of meaning—spiritual death. Such total dissolution of the personality produces an eternal "moment" wherein but one thing is needful: to dissolve one's being into the Being of God as mediated by the prophet—the master of the techniques of ecstasy (Eliade 1964).

What is the relevance of the charismatic moment to the great works of the followers? The practices may serve many purposes having to do with social cohesion, identity formation, initiation, boundary maintenance, and so on, but they also perform crucial psychological functions for the members. It seems that such rituals are needed by the followers as proof of the validity of their vision and of the legitimacy of their leader. If one is on a quest, how does one know when one has arrived other than by some sign such as a moment of transcendence? The rites, which may be quite mild most of the time, nevertheless are sufficiently ego-shattering often enough to convince the followers that some great power or spirit genuinely moves among them. Charismatic rituals also provide a yardstick against which the followers may evaluate their being, check their progress toward their goals, measure their spiritual advancement, and test the results of their efforts. These are opportunities for the followers to clear away past resentments and to discover each other anew; to experiment with themselves and each other; to "bring myself up to date on myself," as one woman described it; and to "discover something new about God." Sometimes the rituals reveal stumbling blocks on one's path, blocks that were unknown before and that are opportunities for fresh growth. One follower recalled:

> Shortly after I arrived here, I spent some time alone with Lindsey. We talked and made love, and then he sat me opposite him and told me to just stare into his eyes. We sat like that for about half an hour, and as I watched, his face changed into every wise man and monster I'd ever known or thought about. One minute he was this ageless saint pouring his love out to me; the next, he'd be like some killer in a dark alley. I was completely thrown by that. I wondered what the hell I'd come to, and I began to cry. Then he calmed me down and told me that none of what I'd seen was him, that I'd have to sort through all of that before I would ever really see him. . . . that was what I'd come here for, and when I did, I wouldn't need him anymore.

The rites also provide a background of shared transcendence that sustains when the members face crises; having once met God, it is easier to face the devil. Despite the collective, bonded nature of the group, personal and spiritual growth may be a lonely affair in which one's only resource is one's self—the accumulated result of all one's previous experience. To have seen the light may make the darkness a little less threatening; sorrow, a little less annihilating. The energy released by the rite, the intimacy felt, the stripping away of pretense, the joys and tears, the dignity and humility of shared humanness exposed without defense—all of these purify and regenerate. But even if the rites served no social or psychological function at all, they would still be valued simply for what they are—profound and fulfilling experiences.

Returning now to the followers and their quest, there appear to be three main components to the great work—testing, transcendence, and love—and charismatic moments are closely associated with each part. Concerning the first, the great work has a strong element of being a personal test or trial. It is a confrontation with a god, an enlistment in the great struggle between good and evil, a measuring of oneself against some ultimate standard, or an examination of one's deeper self to see how much is real and how much is illusion. A follower described this as follows: "There's always a challenge in Christianity. And living together always presents a challenge. Every day presents a challenge that I might be showing forth Christ in every situation. It's a very strong challenge. There's always a challenge in Christ."

Whereas significant turning points in life, such as leaving home or the midlife crisis, may precipitate involvement with the group, other life tasks, such as marriage and child rearing, may become vehicles for the test. "Getting married and having children . . . that's been the major turning point of my life, really. But it was just part of giving myself to Christ. I could never have done that if I'd not been saved; I wouldn't have done it. You can't bring children into this world unless you've got God in your heart, and I never had that before."

The test is a leap of faith into the unknown, made possible by trust in the leader. Letting go of one's self-control and taking a risk in the pursuit of an impossible ideal—even daring to believe that the impossible ideal is possible—is the stuff of the test. It has an intensely personal, private significance to the follower, as a devotee of Rajneesh explained: "In the end, I don't think anyone who isn't a disciple, *willing to jump into total emptiness,* will ever understand the whole story. If it could be understood intellectually it would not be what it is" (Gordon 1987, 243; my emphasis).

For some the extremity of the task is important, portending great things to come and providing an opportunity to demonstrate to others some depth of their soul:

If he told me to take cyanide, I'd have to say to myself, "Well, he's never put me crook before." I don't believe it will ever happen, of course, but who knows, in that situation? And I don't think I'd ever take it, but again, who knows? But the fact is, he's never put me crook yet. People say, outsiders, this following a guru, it's all a bit ridiculous. And I might tend to agree with them. But I've no doubt my life works much better when I'm around him than when I'm not. I can't explain it, I don't know what he does, and I sometimes doubt if he does either. I think he acts like a catalyst. Just his mere presence provides change. But there's no doubt about the effect on me and my life.

One way of understanding the test is to see it as part of the creative process. As described by Graham Wallas (Wallas 1926), there are four stages to this. In the first—preparation—there is a period of struggle in which the individual attempts to solve a problem by using existing strategies and cognitive structures. In the second stage—surrender— the person gives up the struggle to solve the problem and relaxes the creative efforts. In stage three—illumination—a solution to the prob- lem emerges from cognitive processes out of awareness. In the final stage—clarification—the solution is worked out in practical life. Thus the creative process involves a kind of mental restructuring—an "aha" experience or gestalt switch—in which a new insight solves the prob- lem and remains as a strategy for the solution of similar problems should they arise in future. Surrender to a charismatic leader relates to the second stage of the creative process, coming after a period of search and struggle, and is a necessary preparation for the suspension of one's ordinary mode of thinking that leads to illumination. This has been brilliantly described by the philosopher Kurt Wolff, but as he shows, there is a profound risk in surrender (Wolff 1976).

Hence, probably very few followers surrender unconditionally, or if they do, it is only for the short term. In daily life they go along with what the prophet wants as long as they can see its value. They even go along with what the prophet wants when they cannot see its value, provided they can construe compliance as some kind of test of their faith. But if the results of compliance consistently run counter to their ultimate concerns, they will soon withdraw their allegiance. The com- munal groups in this study had each lost far more members over the years than they had retained (indicating that most followers do indeed leave once they have gained what they came for). Among the groups in this study it was the recent converts—the "young lambs"—who were the most devoted, or at least the most extreme in demonstrating their devotion. For some, surrender had become their highest virtue, and they competed among themselves to prove who was the most surrendered. Surrender to the prophet can be an external measure of one's devotion to God, a test of one's faith, courage, and virtue. To do otherwise is to be "resistant," "sinful," "not ready," or whatever.

The second component of the great work is transcendence. In the great work the follower seeks to go beyond his or her current limits. One way to do this is to transform one's personal and social life. For those who have led conventional lives, the freedom of the group provides a chance to drop out and to experience themselves in new ways. For others who have followed unconventional lifestyles, the structure of the group offers a chance to drop in, to get some stability and order into their lives. A senior member of one group said:

> This place changes lives. That's the key. I've seen people arrive here with nothing, and over the years they'll work on themselves, and we work on them, too, and gradually they bite off bigger and bigger hunks of reality, life challenges, and so forth. Marriage, kids, running a business, becoming a trustee, looking after others. People who you'd say, when they first arrived here, "Well, he'll never amount to much," they change in spite of themselves.

Transcendence means to go "beyond the range or domain or grasp of human experience."[1] Theologian Frederick Streng defined religion as the "means of ultimate transformation" (Streng 1969), and Alan Watts spoke of the "ways of liberation" when he discussed Buddhist and Hindu views (Watts 1961). Most of the followers in this study joined their leaders in order to go beyond their previous states and experience in some way. Heinz Kohut has argued that one's entire life cycle is implied in a program laid down in the nuclear self during infancy (Kohut 1980, 498; 1985, 216). In ordinary life we love and work, but these activities do not fully absorb us. There are times when we become aware of a yearning that goes beyond work and love (Kohut 1985, 38). As historian Wilfred Cantwell Smith has shown, everywhere throughout history, humankind has been aware that we live in a world whose greatness transcends our grasp but does not totally elude us;

---

1. *Concise Oxford English Dictionary*, 1976, 1231. Carl Jung also used the concept when describing the "transcendent function" that enabled the pursuit of "individuation" or self-fulfillment; Samuels, Shorter, and Plant 1986, 150.

that Truth, Beauty, Justice, and Love beckon us imperiously yet graciously (Smith 1979, 130). This suggests a drive toward transcendence, a recurring theme in social science (Maslow 1954, 1968, 1971; Marcus 1961; Bloch 1986; Kung 1974; Teilhard de Chardin 1959). Kohut views life as a heroic struggle toward an integrity unique to each individual, what Ernest Becker has called a "quest for the ideal heroism" (Becker 1962, 180). But it is not achieved easily, and help may be needed from a charismatic leader (Kohut 1971, 316). Further, truly heroic acts of transcendence may seem bizarre and frightening.

In a fascinating sideline to his main work, Kohut studied lone heroic figures such as German resisters to the Nazis. He found that prior to taking their stands, many of them had experienced prophetic dreams and even full-blown hallucinations in which God spoke to them. Yet clearly these people were not psychotic. Rather, they needed support during a moral crisis, so they created an image of a Godlike figure —presumably a projection from their unconscious—that gave them strength (Kohut 1985, 6–7). Kohut argued that the ability to create, in extreme situations, the fantasy of being supported by a Godlike omnipotent figure is one of the assets of a healthy personality (Kohut 1977, 46; 1985, 6–8; see also La Barre 1980, 42–43). The crucial difference between the fantasies of creative heroes in the throes of self-transcendence, and the delusions of disturbed individuals, is the peace that creative resolution brings with it. The consummate peace achieved by the hero, enabling him even to face death calmly, comes from the fulfillment of the agenda laid down in his self during infancy and purposefully pursued thereafter (Kohut 1985, 27, 49). This is the psychological meaning of saving one's soul while losing one's life.

All this suggests that the followers may be attempting to fulfill a life plan involving creativity and self-transcendence of a high order. If that is so, then the apparently bizarre behaviors in which they sometimes indulge may make sense. Perhaps we would understand them better if we could expose their underlying agendas. As explained in Chapter 7, two questions asked of the followers in this study seemed to reveal their deeper agendas: "What has been your major change or achievement in your time here [with the leader]?" and "If something happened that forced you to leave the group and [the leader] and you could never return, what would be your most enduring memory?" When responding to these items, the followers consistently spoke of the quality of love in their lives: love of the leader, their friends, their partners, and families, and of the loving peace of mind that they had been able to achieve within themselves. In anticipation that love might emerge as a motive for charismatic involvement, another question was asked of the followers: "What has been your greatest experience of loving, either around [the leader] or since you have been in the group?" This elicited some extraordinary responses. The one that best illustrates the points just covered, especially the elements of testing and transcendence, was the following (paraphrased) anecdote.

John and Mary Miller shared a medical problem that made having children dangerous for them. Because their blood types were opposite—she was Rh negative and he was Rh positive—there was a chance that if she became pregnant, her antibodies might attack the baby's blood cells and cause the infant's death. They didn't know this when they married, but after the birth of their first child, tests revealed the incompatibility in their blood types and they were warned that having more children might be dangerous. They did have another baby, without significant problems, but with their third child they started to have difficulties. Their doctor told them, "If you go on, you're heading for big problems. You'd best not have any more."

John and Mary were radical Christians and believed that contraception was a sin. However, they saw no alternative. Reluctantly they practiced birth control. Some years later, when they met Arnold Harper, they eagerly joined his church. However, this church also was a radical Christian group that believed contraception was sinful. They talked the matter over with Arnold, who finally asked them, "Well, why don't you trust God?"

Together they prayed and thought about Arnold's words. In time John came to feel that they should abandon birth control and leave matters up to God. Mary, who had to carry the child, took much longer to decide, but eventually she, too, agreed, saying, "Yes, I will. I'll trust God." Soon she was pregnant.

In those days intrauterine medical procedures were still very experimental. Mary underwent frequent amniocentesis to measure the antibodies in her baby's blood. When she was six months pregnant, the antibody count reached dangerous levels and the doctors told them that the birth would have to be induced in order to avoid risking the child's life.

Mary was admitted to hospital, placed on an intravenous drip, and electrodes to measure the infant's heartbeat were placed on her baby's scalp. John sat alongside her, listening to the regular "blip, blip, blip" of the fetal heart monitor and watching the printout. After twenty-four hours of this, Mary was becoming exhausted and the baby's heartbeat was slowing down. Suddenly the machine went silent. The nurse in attendance leaped up and called for assistance. The infant's heart had stopped, and a cesarean would have to be performed immediately to save the child's life. Mary was rushed into surgery and John was sent to the waiting room.

Alone, John paced the floor in the waiting room. He heard a voice, not an audible voice, but he knew God spoke to him, saying, "John, what if I take your baby?"

John replied in a whisper, "Lord, we've trusted you for this baby. We've gone out on a limb for this baby. We've believed you for this baby. The church is praying for this. You can't." Then, after a time, he said, "All right, if you want to take that baby, you take it, Lord."

And then God spoke again. "John, what if I take your wife?"

Now he burst into tears, crying, "Oh, please, Lord, you can't do that. I've committed my life to her. I gave her my life. She means everything to me." John struggled with this for some minutes before at last he felt able to say, "Right, Lord, if you must take her, you take her, too."

After John said this, a strange rapture came over him, which he later described as "a peace [that] came into my heart that was unbelievable. Unbelievable. It was just a peace, and a relief, and a joy. . . . That experience has never left me. The peace that came to my heart when I yielded, call it a high, call it what you like, it's something that I don't think I've experienced the depth of it, or the height of it, since, or before."

A few seconds later a nurse wheeled a stand down the corridor, calling out, "Mr Miller." John rushed out and found the nurse who had sat with them in the ward, and who had been quite hard at times, wheeling an incubator with a baby in it, her eyes brimming with tears. "He's alive, he's alive." She rushed around a corner before John could ask about his wife.

Slowly he walked toward the operating room, where he met the surgeons coming out. They told him that his wife was exhausted, drugged, and drowsy, but alive. He whispered, "Thank you, Lord." Later he was told that the cesarean had been a very near thing and that at one point the medical team thought they had lost Mary.

In considering this anecdote as an example of what Kohut implies may have been a creative, heroic act, perhaps the most important point to consider is that John and Mary must have known before they joined Arnold's church that their medical problem would be bound to emerge as an issue sooner or later. Despite this, they joined. The particular nature of their problem probably has little significance; certainly they had little control over it. Yet it is their hunger to be tested, to risk all for God, that stands out. Some might say that this couple was both extremely lucky and very foolish, but that is not the point. Besides, they went on to have more children; the Rh problem corrected itself in time. They felt, for their own reasons, that only a life lived in total accordance with God's will was worth living. No other life was possible for them, and they yearned to be tested.

The third component of the great work is love; the changes the followers make to their lives are expressions of love in some form. Love may involve living a better life, doing good works, serving a noble ideal, or marrying and raising a family. With love, each day is a day lived with God, growing closer to Him, renewing one's commitment to God and the people one is close to.

Three recent studies have focused on love in charismatic groups. Each showed that intense feelings of love distinguished charismatic social relations from other kinds of relationships, giving them their unique flavor. Benjamin Zablocki studied American communes and measured networks of dyadic love (Zablocki 1980, 172–79). What was "undoubtedly the most significant" finding of the study was the "love density effect" (Zablocki 1980, 355), such that the greater the amount of love present in a commune, the less stable that commune was, unless it had a resident charismatic leader. So reliable was this effect that Zablocki was able to deduce from it a "social thermometer" by which he could measure the degree of love in a commune and then predict what proportion of its membership would still be present one year later, and even whether or not the commune itself would still exist (Zablocki 1980, 168–69). Raymond Bradley's research (subtitled *A Study of Love and Power, Wholeness and Transformation*) divided communes into four basic types, depending upon the amount of charisma present (Bradley 1987, 49–75). He measured correlations of love and power with charisma such that the greater the intensity of charisma in a particular group, the more intense were the loving and power relations within that group. Bradley argued that great power was needed to contain the inherently destabilizing effect of intense love. Charles Lindholm's study was an effort to review and integrate previous research into charisma (Lindholm 1990). Lindholm presented three case studies—Adolf Hitler, Charles Manson, and Jim Jones—and related each to shamanism (Wilson 1975). He analyzed the relationship of love to charisma, and even discussed romantic love as an alternative to, and substitute for, charisma. To Lindholm, love was central to charisma, and *"the hidden purpose of the charismatic group is not to 'succeed' but to experience itself"* (Lindholm 1990, 110; my emphasis).

These three works, taken together, suggest that beneath the multitude of rationales that members of charismatic groups give to explain their reasons for joining, there lies another, perhaps unconsciously held, agenda. This agenda is to experience intense love. This makes the relationship between charisma and love purposive. That is, members join charismatic groups for love rather than for the stated aims of the groups. The stated aims of the groups may determine which particular group an individual will choose to join; they are important from the perspective of values—a Christian will not join a group whose values conflict with Christianity.

Most of the followers in this study saw love as an ultimate goal of their movements, and the groups really were, as far as one could tell, very loving, considerate, and caring, placing great value on children, commitment, group activities, relationships, support for the needy, and other aspects of life one normally associates with love. In addition, several of the groups offered charitable assistance and outreach programs that were an extension—in some cases a costly extension—of their loving stance. Yet for all that, there were some clear limits placed by the groups on their loving. One commune shunned dissidents and ex-members in the manner of the Amish (Hostetler 1980). Another opposed abortion in *all* circumstances. A third refused to allow single parents and divorced persons to join the commune. Ex-members also told their stories, one saying, "This is a very loving group of people, but if anyone criticizes the leader or says they're leaving, they soon find out how unloving they can be." Another added, "When you leave here, you find out who your friends *were*."

Love means different things to different people. There may be little relationship between one's idea of love, one's feelings of love, and how one expresses love in daily life. This relates to one of the puzzles of charismatic groups: Why do they so often end in a very unloving manner? Some leaders who have claimed to have an extraordinary capacity for love have gone on to destroy their followers; typical is Jim Jones, who routinely told his followers, "You'll never be loved again like I love you" (Lindholm 1990, 144), Jones restated his limitless love even as he moved among his dying followers at Jonestown (Reiterman and Jacobs 1982, 560). That Jones did love his followers seems indisputable; the assistance given to the poor and needy by his People's Temple was proportionately much greater than the assistance provided by similar church and humanitarian groups (Richardson, Stewart, and Simmonds 1979).

Jones often struggled mightily to help people. Yet he, and many other charismatic leaders, unconsciously adopted policies that resulted in suffering—for example, the violence of Synanon, the collapse of Rajneeshpuram, the sexual excesses of the Children of God, and the various abuses of the Scientology movement (Olin 1980; Milne 1986; Gordon 1987; Davis and Davis 1984; Miller 1987; Lamont 1986). It is as if love and hate toward the followers coexist in the minds of these leaders. To dismiss the leaders as misguided or deranged does not inform. Hence a background question in this study was What is it about the nature of charismatic love that renders it so potentially dangerous? Zablocki has shown that intense love in a commune renders it unstable; Bradley measured the strength of the power relations necessary to control love; Lindholm associated the powerful appeals of Hitler, Manson, and Jones with their abilities to inspire love. But what is so problematic about love?

One possible answer is that the love of the leader for the follower is not real love; that is, it is narcissistic. The leader loves the follower not for his or her self but as an extension of the leader's ego. This may well be true, and the follower's view may be equally distorted. To love the prophet as a symbol of one's ultimate concerns is to be blind to his actual person (and the inflated testimonies of the followers demonstrate this). Hence both leader and follower may share only a narcissistic or self-centered love. This may develop into a more mature love in time but it usually doesn't because most followers leave the prophet within a few years.

However, this explanation—that narcissism pervades both sides of the leader-follower relationship—while it probably has some truth, implies that charismatic love is doomed from the start because it is inherently pathological or immature, and only rarely results in mature, loving relationships. This is unlikely, given the mostly normal personalities of the followers. Also, one does meet followers whose relationships with their leaders have grown—through years of testing and shared experience—from the early romance of seeing the leader as God's intermediary to a less invested and inflated, and a more pragmatic and realistic, friendship. So the question remains: What is it about charismatic love (not pseudo love) that makes it so dangerous?

An account of an altered state recalled by a follower in this study may answer this question. The suggestion basically is that love may be so intensely experienced in charismatic groups as to transcend worldly, and even human, concerns. We recognize that people will risk their lives and even die for those they love. According to Kohut, this is because of a transformation of narcissism in which one's self is replaced as the object of primary narcissism and one's ideals and values become the objects of a "cosmic narcissism" (Kohut 1966, 1976, 1985). In ordinary life this may mean taking a stance of selflessness toward one's beloved—typically a spouse or child—that seeks satisfaction in terms of their, rather than one's own, good (or even one's own survival). But in a charismatic movement the love that is generated may transport the group to an otherworldly or world-rejecting state (Weber 1946, 323–59). In this state, one's view of the world may change so drastically that common ethical and moral concerns lose their significance. As Hugh Prather so eloquently expressed it: "It is not that there is no evil, accidents, deformity, pettiness, hatred. It's that there is a broader view. Evil exists in the part. Perfection exists in the whole. Discord is seeing near-sightedly. And I can choose this broader view—not that I always should—but I always can" (Prather 1970).

The following account, which echoes Durkheim's "outside and above ordinary morals" (Durkheim 1965, 247), shows how this may occur.

I had one experience that I still don't really understand. It's still a bit of a question mark for me.

I've done a lot of meditating . . . when I started [that time], the first thing I became aware of was that I felt anxious. And that was quite a surprise because it [meditation] usually calms me down. . . . I felt uncomfortable. . . . When you get into something like that, the thing to do, of course, is to continue and find out what it's about. It wasn't a big deal, but I thought, "Oh, well, I wonder what that's about," and carried on. But I realized later that that initial anxiety was in some way connected to what came next.

I remember having this oddness creep over me and wondering what it might be. And then I was hit by it, this real powerful, unconditional loving for [the leader]. It took me a long time to recognize it as love, actually, because I'd never known anything like it before. And it wasn't for what he stood for, or what he'd achieved, or what I stood to gain in the future through him, or what we'd shared in the past; it was a core of unconditional loving for him — person to person. The sheer physicalness of it was amazing. The only image I actually had in the entire time . . . was of a kind of a close-up of his leg, of the calf and shin, and of the hairs and the texture of his skin. It wasn't a hallucination, it wasn't anything, really, just like a very vivid thought, but with real love for the, the kind of "meat" of the man. It was absolutely specific and physical, and I was totally open.

Once I let it happen, it became utterly blissful. But to start with, it was so unfamiliar. And that's what threw me. It took me a long time to work out just that it was pleasurable. At first I was just lost. Strangely, I remember thinking that I'd got into something like it a bit when my mother died. But I'd managed to shut it out. But I remembered that when it happened. And I realized that I had it for [the leader], and I'd had it for my mother, but it really, it's, we probably all have it for everyone down deep, but we block it out because it's so raw and open. I'd say that we don't love "because" of this or that; we just have this loving. And that's what's so scary about it. If I say I love someone "because" they're attractive or sexy or something, then I'm justifying myself, it's a defense. I'm kind of putting my love in a box, trying to guard it with reasonableness, to appear mature and tough. But if I say that I have within me a core of basic trusting love for the world, that asks no questions and . . . is always there somewhere in the background, then that's scary because it might get out of control, or I might show it to the wrong person. . . . I'm vulnerable.

Then my mind flipped in, and the two things that came up were "Oh, God, does this mean that I really am just a brainwashed, hypnotized, devotee?" and "Does this mean I'm really a homosexual?" 'Cause it felt deeper than I'd ever been before, so it must be more revealing. . . . This was how I was thinking at the time. And I'm wondering if that's what I'm really like, some kind of deep block removed and I'm really queer? Panic. And of course it doesn't mean either of those things, but they're ways we have of terrorizing ourselves about this thing.

Next I thought, "In this mood, if someone burst through the door and killed me, I could just go on loving them." I spent a bit of time wondering would I, could I, that sort of thing, but it still felt okay. I thought it was probably true, but it was still only a thought.

But then it got spooky, because my next thought was "If someone burst through the door and started to kill my kids, I would just accept that, too, and go on loving them; the kids, the murder, the whole thing." And that's when I started to freak out, because I thought I was starting to lose it, to get lost in it, and maybe I'd never come back. And I can't prove this because it wasn't put to the test, and I hope it never is, but I felt sure that it was so. Or I was terrified it was. And even now I think it probably is, in that state. It wasn't indifference or callousness, but it was kind of inhuman, love at a cosmic level, the kind of love God must have. I could accept anything that could happen as basically okay and appropriate. I was totally open and in love with it all, but it freaked me out, 'cause it's like we humans aren't supposed to feel like that, at least not at our present stage of development. It felt like I'd opened a door that wasn't supposed to be opened. Or I'd intruded where I didn't belong, someplace where everything, the scale of everything, was much bigger than me, the realm of the gods or something, I don't know, but I was helpless.

What else? I had lots of insights . . . and a very definite sense of completion. "It's over; it's complete; that's it; there can be no more." And I'm not sure what that was about, but it wasn't the mystical sense of "I'm home" or arrival that you read about. It was a sense of completion; there could be nothing more than this to find. And of something I'd been looking for but didn't know I was looking for it. But it wasn't enlightenment or anything like that; I didn't meet God or anything. There were no visions or voices; and I'm still pretty much the same person I used to be, so it's not changed me much. Yet it was one of the big experiences of my life, really.

If I tried to push it away, it just got worse. I could let myself have a little bit of it and it was okay, but then the thought of my kids being killed would creep in and I'd try to push it away again, but I knew it was okay, and that was not right, so I'd get confused. If I'd hallucinated, I'd have been able to say, "Okay, this is impossible, get a grip on yourself." But it wasn't even scary in the usual way. I just had no frame of reference for it. There was this inner unease. . . .

I got up and walked outside, and my wife came up to me, and I just collapsed into her arms and said, "Thank God you've come. . . ."

I worried about it for a long time afterward. I was afraid I was some kind of monster. . . . And I'd say I'm still trying to figure it out two years later.

I think I used [the leader] as a symbol, but we all probably feel this way about everything, but we block it off. I just found myself having it, that's all. It was just an outpouring, but I think we all have it inside us somewhere.

Perhaps here is the "one thing needful." Like Mary at the feet of her man-God (Luke 10:38–42), the follower ultimately seeks but one thing: to "dwell in the house of the Lord all my days, to gaze upon the beauty of the Lord" (Psalms 27:4). Nothing is desired here, and not even death can touch us. Philosopher Ernst Bloch calls this Utopia, in which man is finally naturalized and nature is humanized (Bloch 1986). In his vast study *The Principle of Hope*, Bloch argues that an aspiring hopefulness, present in almost all human behavior, leads to a "One Thing that is outstanding and needful." The final will is to be truly present, to enter into the here and now as oneself, to enter fully into life without postponement or distance (Bloch 1986). Yet Lindholm argues that "In essence it [the charismatic experience] has no substantive content beyond being an immediate ecstatic experience, providing a visceral, transcendent moment that is outside of and opposed to the alienation and isolation of the mundane world—a memory upon which ordinary life can be constructed" (Lindholm 1990, 189).

If, as is likely, the account above describes the experiential core of charisma, then Lindholm is clearly wrong in saying that charisma has "no substantive content." (If that is all charisma is, why does it have such power to grip people, some of whom sacrifice even their lives for it?) It seems, rather, that the charismatic experience signifies an ecstatic encounter with one's ultimate concerns in a manner that we are unable —and perhaps unwise—to sustain, but that is available to us from time to time. Charisma is too problematic to give us paradise, but it may perhaps give us a glimpse of paradise, of the "one thing needful."

9

The Soul of the Prophet

Heavens how that man can talk. He has the faith. He can get himself to believe anything, anything!

—Joseph Conrad
Heart of Darkness

As described in Chapter 4, every leader in this study seemed to have split off part of his or her self in order to pursue his or her vision. Some had done so completely, others incompletely, but each seemed to have done so to a much greater extent than "normal" people. As a result, each appeared as a paradoxical, contradictory, and unpredictable being.

This splitting of the personality in narcissistic individuals is discussed by Heinz Kohut, who views it as pathological and points to the danger of "fragmentation" when the process has been carried too far (Kohut 1971, 1977). But such splitting happens as a normal part of growth. The tripartite structure of the mind—id, ego, and superego—is merely a splitting of the psyche in response to the external world. Other splits occur when children identify with one gender and repress the other, and later when they cultivate a persona and an identity, a true self and a shadow self, and later still when developing social roles.

Within broad limits, the mind develops freely and flexibly. There seems to be no "true" course for its development, no final form it inclines toward. Rather, it is free to develop in whichever way it may. The final structure of the mind is primarily influenced by the child's love relations (Parens 1972), and almost any outcome is theoretically possible, provided the right environmental circumstances prevail. Our preferences for one personality type over another result from moral choices, not genetic predisposition. Who is to say that the repressed, civilized "normal" man or woman is more natural than the psychopath?

However, this process is not merely random. It is subject to dialectical principles. If one has an impoverished concept of external reality, then one must also have a correspondingly impoverished concept of one's inner reality, for the two define each other as opposites (Gergen and Morowski 1980). Hence one may have a narcissistic view of the world and an inflated sense of self, but one's sense of self in this instance will be quite unlike the sense of self held by another with a more realistic view of the world. It may be grandiose, yet lack the complexity and depth that come from interaction with *real* others. The upshot is that the creative fragmentation of the narcissistic mind may take it into areas wholly beyond the scope of "normals" and may lead to extraordinary talents. Uncanny modes of thinking and feeling are two possibilities.

In a study of primitive thought processes ("primary process"), Pinchas Noy has explained how the former may occur (Noy 1969). Basically, it seems that some creative individuals are able to regress at will to more primitive, even infantile, ways of thinking. They may develop primitive thought processes in a way that subtly combines them with mature thought processes so as to create rational modes of irrationality, irrational modes of rationality, and startling blends of both. We almost can't conceive what this might be like, but the results appear before us all the time as art. As for unusual modes of feeling, Charles Brenner has shown that emotions do not develop according to an inflexible genetic logic but in response to one's experiences in life (Brenner 1974). For example, rage develops quite early as a consequence of frustration, shame appears later, and guilt later still and only after the development of ideals and a sense of conscience. Brenner concludes that one's childhood memories, wishes, and fears must greatly influence one's emotions in later life. The implication here is that a narcissistic development should lead to unusual emotional states.

Could something of this sort explain the hypnotic "presence" and empathy, the vision and uncanny "knowing" of charismatics? There is a certain fascinating weightlessness to these individuals that seems to echo something far off and high above. James Gordon has described Rajneesh by saying, "he saw something far beyond emotions and intellect" (Gordon 1987, 52), and Laura Hall has described the "inner radiance" of the charismatics she studied (Hall 1983, 79). When scholars use such terms, we must grant that there is something objective about what they are describing. The followers are not deluded about their leaders; they are describing something real—in clumsy terms, perhaps, and seen through the screens of their own projections, but real nevertheless.

A useful way into this is through a case study reported by Gilbert Rose. It involved a patient of his named Ariel, a student in her twenties who sought help for depression (Rose 1972). In adolescence she had experienced a mystical illumination after reading Thomas Mann's *Dr. Faustus*, after which she lost her former equilibrium. The hero of the novel obsessed her, and she developed a fetish about bright light. She claimed that it excited her sexually, so much so that she eventually felt compelled to avoid light completely for fear that if she didn't, she might become so aroused that she would be unable to control her feelings and would remain forever in a trancelike state. She also became hyperempathic. If she accidentally hurt another, she would weep or say "ouch." If she conversed with a friend, then looked in a mirror, she would be surprised to discover herself instead of the friend. Sometimes she wandered off alone in the early morning hours. In tough neighbourhoods she would strike up conversations with strange men. But her air of unearthly innocence so disarmed them of any hostile or sexual intent that she often reduced them to tearful confessions of their own unhappiness. She became convinced that artificial divisions between people ought to be abolished, and deeply committed to the civil rights movement. She worked long hours at considerable sacrifice for this cause. Her response to an LSD trip was also peculiar. She enjoyed the actual experience but was terrorized by subsequent flashbacks. She protected herself by developing vivid fantasies of fusing with her surroundings. In her delusions she believed that merging with the walls, investing herself in everything around her, would give her control over her environment and prevent it from assaulting her.

Rose concluded that Ariel had never been experienced as a whole person by her parents, and thus she had not experienced her own identity or those of others. After working with her, he developed a theory of what he called "fusion states"—intense identifications that occur when the ego suspends its distinction between self and others. One masters something by fusing with it as Ariel did, and as we all do when mastering a new skill, such as learning to ride a bicycle. Rose suggested that merging with something in order to reemerge once one has mastered it is part of the process of psychological growth. It enables us to transcend our limits and expand our reality. Thus, personal growth may involve many microscopic creative acts of fusion with others. Hence the unusual talents of the prophet may derive from an equally unusual developmental process through which his mind has achieved a unique thinking style and has experienced strange emotions. This ability to lose oneself in another, or even in an idea or physical object, may have fantastic consequences. Ariel's effect on strange men in darkened alleys affords us a glimpse of what such a talent may be like. Such magical qualities must come from somewhere. The prophet's lightness and timelessness of being, which bespeak spiritual authority, may evolve quite naturally from such unnatural events.

This creative fragmentation of the prophet's mind shows itself most clearly in his personality splits, where aspects of his self are rejected yet remain active outside awareness. One result is the contradiction of the grandiose messenger of God who at times behaves in a petty, vindictive way toward those beneath him. Prophets are riddled with such paradoxes. For example, the leader's need for the followers is much greater than the followers' need for their leader. Martin Sheppard described this as the "neediness paradox" when writing of Fritz Perls (Sheppard 1976, 120–21). Some leaders have admitted that this is so—typically, Charles Manson, who acknowledged that "something inside me needed them more than they thought they needed me" (Emmons 1988, 183). Other leaders clearly needed their followers to validate their belief in themselves, sensing that without their followers, they would be nothing—most clearly, J. H. Noyes, founder of the Oneida community (Foster 1984a, 114). Yet virtually none, apart from Manson, ever recognize or speak about their need. Prophets also are intensely private, secretive people. They expect transparent honesty from their followers, but they almost never reveal their own deeper motives; examples include Fritz Perls's reluctance to be analyzed (Gaines 1979, 87), Kathryn Kuhlman's refusal to reveal her inner thoughts (Buckingham 1976), and L. Ron Hubbard's vast secret life (Miller 1987).

Then there is the paradox of aloofness. Prophets expect and receive from their followers intimate engagement while remaining personally distant. Again, Fritz Perls is perhaps the best example, especially because he was a therapist whose work drew him into close relations with others (Gaines 1979). Strangely, many charismatics are not exhibitionistic by nature; J. H. Noyes was very retiring (Thomas 1977; Foster 1984a), and even Perls has been described as basically a shy person (Gaines 1979). Rather, they seem driven to thrust themselves forward willfully, even rigidly. Kohut speaks of rigidity as part of the charismatic personality; it is as if there is a stereotyped act that the leader plays out because he believes he must, but it doesn't always come naturally (Kohut 1971, 1976, 1977).

A curious thing happens when a prophet is denied his role—he appears quite lost. Hugh Milne has described how Rajneesh became an empty shadow of his self when his role began to collapse (Milne 1986, 232–33), and L. Ron Hubbard's sense of personal devastation— "I want to die"—and proclamations of "I've been betrayed" reveal something similar (Miller 1987); Adolf Hitler's pathetic appeal, "If only I had someone to take care of me," may signify this, too (Lindholm 1990, 106–07). But the most intriguing of the leader's contradictions is his mastery of the "big lie," his knack for telling whoppers. This peculiarity deserves detailed illustration. Whether it is Madame Blavatsky's myth of Tibet, Paul Twitchell's fantasy of "Eck," Joseph Smith's gold plates, or any of dozens of other falsehoods exposed over the years, lying on a grand scale has been one of the most consistent behaviors of prophets. What is seldom realized, however, is that the prophet may come to believe these lies just as strongly as the followers do. This seems absurd, but it may explain what happened when, for example, Jim Jones became morbidly preoccupied with security after he had faked an assassination attempt against himself (Reiterman and Jacobs 1982, 203). Jones and the rest were great liars who may have convinced even themselves, but by far the best was L. Ron Hubbard.

Hubbard claimed—among many other fibs—to have earned advanced degrees from prestigious universities, to have traveled through several countries as a young adventurer, to have been a successful writer in Hollywood, and to have been variously an atomic scientist, an explorer, and an undercover agent. None of this was true (Miller 1987).

It is tempting to dismiss Hubbard as a pathological liar, a "barefaced messiah," as a biographer put it (Miller 1987). Yet Hubbard's view of his lies is complex. He saw virtue in falsehood when it led to desired ends and, importantly, these ends did not always involve mere personal gain. He stated his position many times. "Truth is what is true for you," he wrote in a dictionary he authored, and elsewhere he claimed, "If there is anyone in the world calculated to believe what he wants to believe it is I" (Miller 1987, 348, 231). Hubbard's determination to place personal truth before objective truth recurs over and over in his utterances. Hence, when he lied about something, he was also asserting, in a premeditated, deliberate way, his personal ascendancy over the world and over history. He could be egotistical, out of control, impulsive, cruel, and shallow, but beneath it all there was a sense of mission, a will to reshape the world in his own image.

This may seem to be reading too much into Hubbard's actions. Yet not only did he seriously expect to be taken seriously, he was baffled and angered when disbelieved. He couldn't understand when others refused to take him seriously because *he took himself so seriously that he believed his own lies.* "You don't understand," he once told an aide. "I'm fighting a battle here. I might lose some people on the way but I'm going to win" (Miller 1987). To Hubbard, his friends, wife, family, and even reality itself, were all secondary to his need to stamp his truth on the world.

What is the evidence that Hubbard believed his own lies? Several remarkable episodes stand out. The first is when he gave permission to a junior follower to write his biography from actual historical records that were stored in an attic. These included his school report cards, his military service documentation, and so on. Hubbard must have known that an investigation of his papers would reveal him to be a fraud, yet he gave permission for the project to go ahead (Miller 1987, 3). Had he lost touch with reality? Unlikely; he could be sharp enough to avoid the authorities when he had to, typically when he refused to travel to Australia to defend Scientology before a government inquiry. Did he have some deranged idea of his past? Perhaps, but he was capable of writing "Falsehood must become exposed by truth, and truth, though fought, always in the end prevails" (Lamont 1986, frontispiece). Other examples of such behavior occurred when he applied to the U.S. Navy for war medals he had never earned (Miller 1987, 323) and when he mounted an expedition to search the Caribbean for gold he believed he had buried in previous lifetimes (Miller 1987, 267). He seems quite literally to have believed these fabrications of his own mind (Miller 1987, 67, 362). How? Why?

Hubbard believed that words had magical abilities to effect reality. He never allowed anyone to say anything negative about him (Miller 1987, 210), seemingly afraid that he might be harmed by such words.

When he attempted to secure an increase in his veteran's pension, he claimed to have a variety of ailments resulting from his military service. However, he was so concerned about the effect that his false claims might have on his health that he wrote "affirmations" in his journals that were intended to counter any bad effects: "When you tell people you are ill it has no ill effect upon your health," "No matter what lies you may tell others they have no physical effects upon you of any kind," "In Veterans' Administration examinations you'll tell them how sick you are, you'll look sick when you [say] it, you'll return to health one hour after the examination and laugh at them," "Your shoulder never hurts," "Your ulcers are all well and never bother you" (Miller 1987, 132). Thus, years before Hubbard founded Scientology, he had arrived at a set of beliefs about the power of words and intentions similar to "New Thought" (Braden 1963). He was so convinced of this power that he feared it might backfire upon him if he misused it. Hence he countered one affirmation with another, an intention with its opposite, a lie with a truth, not because he was afraid of being caught out but because he feared the power of words and thought. Ominously, his affirmations from this time include "Men are your slaves" and "You have the right to be merciless." When he spoke in this way, he was using words to make love to an image of himself. Beneath his freewheeling, lying exterior was a rigid, driven, superstitious mind-set desperate to win every time.

Hubbard's belief bespeaks an infantile, magical view of the world wherein one need only wish to make it so. How such a worldview can be adapted to the adult world was demonstrated at a meeting of one of the groups in this study. The leader had recently made several foolish financial decisions and had lost his followers a great deal of money. They called him to account and he tried to lie his way out. At first only a couple of his followers accepted his explanation, but he courted and praised them, and soon others were tempted to believe also. As more and more waverers were won over, he picked on a few scapegoats among those opposing him and criticized them for stirring things up. These were problem disciples—Judases kept in train for just such emergencies—who were looked down upon by most members. The present difficulties, he explained, were "all their fault" because of their undermining negativism. Now the true believers, not wanting to be associated with what was beginning to look like an out-group, defected to the leader's camp. When he had a clear majority on his side, he changed the discussion into how best to accommodate the misguided few, whom he magnanimously forgave. When he had won everyone over, he merely went along with the wishes of the majority. By wishing hard enough, he had made it so; an infantile hallucinatory wish fulfillment had become an adult socially manipulated wish fulfillment. (But not all of the followers were persuaded. One drew my attention to what was happening early on when she said, "Watch him; he's convincing others so he can believe it himself." Another subsequently explained her behavior as "I started to cringe in embarrassment. I didn't want to see him exposed or rejected. It was very threatening for me to see him challenged. I opted for peace at any price.")

This magical mind-set can be enormously appealing to onlookers. It reminds them of their own lost innocence and grandiosity. It also leads to a novel slant on life, creative insights into problems, and utopian visions of what could be. But more than all else, it is the most powerful proof to intelligent minds that the leader really is special. Certainly some prophets exploit sleight-of-hand miracles to win over simple folk, but even educated, critical people find this sheer magical "otherness" of the leader fascinating, and may accept it as evidence that he is guided by some great power.

To summarize thus far, the narcissistic mind develops differently from others. Because of this it may achieve unusual powers, highly original thought processes, and ecstatic feeling states. These may be such as to give the leader a fundamentally different—seemingly alien —psychology. The evidence for this comes from the unusual powers of such figures (which must be explicable in some way), the odd splitting of their personalities that allows them to function as gods and heroes, and the residual magical mind-set they retain from childhood. A central part of all this is the leader's peculiar experience of, and transcendence of, time.

Time is purely a mental construct—it does not exist in the universe. There, change exists, movement exists, but only the mind collates the sense data of change and movement to experience them as time (just as color does not exist in the world but frequencies of light waves do). But as Robert Ellwood has shown (Ellwood 1973a, 86), time has been a fundamental problem for religion. It is all very well for the mystic to have a peak experience in which time falls away and only God is alive in His timeless being, but then one has to return to live through time, to be born, to suffer, and to die, to experience war, loss, and disease. Yet suppose one could retain a sense of timelessness? What might life be like for one who knows eternity?

It is well known that certain individuals may, in response to crisis or anxiety, alter their experience of time; typical is the near-death experience when "time stood still" or "my whole life flashed before my eyes." Other examples include epileptic seizures and some psychotic conditions. What seems to be happening is that the sense of time is manipulated by the mind to defend against a threat. Freud has associated this with the primary narcissism of the infant and with certain trances and ecstasies. Hans Loewald has related it to creativity, showing how in some instances this ability may become "the starting point for novel linking processes which create new meanings" (Loewald 1972, 409). He suggests that this corresponds to a hallucinatory wish fulfillment that recaptures the sense of omnipotent perfection of the narcissistic child (Loewald 1962, 265–66).

To suggest a modest yet familiar example of how this may occur, one may come to believe that certain painful events—say, a spouse's infidelity or a parent's betrayal—really did not occur, in order to maintain the "vital lie" of a loving family with all its symbolic associations and gratifications. One may blank out whole chunks of experience and invent fantasy memories that protect and support. Some people do this as a way of dealing with painful childhood experiences, expanding their sense of the good times and contracting their sense of the bad times (or vice versa) according to their current needs. Sometimes whole groups of people may do this; the term "collective amnesia" is applied to groups eager to forget a stain on their past. Perhaps what is being manipulated here is memory rather than the sense of time, but the two are closely interwoven.

Our knowledge of what is true or false depends ultimately upon our recollection of the past. One cannot even know who one is other than by referring to one's memory. If someone says that her name is Jill, she does so by recalling times in the past when she was called Jill. Or she can test her belief by asking others who know her, assuming that she can remember who they are, that she can recall them as usually telling the truth, and that her remembrance of the world is that the future is generally like the past, and hence she can perform such tests without the laws of the universe suddenly changing. In short, all one's meanings and identity depend in important ways upon memory.

Is it possible that the narcissistic mind locates its meanings as much in the future as the past? In the telling of a great lie, the lie would not be felt as false because it would not be compared with facts located in memory. Rather, it would be compared with "facts" from an imagined, yet-to-become future *that is experienced as just as real as the past.*

Two things must be done if one is to believe one's own lies. First, at the time of telling one must distort one's sense of time such that the hoped-for future is experienced as being just as real as the lived-and-remembered past. To do this, one must identify with it in something like the manner of Ariel's hyperempathy for those around her (if she accidentally hurt them, she would respond "ouch"), or in the manner of her identification with the walls and her surroundings, fusing with them, merging herself into them, in order to control them. One brings the future to life by investing one's entire being in it, by holding nothing of one's self back from it. That it is not yet, and has never been, counts for little. It is, after all, God's creation, His to bring into being or to reject. Perhaps God can be persuaded—by an act of faith and the utterance of magical words, incantations, and affirmations—to bring His future into being. And in the mystery of the cosmos, who can say that the human past is truer than God's future?

Second, one must fracture one's sense of the past such that all the countervailing facts in memory are rendered vague and indistinct. In order to do this, one must distort one's sense of self, for that, too, is rooted in memory (Sacks 1985). But the prophet's sense of self was distorted long ago. It was split off—creatively fragmented—in order to adapt to unusual circumstances. By developing in this way, which from our perspective must seem like sacrificing the integrity of one's self, the prophet gains tremendous freedom—the weightlessness of one who has transcended his center or slipped his psychic anchor chain. There is nothing to hold him back now. He is free to soar over infinity and eternity and the entire range of all the mind can conceive, to manipulate time, and to wish and make it so. Fusion states of intense identification with others, regression to primitive modes of thinking and infantile emotional states, unearthly innocence combined with uncanny knowing and a hypnotic presence, oneness with the deity— these may be the fantastic consequences of narcissistic adaptation. And yet he lives in the shadow of that terrible truth: "Mommy will not love me unless I am God."

To use these talents, to talk oneself into believing *"anything, any-*

thing!" may be rather like subtly shifting gears. One disidentifies with one's past and identifies with one's future. Losing oneself in a lie of the future might be rather like losing oneself in a lover; one merely surrenders and the self-in-other comes to life with all its awe and mystery. The prophet has no supernatural powers, but the truth is much stranger. Because of the peculiarities of his psychological development he thinks, feels, and sees the world and himself differently from others. What he knows as reality has some of the qualities of a dream, with fluid boundaries between the real and the unreal, self and other, past and future, God and humankind. We may all share this experience at times of great intimacy or in moments of truth, but not on a daily basis. The prophet does not understand this difference. At first he assumes that we all think and feel the same. Only much later, after having created a self-flattering doctrine to explain the difference in terms of his calling and mission, does he recognize what is special about him. "In my soul I am free," said Paul Twitchell of Eckankar (Steiger 1968), giving us an apt metaphor for this inner spacelessness and wildness of mind.

10

Stage Five | Decline or Fall?

Men, briefly inspired, are doomed to become "rational" once more. Some-times it's a simple matter of economics. With the evolution of an agricul-tural economy the fiery shaman of the hunting and gathering societies gave way to the sensibly orthodox priest. Charismatic leadership gave way to traditionalism; imaginatively individual guidance and inspiration yielded to enduring institutions and material interests. Camus has pointed out that today's revolutionary must become tomorrow's heretic if he is not to become tomorrow's oppressor. Every post-revolutionary reign of terror teaches this, and yet we never seem able to learn.

—Sheldon Kopp
Guru

In the second chapter of this book the two kinds of prophetic personali-ties—the messianic and charismatic types—were described. In later chapters this distinction was not developed because in the real world their behaviors are often very similar, being determined more by cir-cumstance than by personality. However, when reviewing the entire lives of prophets, one sees more clearly the differences between the two (see the list at the end of this chapter). In this study, four of the twenty leaders were approaching the ends of their lives and three were deceased. This chapter presents insights derived from these seven leaders and applies them to other, better-known prophets.

An important difference between the two types concerns antisocial behaviors. Of the three deceased leaders, the two charismatic personal-ities—William Hart and Lindsey Amherst—had had major scandals associated with them, but the messianic personality—Harry Hunting-ton—died free from scandal. The messianic prophets generally antici-pated their declines (as much as one can); Kit van Voon departed from his group to allow the new generation to establish themselves, and Arnold Harper set up a council of elders to run his community after

176

his death. (Harry Huntington was killed in an accident before he could plan for his demise.) In contrast, the stance of the charismatic types was to attempt to retain as much power as possible for as long as possible—Lindsey Amherst died disillusioned with the way his group had come to ignore him, refusing to involve himself in the community's affairs, and Fred Thomson continues to send from his jail cell somewhat pathetic but highly manipulative letters to those he regards as his faithful followers, despite having been rejected by almost all of these people. Of the other leaders of this study (not mentioned above) who have served jail terms (that are known about), the one who had served time for what was clearly a crime (robbery) was charismatic, whereas the only messianic leader who had spent time in jail did so in his youth for what would be regarded by most people today as a victimless crime arising more from society's values than from any malign intent on his part—his crime was homosexuality, which he suppressed for the rest of his life, marrying and adopting children. At least one other leader in this study could have served a jail term, had he been caught, for manufacturing illegal drugs; he was a charismatic.

Thus an important distinction between charismatic and messianic types is their relative stability over the years. The messianic types were not prey to the kind of erratic and provocative behaviors to which the charismatic types were prone. This antisocial instability of the charismatic needs some explanation. It was not merely a feature of the final stage; it recurred throughout their lives. The messianic prophets' orientation to an external God kept them in touch with reality and in rough conformity with society's norms, whereas the orientation to an inner God on the part of charismatic prophets inclined them toward conflict with society and hastened their demise. The messianic type seeks to realize the higher order of God, and this may lead him or her into conflict with the prevailing order of society; the charismatic type is trying to express something that is fundamentally opposed to *any* order, something primitive, nascent, and unrestrained (Dow 1978). This leads charismatics into conflict with convention frequently and disastrously. The messianic type usually adopts the posture of being merely a vehicle for God or God's mouthpiece. This enables him to admit mistakes, to compromise, and to advance a less total claim. If the messianic leader fails, it is only God's vehicle that is at fault. Hence the messianic type really advances no special claim for himself other than the possession of God's grace. But the charismatic type is, by Max

Weber's definition, "exemplary" and usually claims to be God in one guise or another. This is a more precarious and seductive role; if he fails, then God has failed, and if he succeeds, then he has proof that he really is God and may become ever more grandiose and self-indulgent, a clear recipe for failure. Nevertheless, both messianic and charismatic types are largely motivated by hostility, and this could emerge as anti-social behavior at any time.

From Jesus to Jonestown, the most consistent thing about prophets has been their failure. The Old Testament prophets were mostly ignored, but they may have been lucky for all that; crucifixion, torture, lynching, and jail have been the fates of others. Prophets are dangerous, and they have been treated accordingly. But as "the oak is felled by the acorn" (Kopp 1971, 7), so the cause of the prophet's success —his narcissistically closed world—contains the seeds of his failure (Bartlett 1988, 11; Johnson 1979). The precariousness of the divine role (Johnson 1979; Wallis 1982), coupled with a failure to consult or delegate, fear of rivals, lack of genuine empathy, and unrealistic estimates of one's own abilities, virtually dooms him from the start. Perhaps deep down the prophet senses that he will fail, and this awareness drives him harder than he would otherwise go. This might account for the frantic pace at which many conduct their missions, even into old age, trying to achieve as much as they can in a time they sense will be brief. For all the prophet's narcissistic unreality, he can be eerily realistic at times.

Sometimes the prophet's arbitrary excesses, stemming from his grandiosity, place him on a collision course with reality. Joseph Smith at the head of his private army (Foster 1984a, 127), J. H. Noyes appointing his wayward and unreliable son as his successor (S. C. Olin 1980), Jim Jones craving fame at any price (Reiterman and Jacobs 1982, 68), and Fritz Perls's interference in the lives of others beyond his role as therapist (Gaines 1979, 381) are actions likely to lead to conflict and the alienation of the followers. Yet despite this the prophet is often able to retain control and outmaneuver opponents. It takes a particularly severe emotional upset to seriously weaken him (or sheer old age, as with J. H. Noyes; S. C. Olin 1980). In the case of Chuck Dederich it seems that the death of his wife spelled the beginning of the end (W. F. Olin 1980). In Jim Jones's case the death of his mother and a custody battle may have tipped him over the edge (Reiterman and Jacobs 1982, 395). Benjamin Zablocki noted the significance of child custody struggles in his communal sample (Zablocki 1980, 65). However, this effect is not clear-cut; it is likely that the death of Moses Berg's mother removed a restraint that allowed him to ascend to his prophetic status, yet with increasingly antisocial behaviors (Wallis 1982; Davis and Davis 1984).

Sex is invariably problematic. Six of the leaders in this study have had sexual scandals associated them. Four of these six were charismatic types, and of the remaining two, the case of one (mentioned above) really involved a crime of values rather than sex as such (the other was jailed for his crimes). Hence the charismatic types again showed up strongest. It is ironic that, generally, leaders who espouse sexual freedom and cultivate a retinue of sexually available followers tend to fall victim to their own images; typical is the Polynesian prophet Yali, who used to charge his female followers five shillings a time for his sexual favors but—incredibly—was eventually imprisoned for rape (Burridge 1969, 161). Charges of sexual misconduct are sometimes used by authorities to bring down a leader when all else has failed.

This points to the role of the followers in their leader's demise. Far from being uncritical and unquestioning of the leader, the followers are frequently skeptical, suspicious, and even hostile on occasions; we sometimes hate those we love for the power we give them over us (Abse and Ulman 1977; Camic 1980; Otto, quoted in Camic 1980; Slater 1961, quoted in Camic 1980). The central ingredient in their relationship is trust; the followers will pay almost any price, accept almost any humiliation, for a higher purpose, but when trust is lost, every sacrifice is recalled as a score to be settled. The followers usually fail to see that the charismatic leader demands trust in his person, not just in his vision or in the movement. Like a general during war, he may willingly sacrifice his troops without feeling that he has betrayed them. They, of course, see things differently.

The intense lifestyle of the cult cannot be maintained (Melton 1987). When virtually every behavior is construed as a test of one's commitment, a phony conformity develops that runs counter to the group's espoused values (W. F. Olin 1980). Then exhaustion sets in, cynicism and contempt grow, and with them resistance to the leader. Now the leader may move the group toward authoritarianism (Zablocki 1980, 47) and supernatural beliefs (Robbins 1988, 124), both of which function as social control mechanisms but also increase the risk of mistakes.

By far the most common cause of trouble in modern groups has been failure of second-order leadership in authoritarian, supernaturalist groups such as the Rajneesh and Hare Krishna movements (Melton 1987). Or the leader's charisma may be eroded by the process of routinization, leaving a power vacuum for malcontents to exploit (S. C. Olin 1980). Social isolates recruited into the group may bring with them troubles that undermine authority later on (Robbins 1988, 86), or opponents and "career apostates" may precipitate collapse from outside; it has been suggested that the activities of the group of "concerned relatives" were at least partly responsible for the Jonestown tragedy (Foster 1984b). Finally, there may come the revelation of a destructive doctrine, such as the sacred prostitution of the Children of God (Davis and Davis 1984) or the polygamy of the Mormons, that eclipses the good work of the group and creates enemies.

What of the leader's state of mind at the end? The prophet on the verge of a nervous breakdown doesn't usually go psychotic (see chapter 3), he just becomes increasingly unreal. Hugh Milne described Rajneesh in this state as empty and hollow (Milne 1986, 249–50), and Lawrence Foster has written of Joseph Smith's inability to understand what had happened to him near the end (Foster 1992, 17). Typically the leader blames others and refuses to accept responsibility for personal failings, as Charles Manson did (Lindholm 1990, 132), crying that "no one understands me," and as Moses Berg did (Davis and Davis 1984, 25); and, retaining his grandiose self-confidence to the end, as Adolf Hitler did (Waite 1977, 502). Now his delusions are apparent for anyone who knows him well to see; his wisdom is banal, his self-certainty appears as bombast, and his social mastery as crude manipulation. The prophet has lost his magic key to the garden and now gropes blindly, searching like an alcoholic for the bottle hidden by his children. The effect is shocking, pathetic, even disgusting to the followers, who wonder how they could ever have believed in him. There is no dignity now; no warmth or even contact, just a compulsive sham as his world unravels. The charismatic prophet who has "become the message" faces failure as a mere persona, a mask lacking humanness. His only friends are his tears. Trapped in his role, the leader can only try and try again all the tricks that once so inspired the followers, becoming a sad cartoon of all he once was.

The prophet's credibility founders most over his failure to be truly human, that is, to reflect on his behavior, to doubt himself, to concede error, and to show genuine regret for hurt to others. This lack unnerves and embarrasses the followers. They bring with them enormous good-will and loyalty, but when the leader shows not mere refusal but sheer inability to admit any insufficiency, when vain boasting and ranting, naive invincibility alternate with bouts of self-pity and paranoid fanta-sies, and when the followers sense that the leader's fancies are more important to him than their welfare, their affections change. Like Raj-neesh blaming all his misfortunes on Sheela, unaware that in doing so he was alienating the very devotees he was struggling to retain, the leader cannot see the effect he is having, and this blindness further erodes his credibility. Even the most loyal soon begin to question. To continue working for him then becomes a conspiracy to protect him from facing his own delusions. Like Heinz Kohut's patients, the leader defends his brittle strengths in an increasingly grotesque and inflexible way; the nearer he comes to the core of his pathology, the more cata-strophic and extreme his reactions become (Kohut 1971, 1977).

This precipitates a psychological and spiritual crisis for the follow-ers. Very few enter into a conspiracy to perpetuate the leader's vision at the risk of their own welfare. These are the truly needy and those who have bonded to the leader so closely that they no longer desire to live without him. When faced with his failures and denials, they ask themselves "What is he really trying to teach us here?" They continue to look for spiritual lessons in the leader's behavior, to collude with his delusions, but they do so in a hollow, desperate way. Most follow-ers react to the leader's failure with hurt, anger, and a sense of betrayal. At best they may merely reject him, and at worst they may kill him. Their response is extreme not just because they feel tricked but because in failing them, the leader deprives them of the possibility of transcen-dence. As Lawrence Foster has said, "there is no greater bitterness than that of the person who genuinely believed or wanted to believe, only to have his or her high hopes dashed" (Foster 1984b, 53). The prophet has led them to wild dreams that (they now feel) no one should be tempted to, encouraged them to freedoms they had abandoned years before, and aroused them to hope on a scale they would never have risked without him. The followers have exposed their most tender feelings to the prophet, allowing him "to know my heart as only God knows it." To discover that the leader really didn't really love them at all, that his love was just a sham, is a cruel disappointment. Now the irrationality of the crowd rebounds onto the leader, who has encouraged its dependency and hero worship. The followers reconstitute themselves by reviling the leader, but they are no longer a charismatic group, and in breaking the illusion of the leader's power, they break their own as well.

Because of all of this, several scholars have argued that failure is inevitable, both for prophets and for charismatic leaders generally (Bartlett 1988, 50; Berger 1981, 388; Kopp 1971). This is too harsh. Granted that no prophet has yet ushered in the kingdom of heaven, nevertheless quite a few have led successful movements and died with their integrity intact; examples include Phineas Quimby, Kathryn Kuhlman, Father Divine, Ann Lee, Prabhupada, and Muhammad. This study includes two such leaders—Harry Huntington and Kit van Voon —who left behind them viable communes and teachings that ensured them places of honor in the memories of their followers.[1] These were all messianic leaders, however; the fates of charismatic types such as Bhagwan Shree Rajneesh, Chuck Dederich, L. Ron Hubbard, J. H. Noyes, Jim Jones, and Charles Manson are much different.

Do such figures share a secret death wish? Some seem to (Foster 1992, 16; Miller 1987, 266). Jim Jones experimented with poisons as a youngster, and later his "white nights" were rehearsals for the final tragedy. But it is also possible that Jones was merely morbid, and later —sensing he would fail—prepared himself for the worst and was finally obliged to resort to it. His commune in the jungle was on the brink of collapse when he staged the mass suicide, and having abandoned the United States, Jones had nowhere left to flee. Rather than harboring a death wish, Jones may have brought down the holocaust to avoid facing his failure (Reiterman and Jacobs 1982, 365). Most charismatic leaders' egos are too grandiose to include a death wish, and the notion doesn't sit well with the concept of narcissism and the leader's need to feel omnipotent.

Messianic prophets are not immune to the pull of disaster; among the leaders in this study there is one messianic personality who is currently serving time in jail. Kenelm Burridge notes that virtually all prophets seem to succumb sooner or later (Burridge 1969, 153–64), and Kohut explains this by saying that the push of ambition outpaces the pull of ideals (Kohut 1966, 1976); he also reminds us that there are no pure types. Yet for all that, it is instructive to compare the incidence of

1. See Weber (1946; 1968b) for an account of succession and transition of charismatic authority.

charismatic failure with the incidence of flawed leadership generally, which Robert Hogan and his associates estimate at between 60 and 75 percent (Hogan, Raskin, and Fazzini 1990); it seems that good leadership of any kind is rare.

As for the charismatic types, perhaps they do succeed, but in a different way (Kopp 1976). Perhaps the Dionysian release that they express, and the lack of discipline that accompanies it (Dow 1978), have a place also. These leaders traverse a dimension of human experience that may need to be reexplored from time to time. Perhaps for some, as M. Scott Peck has written, "the path to holiness lies through questioning *everything*" (Peck 1978, 193). For the charismatic prophet is both moth and flame, quest and grail. Perhaps the best expression of this mentality comes from Heinrich Suso; a fourteenth-century mystic who has left us the following account of his conversation with a spirit entity whom we may recognize as a prophet figure:

> Whence have you come?
> I come from nowhere.
> Tell me, what are you?
> I am not.
> What do you wish?
> I do not wish.
> This is a miracle! Tell me, what is your name?
> I am called "Nameless Wildness."
> Where does your insight lead to?
> To untrammelled freedom.
> Tell me, what do you call untrammelled freedom?
> When a man lives according to all his caprices without
>   distinguishing between God and himself, and without
>   looking before or after. (quoted in Zerzan 1988, 14)

• • •

The following list summarizes the differences between messianic and charismatic prophets.

1. The messianic type has an external source of inspiration or location of God; the charismatic type locates God within.

2. The messianic type arises in the context of belief in a personal God, whereas the charismatic type arises in a context of belief in an impersonal divine force.

3. The messianic teaches by decree or revelation; the charismatic teaches by example.

4. The messianic prophet can envisage, describe, and communicate with his God (who has "object" qualities); the charismatic experiences God more as a subtle tension, pressure, or drive (lacking in "object" qualities).

5. The origin of the motivation of the messianic leader is the archaic fantasy "You are perfect and I am part of you." The origin of the motivation of the charismatic leader is the fantasy "I and the father [or mother] are one."

6. The psychic orientation of the messianic is toward the external world. It is self-checking and is related to reality; virtue and excellence come from what he *does*. The orientation of the charismatic prophet is unrelated to reality and is not self-checking; virtue and excellence— divinity, even—come from what he *is*.

7. The messianic leader is likely to be described as highly consistent; the most consistent thing about the charismatic is his inconsistency.

8. The messianic makes relatively modest claims about himself (e.g., to be the mouthpiece of God), whereas the charismatic advances grandiose claims ("I am God").

9. The messianic leader's ambitions are ultimately directed toward the well-being of others; the charismatic's ambitions are ultimately egocentric and antisocial.

10. The messianic prophet is likely to accept a gradual decline in his power, whereas the charismatic eventually falls from grace.

11. The messianic revelation is marked by stability—one truth is promoted—whereas the charismatic style is unstable—there may be as many truths as suit.

12. The messianic vision leads directly to new laws; release ultimately serves the purpose of restraint. The charismatic vision takes laws away; release is its own justification.

13. To the messianic, God's work is the most important goal, whereas for the charismatic, recognition is most important.

14. The messianic tends to be unworldly, to withdraw from the corruption of the world and to be correspondingly innocent of it, whereas the charismatic embraces the world's corruption as a justification of his own amorality and opportunism.

15. For the messianic the highest ethic concerns notions of truth and duty, whereas the charismatic's highest ethic is expressed in terms of freedom and love.

||

Conclusions

I found myself back in the sepulchral city, resenting the sight of people hurrying through the streets to filch a little money from each other, to devour their infamous cookery, to gulp their unwholesome beer, to dream their insignificant and silly dreams. They trespassed upon my thoughts. They were intruders whose knowledge of life was to me an irritating pretence, because I felt so sure they could not possibly know the things I knew. Their bearing, which was simply the bearing of commonplace individuals going about their business in the assurance of perfect safety, was offensive to me like the outrageous flauntings of folly in the face of a danger it is unable to comprehend. I had no particular desire to enlighten them, but I had some difficulty in restraining myself from laughing in their faces so full of stupid importance.

—Joseph Conrad
Heart of Darkness

We describe someone as charismatic when that person embodies our ultimate concerns or the ultimate concerns of others. These concerns reflect our extraordinary psychological needs. Hence the pop star elicits the extraordinary needs of the adolescent by projecting "something I have never seen in my life . . . a halo around his head of stars. . . . I can't snap out of it . . . fascinating."[1] The politician resonates with a quite different set of extraordinary needs, perhaps even the need for someone who "has got everything to be a king . . . a genius . . . Adolf Hitler, I love you" (Heiber 1962, 48, 78, 80). Hitler's power was such that when, during the Nuremberg trials, von Ribbentrop was shown a film of him, he burst into tears and exclaimed, "Can't you see how he swept people off their feet? Do you know, even with all I know, if

1. Hesse 1970; said by a beauty queen of her date with Frank Sinatra. Quoted in Becker 1973.

Hitler should come to me in this cell now and say 'Do this!'—I would still do it" (Gilbert 1950, 195–96). The businessman Lee Iacocca, with his "clear bright look of a seeker of wisdom and truth . . . up-turned chin and that grin of impetuous youth . . . Oh, I believe in you" (from the hit musical *How to Succeed in Business Without Really Trying*), has been the subject of at least one major study of charisma (Westley and Mintzberg 1988). Intellectual prophets such as Sigmund Freud, J. B. Watson, Max Weber, and others have also been described as charismatic by their disciples (see Kohut 1977; Singer 1961; Malcolm 1980; Stark 1968, 1969, 1977). A typical example is quoted below.

> Psychology at Cornell . . . revolved around and was almost bounded up by the personality of E. B. Titchener. . . . And what a man Titchener was! He always seemed to me the nearest approach to genius of anyone with whom I have been closely associated. I used to watch my conversations with him, hoping I might gain an insight into why his thought was so much better than mine . . . how [could] Titchener so dominate and control [us]. . . . He did it by the magic of his personality, by his social charm . . . you decided eventually from his brilliance, his erudition, and his long list of honours that he was a Great Man. (Boring 1961)

Hence charisma may involve the educated and the uneducated, the clever and the stupid, male and female, rich and poor, believers and unbelievers, those with good intentions and those with evil intentions. Notice also how the accounts become more naturalistic and rational, less transcendent and mystical, according to the sophistication of each follower—Jesus is God, Vivekananda transcends genius, Hitler is a genius, Titchener approached genius.

Charisma is a revolutionary spiritual power, and for the follower it is the spiritualizing of a relationship based upon extraordinary needs and ultimate concerns. The leader signals utopia and becomes a magnet for those on a quest, for whom

> the path leads via the little waking dreams to the strong ones, via the wavering dreams that can be abused to the rigorous ones, via the shifting castles in the air to the *One Thing* that is outstanding and needful. . . . The final will is to be truly present so that the lived moment belongs to us and we to it, and "stay awhile" could be said of it. Man wants at last to enter into the Here and Now as himself, wants to enter his full life without postponement and distance. (Bloch 1986, 16)

The hope of this utopia is that mankind becomes naturalized while nature is humanized, that transcendence coexists with the energy, focus, and structure of normal consciousness. Everyone seeks and everyone follows. Seeking is actually a kind of listening, and following at a distance is what we all do in daily life (Little 1985). However, each follower has his or her own vision that derives from the agenda of the nuclear self (Kohut 1971, 1977). The follower's bold dreams of salvation and enlightenment, perhaps expressed at first in high-flown mumbo jumbo, are later transmuted into a mundane great work and eventually become realized in the spiritual community as a successful testing of oneself against an ultimate standard, as life tasks undertaken in a mood of total commitment, or as an examination of oneself that is unconditional and questioning of everything, as he or she shouts "*YES!*" to God.

Tales of the supernatural prowess of charismatic prophets are merely metaphors for something real and felt, yet inexplicable to the followers. The magical mind set of the prophet is so uncanny that it seems divine, and for some followers the clearest way to convey this is to invent a fable, an "as if" story that says, in effect, "It was *as if* he had performed such-and-such a miracle, for if he had, we would have been no more impressed." To the followers, the leader's charisma represents the triumph of the personal over the rational and the theoretical, over custom and tradition; and their fables, metaphors, and miracle stories of the leader communicate by analogy the awe, power, and love inspired by him. (Perhaps it is an open question as to whether the metaphors of psychology describe it better.) Anyone who treats these matters seriously will end up using similarly flawed concepts.

The leader also is on a quest, but of a quite different sort. His earliest history has left him with a "memory and vision of paradise" (Heinberg 1991) and a personality adept at manipulating others. He retains his infantile grandiosity and exhibitionism by skillful use of empathy and memory, traits that are acute in young children but have been socialized down in the normal adult. As a child he may have had a commanding seriousness and substantiveness that marked him out as a future leader. As an adult he becomes a charismatic leader at least in part because he is afraid that if he doesn't, nobody will love him. He is resourceful and energetic because his mind is not conflicted with the doubts and fears that beset others. His ultimate statement, made by those religious charismatics who are secure enough in their followings to be able to claim it, is "I am God."

Once the prophet's mission becomes clear, all that remains is to fulfill it. In the belief that he is the source of ultimate good for others, he makes a charismatic claim to their obedience. This claim, and the fascinating effect of his personal style, arouse faith, hope, and love among those with similar values, and also echo their own abandoned narcissism. For a few with sufficient awareness, courage, and opportunity, this becomes a call to join him in a great work of transformation. The charismatic relationship is characterized in its earliest stages by trust and surrender, but in time the follower projects his or her ultimate concerns onto the leader. From that point onward their needs fuse, their boundaries melt away, and, for the follower, interaction with the "other" virtually becomes interaction with one's own deeper self. There may be mistakes, false starts, and strategic reversals, but beneath the rhetoric of world transformation the mission and the great work proceed as an exploration of love—largely through rituals of a somewhat sexual cast—and the practical aspects of the followers' lives. Thus, the prophet's mission has a dual focus. On the one hand there is the creation of an earthly heaven. To this end the followers are driven and inspired to sacrifice and hard work. On the other hand there are the rituals of transcendence, the charismatic moments. This blend of the conservative and the radical allows the members to create a community that transcends individuals yet doesn't crush them, that enables them to feel closer to each other, to feel powerful, cooperative, and intimate while connected to something greater than themselves.

But is the prophet really an enlightened, spiritual being? If this question asks whether the prophet has personally experienced with the fullness of his being—with his feelings and in his relationships—a spiritual reality, then the answer appears to be no. Indeed, quite the opposite is true; it is the very shallowness of the prophet's feelings and relationships, his pervasive narcissism, that prevents him from ever entering into a genuine relationship with another, or ever having anything other than pseudo feelings for others. Further, it is his vague awareness that this is so, that something is profoundly wrong, that drives the prophet to try to solve for others some problem he has been unable to solve for himself. Yet there must be more to this, for clearly prophets must at times feel *some* spiritual stirrings. But they are such intensely private, secretive beings that we may never know what such feelings involve. What might the inner life of the prophet look like if we could see it clearly, or if he could talk of it honestly, devoid of all posturing, egoism, and grandiosity? Is this not merely another human like ourselves, struggling to find meaning in life? Perhaps the reality behind the myth is as unremarkable as the next person's, but we may never know.

Believers find this hard to stomach. How could anyone discover a profound spiritual insight and not be affected by it? The answer to this contradiction is that there is a religious vocabulary that has properties similar to the "languages" of modern art and popular music and, like them, can be creatively recombined in endless variations, in ways no more meaningful than the way a pop songwriter moves product. A little dualism here, a touch of New Thought or mysticism there, some derivative meditation practices with a new twist, and some moral rules derived from an esoteric religious tradition, all packaged with intelligence, sensitivity, and an inspiration born of genuine conviction, and soon one has a new religion. No matter how bizarre a cosmogony is, there will always be some who accept it, for it is the singer, not the song, that they really respond to. The leader's ability to perceive or think differently is more important than his message (Bohm 1993, 42). His ability to ask strategic questions—as Werner Erhard asked his associates, "How do I know I'm *not* the reincarnation of Jesus Christ?" —recontextualizes their lives so persuasively that he opens up hitherto unseen possibilities for them, and prods them to confront difficult issues in promising ways that avoid old pitfalls and conflicts. Prophets are seldom original and their message is usually banal, but they are great repackagers. L. Ron Hubbard repackaged Scientology from occultism, and est/Forum was a repackaging of Scientology by Werner Erhard, but few Scientologists or estians ever see the connections, and both leaders seem to have gained little from their teachings. This is what the followers of Erhard found so unsettling; he was the great pop artist of spirituality yet was unable to apply his insights to himself (Pressman 1993, 97). This virtually universal principle has been dubbed "Esalen's Law" and runs "One teaches best that which one most needs to learn" (Anderson 1983). In a similar vein, Chogyam Trungpa has advised that "ego can convert *anything* to its own ends, *even spirituality*" (Trungpa 1973, 55).

The messiah is not a professional performer; rather, he is an inspired amateur. Hence, there is often a pathetic pretentiousness to these leaders, many of whom are quite unworldly. The prophet's ego is unrestrained, and when his grandiosity overrides his common sense, the effect is risible. When God's messenger lives off welfare, as one of the leaders in this study did, or when the enlightened master talks naive nonsense about science and philosophy, unaware of his ignorance, sophisticated followers get frankly embarrassed. An Australian guru who refused to participate in this study because, as he told me by letter, "your life as you are living it is empty of real meaning" (he knows nothing about my life), recently contributed "something new and original to . . . psychology [which] no psychologist is going to believe or understand." What was this epochal revelation? It was that the subject of psychology is not its object.[2]

The charismatic prophet blends love and hate in a larger-than-life way. He attaches himself to a social or religious conflict from which he offers salvation and articulates a vision of truth and love. But his love is also a vehicle for his hate. His talk of love and truth serves three needs. It helps him achieve an inner equilibrium, for he dimly senses the powerful antagonism that drives him. It also attracts followers—who don't usually sense his underlying hostility, and without whom he cannot feel whole. Last, it enables him to vent his hatred, to criticize, oppose, attack, and destroy, without having to acknowledge this side of himself. He wages war, but in a good cause. He thrives on conflict because it weakens others while it allows him to express his hostility in a virtuous way.

How, then, are we to evaluate prophetic charisma? Scholars tend to view it in an "unrelentingly negative light," but such judgments merely reflect their moral bias (Lindholm 1990, 74). After a detailed analysis of the leading theories of charisma, Charles Lindholm concluded that "The moral opprobrium in which these theorists hold charisma is . . . not grounded in their material but is instead an artefact of their desire to uphold the civilised world and its values without any way of justifying them" (Lindholm 1990, 69).

Because prophetic charisma is "part of our human condition" (Lindholm 1990, 189) that by its nature is opposed to whatever is conventional, in evaluating it we shouldn't begin by assuming conventional values and then proceed to the inevitable conclusion that charisma is in some way evil or wrong. Rather, we should be tentative, judging charisma both in its own terms and according to enduring values. Kohut defended amoral creativity in the belief that living out the

2. Barry Long n.d., 87–88. Also personal communication (1992).

agenda of one's nuclear self leads inevitably to socially beneficial results even though society may at first disapprove. He argued that
because social values change, mere agreement with a particular moral
or ethical system counts for little (Kohut 1980, 498). This approach is
consistent with Rajneesh's dictum that "authenticity *is* morality" and
attempts to judge charisma on its own terms. But it implies that means
outweigh ends, and may be repugnant to many.

To evaluate prophetic charisma by some external ethic, we must
first clarify its essential nature—the meaning of "pure" charisma. The
key theme of charisma is release from both internal (conscience) and
external (social and economic) restraints; release from "traditional or
rational everyday economising" (Weber 1946, 362); release from custom, law, tradition, and all notions of sanctity (Weber 1968a, 1117); and
release from "ordinary worldly attachments and duties of occupational
and family life" (Weber 1968a, 1113). Pure charisma "revolutionises
men from within" (Weber 1968a, 1116) by freeing emotional and in-
stinctive elements previously repressed by convention (Dow 1978, 85).
It is an "emotional life-force" antagonistic to the dreary constraints of
convention that replaces conformity with passion (Weber 1946, 115),
and that has an unconditional orientation to absolute values (Weber
1946, 117; Dow 1978). Release comes after the follower recognizes in
the prophet forces that also exist within himself. The follower's devotion to the leader frees these forces within. Release results in ecstasy
(Weber 1968a, 401), and leads to rebirth and "self-deification" (Weber
1968a, 535). The actions of the leader that produce ecstasy may include
rituals involving sex, drugs, and music—orgies. These work by breaking down the inhibitions that normally restrain the forces within
(Weber 1968a, 535). This association of charisma with ecstasy is essentially Dionysian, and exposes the elemental and demonic nature of
charisma. Like Dionysus, charisma represents the incarnate life force,
the "thrust of the sap in the tree and the blood in the veins"
(Arrowsmith 1958, 537). The prophet who releases this force represents
divine grace devoid of morality (Arrowsmith 1958, 537). The force is
elemental rather than ethical; it is not devilish but "the reality of care-
less power" (Arrowsmith 1958, 537).

Having thus grasped the meaning of pure charisma, we may now
choose an ethical stance from which to evaluate its amoral nature. Max
Weber took a stand on classical democratic theory (Bachrach 1967,
324–25), from which he concluded that while the unrestrained release

of charisma can be a vehicle for personal freedom, it may also lead to a kind of imprisonment in which maturity and disciplined achievement are impossible (Dow 1978). Charisma may lead to personal growth, but it is too undisciplined and irresponsible to serve as a model for any kind of viable society. Weber would seem to have history on his side, at least Christian history. When the fires of the early cult died down, it took the reformer Paul, and later Emperor Constantine, to succeed where Jesus and his followers had failed. Thus charisma would seem to be a necessary and inevitable part of human growth, albeit a transitory part. We may not always approve of it, but we need it just the same, for "we shall not cease from exploration." Perhaps it will always be so.

This linkage of new religious movements with the early Christian cult and the foundations of Western values will no doubt be difficult for some to accept. A paradox underlying this study is the steadfast refusal by many—including some "experts"—to recognize the significance of these movements. For in the history of religion the original Christian community is just one more cult, Jesus just one more miracle worker. If one wishes to know the inner meaning of Christianity, then one of the necessary requirements, along with study of the Bible and so on, is an understanding of charismatic prophets and their followers. This is best achieved by immersion in such a group; study is the easy part—there is no risk involved. But one who merely studies what Jesus supposedly said has at best a poor understanding of who Jesus was, what he meant, and what was driving him. Hence the clergy criticize cults without seeing that Jesus at the well, the forgiveness of Mary Magdalene, the fishing for men, and so on and on, recur daily at the margins of society. Scholars pore over the minutiae of the early Christian cult, filtered through God knows what adulterations, yet dismiss the adventures of contemporary cultists. In a recent study of a fundamentalist Christian cult the author—a clergyman—concluded by listing some warning signs for religious groups to watch out for. The first of them is given below.

When the life of a group is dominated by the insights or "revelations" or "words of knowledge" or "prophecies" of one or a few people, and where these utterances are assigned a higher priority than the normal process of reading, discussion and reflection. This is by its nature dangerous. It denies those who do not have such "special gifts" the capacity to make the same decisions. Once such a division occurs within the life of the community, where a tiny minority acquires the unquestioned right to state the word of God, it puts the rest into a dependency relationship which inevitably begins to cramp their growth to maturity. It also puts an excessive emphasis on the importance of special spiritual gifts. (Millikan 1991, 199)

Surely this description applies to the early Christian community. Isn't this writer merely trying to "uphold the civilised world and its values" (Lindholm 1990, 69) while ignoring the cultish origins of his own faith? Is such willed denial a greater or lesser danger than the cults themselves pose? Perhaps the theory proposed in this book—of ecstasy, transcendence, and the quest for truth and love in charismatic cults—fails to impress such experts, but equally their rejection of it may be explained in terms of their social niche. The authorities who defend orthodoxy are no strangers to ecstasy. Theirs is the ecstasy of social status, the truth of the majority. It is a function of their self-interest to see things "one way," and it is in opposition to such sentiments that charisma thrives. Religion brings out the best and the worst in us; it is an outgrowth of faith but it requires nourishment in real life to mature. To deny the cultish origins of our culture, and to refuse to consider the implications thereof, are the behaviors of those whose spirituality is fearful and conventional, who cannot—*who must not and will not*—understand. The religious life is not for everyone, and it does not encompass everything; perhaps after all it is not even a great thing, but neither is it nothing. If we could only ask the right questions, we might learn much from those who say, "We are more than conquerors. For neither death nor life, neither angels nor demons, neither the present nor the future, nor any powers, neither height nor depth, nor anything else in all creation, can separate us from the love of God" (Romans 8:37–39).

One lesson we may learn from the study of prophetic charisma concerns our understanding of the moral and spiritual basis of culture. Western civilization evolved from, and is still rooted in, Christianity. At the center of this religion is a man, Jesus of Nazareth. We know little about Jesus, but what we do know suggests that he was probably the charismatic leader of a religious cult. It is likely that the founders of other religions were charismatic prophets, too. What we can discover about these leaders may affect our most fundamental ideas about ourselves. Doing this may be like tracking down and reclaiming our lost fathers, to finally come of age beyond mere servility to, or rejection of, the originators of culture. If it turns out that saviors, prophets, and messiahs are extraordinary in something like the way this study suggests—that is, they are not "normal," but neither are they pathological or solely God-inspired—that their peculiar development has enabled them to retain certain traits that, when functional, others identify with the sacred and that everyone once possessed, then we will surely have arrived "where we started, [to] know the place for the first time."

Another lesson concerns what kind of beings we think we are. It seems that we are creatures of divine and devilish passions. The members of new religious movements are in the same position that Jesus' disciples were, and they respond in the same way. They believe that God is on earth and that the millennium is at hand, but they are not fools. Only by holding to this singular belief—that they are participating in the divine drama—are they different from others. They are ourselves, as we might be in the presence of God or whatever ultimate concerns we hold dearest. We might ask ourselves how we would behave if we sincerely believed that God had come to Earth. Suppose I met Jesus—what would be the implications for the rest of my life? Would I abandon my family to follow Him? After all, I wouldn't want to turn my back on Jesus, would I? Would I let Him marry me off to a stranger, as the Reverend Sun Myung Moon does for his followers? Would I abandon my career to live in a rural commune just to be closer to Him? Perhaps Jesus would not ask these things of me, but suppose He did? He did last time He came. Perhaps, if He asked, in His presence, it would all seem all right. God can perform miracles, can't He? He would make it all right, wouldn't He? Perhaps I might break the law for Him. Cult members who do these things say that they are obeying a higher law. Perhaps the justification of the law is that it guides us in the absence of God, and in His presence we have no need of laws. (Secular humanists may smile at this and speak of "misplaced idealism," but they, too, can be recruited to the great struggle between good and evil in times of war.)

So a third question is, What is one's relationship to higher powers or ultimate concerns? How seriously do we take our values? Seriously enough to live and die for them? Most people never have to face the fact that, given the right circumstance, they are capable of *anything!* It is given to few to step over that threshold. None return unchanged, and most are unable to tell of it sensibly. For those who do abandon convention in pursuit of an impossible ideal, their joys, griefs, triumphs and failures, wisdom and foolishness are the inevitable lot of all fallible human beings who thus cast themselves adrift. We may watch them and say, "So would I, if I believed."

Last, there is the lesson of the prophet himself. When we come to know him as he really is, unfiltered by our superstitions and sentiment, we realize that within every great truth there is a great lie, that beside every virtue is a vice, beneath order lies chaos, and at the core of our noblest ideals lies a terrible delusion: that much of what we call "truth" is just a defense against the unknown. As anthropologist Geza Roheim put it, "culture is the fabrication of a child afraid to be alone in the dark." This is the point of the distinction between the historical Jesus and the mythic Christ. To discover that one's culture has been built upon an illusion is not pleasant, but could it have been any other way? Was it perhaps a necessary illusion? A justified illusion? Perhaps it would all be all right, maybe it would even come true, near Him! Oh, we protest, but perhaps in God's presence we would feel differently. Near Him I might discard what I think of as my "self" and discover that I am really quite a different person. I might abandon all restraint, perform "unspeakable rites" in His name and in the sanctity of His power; I might find wild ecstasies, fantastic struggles, total repose. Untroubled by fear, having no heed of care, I might abandon this life to Him, believing that all that has gone before is but a dream, that all will be redeemed in some near/far paradise wherein I and my loved ones always were, now are, and soon will be. As Joseph Conrad concluded in *Heart of Darkness*: "Perhaps in this is the whole difference: perhaps all the wisdom, and all truth, and all sincerity, are just compressed into that inappreciable moment of time in which we step over the threshold of the invisible" (Conrad 1950).

Appendixes

Works Cited

Index

Appendix A | On Theory and Method

In attempting to study charismatic leaders of new religious and quasi-religious movements, a mixed research strategy was chosen. This combined both qualitative and quantitative techniques, as advocated by many theorists (e.g., Clark and Reis 1988; Campbell 1979; Filstead 1979; Glaser and Strauss 1967; Lazerfield 1972; Patton 1980; Reichardt and Cook 1979). Psychometric and life history data were collected from both leaders and followers; existing theories of charisma were used to generate research questions and to guide the analysis of data; and both inductive and deductive methods of analysis were used to find emergent patterns in the data and to explore and extend those patterns, as well as to demonstrate linkages between them. In sum, the variety of data sources, types of data gathering, and analysis methods represented an attempt to provide rigor, control, and triangulation to the study (Denzin 1970).

Three questionnaires were used. The quantitative instrument chosen was the Adjective Checklist (ACL; Gough and Heilbrun 1983), a three hundred-item measure of personality. When using the ACL to describe themselves or some target individual, respondents merely check the adjectives they feel are appropriate. When results are processed, a personality profile is assembled that comprises thirty-seven subscales. Four of the subscales are methodological; fifteen are based on the personality theory of Henry Murray (1938); nine are "topical" scales not drawn from any particular theory and include such subscales as "Counseling readiness" and "Military leadership"; five are derived from the theory of Transactional Analysis developed by Eric Berne (1961); and the remaining four subscales utilize the theory of creativity and intelligence proposed by Welsh (1975). The ACL is a very widely used measure of personality (Buros (1978, vol. 1, xxxvii-xxxix). Normative samples have been calculated for the most commonly studied categories of subjects—adults, students, psychiatric patients, and so forth—and reliabilities are reported to be in the range of 0.7 to 0.9 (Gough and Heilbrun 1983, 31). The ACL has been used in a variety of psychobiographical and observer-rating studies (Gough and Heilbrun 1983, 39–44) and in at least one other major study of a charismatic group (Richardson, Stewart, and Simmonds 1979). Hence the ACL is especially appropriate to the present research because its content derives not from a preexisting theory but from an empirical study of descriptive language. Further, one may use it to develop more specialized scales of whatever traits or behaviors one wishes to study.

The Interview Questionnaire for Leaders was constructed by myself. It comprised ten items intended to get close to the heart of the leaders' self-concepts and ultimate concerns. The first item was the "True Self Method" of Turner and Schutte (1981). In addition to eliciting important information, this item was intended to set the mood for the rest of the interview. Other items were either questions that I had seen in a variety of sources and that seemed likely to develop the lines of inquiry intended, or items I developed based on my reading of the literature on charismatic religious leaders and minority religious groups. For example, the item "Inexpressible Knowledge" was adapted from Foster (1983). It asked the leaders to respond to a statement made by the Mormon prophet Joseph Smith, who, in a sermon a few months before his death, spoke of his inability and refusal to convey his deepest message to his closest followers: "You never knew my heart; no man knows my history. I cannot tell it. I shall never undertake it; if I had not experienced what I have I should not have known it myself" (Foster 1984a, 47). It seemed to me that this statement reflected an experience common to prophets, perhaps indicating an inability or refusal by them to divulge their inner lives. It also seemed to be a useful stimulus item to provoke an open-ended inquiry by the leaders that might take them away from familiar ground, which they were well-practiced at talking about, and into novel areas where their answers might become more spontaneous and revealing. Other examples are the items "If you were asked to pass on your accumulated wisdom in the form of a statement that others might use as a sort of guiding insight to help them live their lives, what would you say?" and "Imagine you have died and been buried and a gravestone has been erected. . . . On the gravestone is written an epitaph. What would it say to accurately sum up your life and work?" These items were not intended to be interview questions in the usual manner; they did not seek specific information. Rather, they were items that seemed to me, based on my sixteen-year association with a charismatic religious leader, to tap some nerve central to the being of the prophetic mentality.

Questions seeking specific demographic information also were asked, and these items either were used at the beginning of each interview to set the mood, or were interwoven with the other items, sometimes to refocus attention or to dampen the emotional intensity of the exchange. The interviews were tape-recorded. The combination of demographic and provocative questions enabled a biography of each leader to be constructed.

The Interview Questionnaire for Followers also was constructed by myself. It comprised eighteen items derived from discussions I had with members of the critical case group. It explored issues I felt were important in understanding the personality of the charismatic leader and his relationship with his followers. It included items such as "Has there been a cycle or pattern to your relationship with the leader?" "What do you find most difficult to discuss with the leader?" and "What would you most like to change about this group?"

The nature of the questionnaires for leaders and followers derived from my growing conviction that a standard life history inventory would not get at the essence of charisma, which lies in subjective experience and is poorly related to objective events. For example, the theory of charisma used herein ought to be consistent with certain birth-order effects involving eldest or only sons. At least one researcher (Zablocki 1980) has set out to study such effects. Nevertheless, birth-order effects turn out to be illusory (Schooler 1972), and while one may remain sympathetic to a modified form of a birth-order effect hypothesis such that charismatic prophets ought to be mostly favored children or those perceived as in some way special, this raises questions about why some children are favored or seen as special while others aren't, and what the experience of such favoritism and specialness means to the child. These questions begin to return us to the subjective focus adopted in this study. Hence it is acceptable to complement the "hard" technology of the ACL with a radically "soft" approach in which questionnaire items serve merely as vehicles for the exploration of subjective experience, arguably the "most radical exercise of reason" (Wolff 1976). More on this below.

The population from which this sample was drawn included leaders of communal, new religious, quasi-therapeutic, and New Age movements, and charismatic Christian churches resident in New Zealand in the years 1989–91, as well as two international leaders with followers in New Zealand who visited that country in the period of this study, and three deceased leaders of communal movements.

Selection of the sample was initially based on two field trips to eighteen communes in New Zealand in September and October 1990. This sample yielded qualitative data on eight leaders (three of whom were deceased) but quantitative data on only five. To increase the sample size, the scope of the study was broadened to include founders of quasi-therapeutic, New Age, and new religious movements. This increased the sample by two leaders for whom both qualitative and quantitative data were obtained. Two visiting American personal growth entrepreneurs with substantial personal followings also were included. Last, the leader of the critical case group and one former Pentecostal pastor were added. This was the sample of fourteen leaders who were the subjects of my doctoral research.

Criteria for selection of leaders were (a) they must have founded or co-founded their group; (b) their leadership must be charismatic, that is, their followers must have a sense of personal loyalty and devotion to them; and (c) the movement must stand outside mainstream society, in opposition to some of its central values.

Each of the leaders was asked to nominate two or more "close friends, associates, or followers" who could be approached to gather data concerning the leader. Four followers of overseas charismatic leaders of alternative religious movements (Rajneesh and Da Avadhoota) also were interviewed because they seemed to have particularly insightful experiences to relate. In all, this resulted in the following participants and data:

1. Eleven leaders were interviewed, and both quantitative and qualitative data were gained from them.

2. Thirty-one nominated followers of these leaders were interviewed, and both qualitative and quantitative data were gained from them.

3. In the case of one of these leaders, a survey of the entire adult membership of his group was undertaken using the ACL. This resulted in a case study of eighty followers and their relationships with their leader.

4. Three deceased leaders were studied via qualitative data gained from eleven of their followers. (Quantitative data were not attempted in these instances because of the advanced age of most of the followers.)

5. Four followers of two overseas leaders were interviewed, and qualitative data were obtained from them.

Many other informants participated in the study. These were spouses, family members, friends, and acquaintances of the various leaders. Conversations with these informants were accepted—and sometimes encouraged—by the leaders. Anyone who had the time and a relevant story to tell was listened to.

After the completion of my dissertation, I moved to Australia and continued this work. Six more leaders and eight followers were studied there, using the same questionnaires as before. This resulted in a final total of 20 leaders and 136 followers.

Seventeen of the leaders were male and three were female. Their average age was 49, and they ranged in age from 37 to 70 with a standard deviation of 9.7 years. Ten held university degrees, three had matriculated, and the remainder had lesser (e.g., trade) or no educational qualifications. Three leaders had bachelor's degrees in religion, one held a bachelor's and a master's degree in English, another had a bachelor's degree in English, one had a double-major bachelor's degree in politics and history, and four subjects had bachelor's degrees in the social sciences. Of the three female leaders, their ages were forty, fifty-four, and seventy; none had a degree but two had trade certificates. Five of the male leaders were currently separated, divorced, or widowed; three were in a relationship; six had never married; and the three deceased subjects were married at the time of death. Of the females, two were married and one had never married.

Sixty-seven of the followers interviewed were male. Their average age was forty-two, with a range from twenty-three to sixty-seven. Nineteen of them held at least one degree, thirty-one had other tertiary or trade qualifications, and seventeen had no educational qualifications. Forty-five were married, fifteen were separated, divorced, or widowed, and seven had never married.

Sixty-five of the followers interviewed were women. Their average age was forty-three, and the range was from twenty-three to fifty-two. Fourteen held a degree and sixteen had other tertiary or trades qualifications; thirty-five had no educational qualifications. Forty were married, twenty were separated, divorced, or widowed, and five had never married.

The length of time each group had been in existence varied from a week to about 20 years, with a mean of 9.5 years. The group that had been in existence for one week was headed by a woman who had functioned informally as a leader in the wider community for several years. When interviewed, she was beginning her second communal group. An earlier communal experiment—with different participants—had been wound up some years earlier. The average number of followers in each group was 65 (including children), with a range from 6 to 280 (including children) and a standard deviation of 69.

Descriptive ideologies of the groups are Human Potential (4); ecological (2); fundamentalist, Pentecostal, or other Christian (5); Eastern religious (3); anarchist (1); Rastafarian (1); New Age (2); and occult (2). Eleven of these groups were communal.

The design of the study was an extension of the designs used by Labak (1972) and Hall (1983). Information concerning the personalities and behaviors of the leaders was obtained from two sources—leaders and followers. In addition, both leaders' and followers' responses were quantified in a directly comparable format using the ACL.

Followers were either directly nominated by leaders or were recruited in the various communes and centers I visited. The criteria for their selection were that they had to have been closely associated with their leader for at least five years, and in that time had had considerable face-to-face contact with that leader, enough to form some idea of the leader's personality.

Data on leaders were gathered in a variety of ways, with most interviews being conducted in their homes. Each interview began with an explanation of the purposes of the study. After this and various administrative tasks, such as informed consent, had been taken care of, leaders were asked several demographic questions and then requested to provide the names of two or more long-standing friends, associates, or followers to serve as sources of information concerning them. Next, leaders were asked to complete the ACL. After this, open-ended questions from the Interview Questionnaire for Leaders were asked in interviews lasting from one to (in one case) fourteen hours.

Nominated followers were approached and interviews were requested with them. Most interviews were conducted in followers' homes and had a format similar to that for the leaders but using the Interview Questionnaire for Followers. Followers and informants not nominated by the leaders were interviewed wherever they were encountered. They were also asked the questions contained in the Interview Questionnaire for Followers.

The leaders chosen for study in phase 2 were small-scale charismatic leaders with at most a few hundred followers. Zablocki (1980) has argued that such groups are ideal for the study of charismatic processes, and claimed we may safely infer from them the basic dynamics of the larger-scale charismatic prophets. However, these leaders are not representative of all so-called prophets. The sickly child whose nightmares become the inspiration for a cargo cult (Burridge 1969, 12), the feebleminded epileptic visionary whose utterances rally others to rebellion (Wilson 1975), and Durkheim's criminal-prophet (Emmet 1958) do not fit this definition. Nor do "pseudo-charismatics" (Benseman and Givant 1975), "totem" leaders (Conger and Kanungo 1988), activist priests, or those curious "rational" charismatics typified (in the political sphere) by Vladimir Lenin and George Washington (Conger and Kanungo 1988). On the other hand, several times in this book reference is made to research on the personality of Adolf Hitler that is too well-developed to ignore (Willner 1984). No doubt the inclusion of Fritz Perls as a charismatic prophet will be argued, despite the fact that he founded a movement and a commune (even devising a prayer), opposed convention, and clearly enjoyed charismatic relations with his followers.

At least as important as the questions asked of the leaders, followers, and informants was the way the interviews were conducted. They were somewhat spontaneous and intuitively based, and arose from my experience as an insider of the critical case group. The methods are not mysterious and will be described, but it is perhaps unlikely that someone who had never been in a relationship with a charismatic leader would have followed quite the same lines of inquiry pursued herein.

The interview techniques were derived from various psychotherapeutic and journalistic procedures. They were aimed at getting past superficial concerns and pat explanations as quickly as possible, and at evoking a reflective stance on the part of subjects. This involved such strategies as the tactical use of silences, repetitions, and ambiguous "Why?" questions; requests for specific examples, instances, and anecdotes to illustrate general points; pacing interviewees' body language and metacommenting on their paralinguistic cues concerning their interests, energies, agitations, and disturbances—the processes rather than the contents of their replies—and trying to reach the sources of these cues; tracing specific feelings and ideas reported by interviewees back through their entire life spans, typically with such questions as "Can you recall the first time you ever felt that way?"; relating answers of questions to unusual or neglected lines of inquiry that seemed likely, given the specific situation, to be profitable, and even using such chestnuts as "What would your mother think if she could hear you speaking now?"; and such other impromptu devices as seemed to keep the interviewees focusing on what Kurt Wolff (1976) has called "existential truths."

In addition, self-disclosure on my part was used to encourage and continue self-disclosure by informants (Jourard and Resnik 1970), and self-monitoring of my responses to their answers was used to detect replies that may have been defensive or evasive. Hence the interviews were fashioned more along the lines of the "research alliance" suggested by Offer and Strozier (1985, 305) and consistent with suggestions made by Oakley (1981) and Kohut (1976, 422) rather than in accordance with any textbook ideal or model.

These interview techniques, the design of the open-ended questions, and the overall strategy for the qualitative portion of this study followed the lines advocated by Wolff (1976). The attempt was to delve as deeply as possible into the hearts and minds of the leaders in the brief time available, and to study their *essential* natures, or their "peculiar spirit" (Kakar 1981, 14). The behaviors, thoughts, and feelings that the leaders had in common with other people (Wolff 1976, 74–77) were not of primary interest. Rather, an attempt was made to develop a specific mood of "surrender" (Wolff 1976), characterized by "empathic closeness with total sectors of another's mind" (Kohut 1976, 384). In this mood, the suspension of received notions might allow for a total or near-total involvement and identification between the interviewer and each leader. From this, I hoped, some of the *essential* nature of the leader's charisma would be revealed, specifically those behaviors, thoughts, and feelings that were uniquely his. The hope was to push past words and theories to their experiential roots (Berger 1980, 191). Hence the study was not just a search for scientific truth. Rather, a mixed strategy was developed in which the scientific facts explored by the quantitative measures were augmented by "existential truths" (Wolff 1976, 128) produced by the qualitative methodology in the manner of such studies as Osgood (1953), Turnbull (1961), Bowen (1954), Lévi-Strauss (1955), and Bateson (1936).

In the interviews I attempted—as much as I was able—to abandon the role of scientific investigator and to enter as fully as possible into the worlds of the leaders. The intention was to avoid seeing them through a web of theoretical concepts, and to seek out some part of myself that responded to each leader's charisma. This involved as much self-observation on my part as it involved observation of the leaders; as Lévi-Strauss has said, time in the field is "a time, above all, of self-interrogation" (Lévi-Strauss, 1955, 374). I chose not to suppress the suspicion that this research was also a search for new light on issues in my own life, for that is the attitude of the charismatic follower (see also Kakar 1981, 12). In sum, a search was undertaken for the essence of the charismatic leader, the part of him that was unique to him, that stood revealed when all else was suspended, and from which he might congruently claim (paraphrasing Beethoven) that "He who understands my music [message] can never know unhappiness again" (Wolff 1976, 86); I also sought some part of myself that might enthusiastically agree.

For quantitative data analysis, the ACL was scored per the manual (Gough and Heilbrun 1983) and comparisons were made with appropriate samples therein. Profiles were calculated using the Excell spreadsheet program, and subsequent statistical analysis was performed using the Systat statistics program (Wilkinson 1975).

Qualitative data analysis involved inductive and deductive procedures, as recommended by Patton (1980). This included intuitive, creative, and analytic skills, and considerable repetition and patience in studying the data. The interview data were examined many times and extensive notes were made. On the basis of these notes, data were sorted into categories according to criteria established in defining the categories. From this process, patterns and linkages emerged, new categories were established, and several old categories were abandoned. Then the quantitative data were consulted to strengthen or extend the categories, and some new patterns were identified. Finally the categories and patterns were prioritized and examined for completeness and accuracy, using the theoretical perspectives of Weber (1946) and Kohut (1976).

During the course of the study a range of issues emerged that proved problematic and thus deserve to be mentioned. In the first place, the gathering of data posed several problems. While some of the leaders were quite happy to talk with me about themselves and their work, most weren't. Their reasons were always the same: they had suffered at the hands of the media and various authorities, and were suspicious of outsiders. They had not always felt this way, but had become less inclined to talk to outsiders as a result of negative experiences. One leader stated that his group had initially welcomed visitors, but had eventually been forced to seal themselves off from the world and post guards at the gates at night. He added that he still allowed trainee social workers and teachers to visit by appointment, but "We don't admit students anymore; there's no one more arrogant than students." He recounted several misadventures to support this claim.

In the face of such resistance, two strategies were found to be useful. First, face-to-face introductions were far more effective than even the most carefully crafted letter. As an older student (aged forty-two) I found that I had much more credibility than a young person might have. Second, I took with me a kit of documents, including my passport and various official letters, that provided the subjects with very tight guarantees of confidentiality.

How successful were these stratagems? In all, eighteen communal and twelve noncommunal groups were contacted, from which satisfactory qualitative and quantitative data on eleven charismatic leaders, and partial qualitative data on three more, were gathered. In a comparable effort, Zablocki (1980) contacted 120 communes but gained satisfactory qualitative and quantitative data on only three resident charismatic leaders (although he gathered a great deal of other relevant data). Bradley (1987) contacted fifty-seven communal groups but gained satisfactory quantitative and qualitative data on only four resident charismatic leaders. It must be said that the aims of these two researchers were somewhat different from those in the present study, but the disparity of results is striking nonetheless. However, the sample for this study was quite different from those of Zablocki and Bradley. The groups in this study were much older and generally larger, with several into their second or third generation.

Another issue found to be problematic concerned the label "charismatic," which I soon learned to avoid but never managed to totally cull from my vocabulary. Several leaders rejected the label. Another headed a group that espoused an anarchistic philosophy that would not recognize charismatic leadership within itself (officially at least; in fact, several members frankly described their spokesman/leader/founder and author of the group's constitution as charismatic). Hall (1983, 61), Bradley (1987), and Zablocki (1980) mention this problem also.

A related issue—that was never really resolved satisfactorily—concerned the relationships of the "followers" to the leaders. Most were clearly in charismatic relationships with their leader, in that they spoke of him in terms of love, awe, and obedience, but some weren't. These were followers whose relationships with their leaders were much more equal. For example, one said that "He [the leader] taught me all I know," yet described himself as a long-time friend of the leader and clearly was not bound by any kind of leader-follower contract, implicit or explicit. They were "best friends" and "supporters" of the leaders. These relationships occurred in the context of organizations whose ideology didn't permit a stated charismatic relationship. Yet in most ways these relationships still seemed charismatic, and the leaders were commanding figures. In considering this matter it is perhaps best to remember that charisma occurs within a matrix of social understandings that take a great variety of forms. The character of the relationships of Churchill and his followers was different from the character of the relationships of Hitler and his followers, yet each was charismatic. Within the countercultural milieu, charismatic followers describe themselves with a variety of adjectives ranging from the "lovers" of Meher Baba, to adherents of est who have "it" and are grateful to Werner Erhard for giving "it" to them. For sake of consistency, in each case where a follower was nominated by a leader, that person was interviewed, but in fact the varieties of followership varied tremendously.

This was especially problematic with the followers of Rajneesh and Da Avadhoota, all of whom had lived with these gurus for years; had meditated, eaten, and slept in the same quarters with these leaders many times; and who felt a close psychic bond with them, even including claims of telepathic communication. Yet from what I was told of the social structures of these groups, it was clear that these followers did not enjoy the same frequent physical access to their leaders as most of the other followers in this study, especially those who lived communally with their leaders.

Another complicating factor is that while the criteria used (see above) ensured that most of the followers identified themselves as followers, several did not. For five followers—four members of the Oceanville community and a historian preparing a history of that community—this was appropriate because they were second-generation members of the community who had been born into their relationships with the leader. However, some of the other followers would probably refuse to describe themselves as followers. This problem is not as great as it may seem, however, because these persons were in fact members of movements headed by the leaders concerned. In all, there were only two nominated followers who were not formal or informal members of movements headed by the leaders; these two would be best described as long-term friends.

The result is a spectrum of followers ranging from those who were relatively distant from their leaders for much of their discipleship, to those whose contact with their leaders had been face-to-face and daily for twenty or more years. This continuum of proximity cannot be reliably measured, but in analyzing the results it was never found to be a problem. When gathering followers' reports of the various leaders' personalities, specific behavioral examples were sought. Where these were lacking, less weight was given to the accounts of the more distant followers. Hence the quality of data gathered concerning the leaders varied from—at one extreme—many lengthy interviews (formal and informal) with the leader and his followers, as well as access to historical documents including military service records and other personal papers dating back to the leader's childhood, and extended discussions with siblings about the early life of the leader—to, at the other extreme, a single one-hour interview with the leader and another one-hour interview with one follower. Such horizontal and vertical variations in the data of the central phenomena under study have been mentioned by others working in this field (e.g., Barker 1984, 84, 89) and have been handled quite successfully by them.

Theoretical issues also emerged that need, if not resolution, at least justification of the stance taken herein. This study unashamedly attempts to address "Why?" questions, which psychology has mostly found difficult to handle (Eacker 1975, 53–54; Westland 1978; Valentine 1982; Frosh 1989). The aim is to find out why charismatic prophets behave as they do; that is, to get at the causes and intentions of their behavior. Depth psychology was selected as the most promising vehicle for such theorizing, despite its "unscientific" nature

(MacMillan 1992; Wallerstein 1988). The position adopted herein is similar to that of Frosh (1989), who argued that psychoanalysis, "despite its frequent wildness," is valuable because it asks questions of great provocativeness. That is, it asks for "the meaning of actions, their significance and intention, and the subjective position they hold within the life of the person concerned" (Frosh 1989, 6–7; see also Gitelson 1954, 178; Edelson 1988, 8).

Generally speaking, depth psychology loses credibility the more observation-distant it becomes. Clinical reports no doubt deserve the same scientific status as reliable observations made by trained observers anywhere, but the metapsychological speculations of analysts are controversial even among the orthodox, and the spectacle of the dozen or more competing "schools" does psychoanalysis no credit. This study attempts to remain as close as possible to the level of observation, venturing into metapsychology only when the material seems to demand it.

The main depth psychological approach used was the "Self-psychology" of Heinz Kohut (1913–81). Self-psychology is seen by some as the "leading paradigm of psychoanalysis" (Ornstein 1978, 1:91), while Kohut is said to have "revitalized" depth psychology (Strozier and Offer, 1985, 73). Kohut studied a difficult class of patients, the narcissistic disorders. From them he developed his main theory: that the dynamic "Self" coalesces in the primitive psyche in early infancy and develops throughout the life span, relatively independent of the tripartite structure of classical psychoanalysis (id, ego, and superego). In studying narcissistic patients Kohut also noticed many parallels between their behaviors and those of powerful leaders. Although he never worked out a systematic theory of charisma, he did discuss it in one paper (Kohut 1976). He made many observations about such leaders as Hitler and Churchill, and left the outlines of such a theory implicit in his voluminous general works. Kohut's approach also has the added advantage of having drawn substantive critiques from the ranks of orthodox analysts and from experts outside psychoanalysis (see, e.g., Hanly and Masson 1976; Crews 1980). Of course, Kohut is by no means the only psychodynamic theorist whose work one might use to develop a theory of charisma; studies by Margaret Mahler (Mahler, Pine, and Bergman 1967), Melanie Klein (1949), D. N. Stern (1985), Anna Freud (1966), John Bowlby (1969), Rene Spitz (1965), Ernst Kris (1952), and D. W. Winnicott (1960) are all relevant. Indeed, Post (1986) has developed a theory of charisma that draws primarily on the work of Otto Kernberg, whom he finds "more congenial" than Kohut (Post 1986, 678).

However this study is not solely, or even primarily, psychoanalytic. Rather, it utilizes the convergence of several streams of psychological theory that share an appreciation for the strengths of naturalistic research and a focus on the entire life span of subjects. This tradition, beginning with Wundt (1916; see Danziger 1980) and including Gordon Allport (1937) and Henry Murray

(1938), also attempts to grapple with depth material in a historical and bio-graphical manner (Runyon 1984; White 1963; Strozier and Offer 1985). Such studies may tend to rely upon agreement rather than statistical proof as the basis of understanding, but they remain "scientific" for all that (Follesdal 1979).

The use of self in research is not new or radical; Freud's self-analysis and Piaget's study of his own children (Boring et al. 1961, 249) being obvious examples. This approach has been refined by researchers such as Jourard and Kormann (1968), who researched the effects of self-disclosure on interviewing and test performance; by Constantine and Constantine (1973, 51), who used interview strategies such as selective silence to elicit information on an emo-tionally loaded subject; and by feminist researchers such as Oakley (1981), who demonstrated the impossibility of the "proper" textbook interview when attempting to study certain subjects. She also critiqued the bias inherent in objectifying such subjects, and argued that "personal involvement is more than a dangerous bias—it is the condition under which people come to know each other and to admit others into their lives" (Oakley 1981, 58). In short, it is accepted in this study that the researcher's own behavior, and even subjective experience (Garfinkel 1967), can be useful adjuncts to inquiry at all stages of research (Gergen and Morawski 1980).

The use of an "inside-outsider" approach to data gathering is not new; Barker (1984), Kakar (1981, 13), and Constantine and Constantine (1973) also have used it. However, the interpretation of such data within the "hermeneutic circle" (Ruether 1981; Follesdal 1979) risks what Berger (1981) has called "the law of sacred biography," in which one unconsciously projects one's own values and self onto the material (Erikson 1968). How well this trap was avoided in this study, only time will tell, but since only a few researchers in this field have taken charismatic prophets seriously, it was decided that regard-less of the risks of subjectivity and projective bias, the attempt to understand such figures was worthwhile. Nonetheless, because one's epistemological stance and values can make a difference, I shall declare my own as "modern," in the sense described by Sass (1988, 556).

The use of retrospective self-report data has been both criticized (Robbins 1988) and defended (Rorer and Widiger 1983; Pervin 1985). Clearly, knowledge of context is crucial when evaluating such data, especially when one forgoes the two-source rule (Reiterman and Jacobs 1982). Some classic studies have relied on self-report data gained from empathy and evaluated with the aid of an inside-outsider understanding of context (see, e.g., Freud's case studies as well as those by Barker 1984; Foster 1983; Constantine and Constantine 1973; and Richardson, Stewart, and Simmonds 1979).

The study abandons hypothesis testing and adopts a discovery-oriented research philosophy (Mahrer 1988). This is consistent with recent critiques of traditional methodologies and the assumptions underlying them (McGuire 1980; Gergen 1985; Harre 1985; Rorer and Widiger 1983; Argyris 1980; Meehl 1978). The motive for dispensing with aspects of traditional methodology is an attempt to "study man in his full humanity," as Wilfred Cantwell Smith has argued: "The proper study of man is by inference. . . . By the exercise of imaginative sympathy, disciplined by intellectual rigour and checked by elaborate procedures, cross-checked by vigorous criticism, it is not impossible to infer what goes on in another's mind and heart" (Smith 1962, 188).

Hence it is assumed that people can give an account of themselves, and that this account, which is as valid as any "objective" social science account, can be apprehended by others who may critically evaluate it and reach an understanding of that person's subjective reality.

Another issue concerns what is involved when researching a specific trait or behavior. While it is possible to treat charisma as a continuous variable (Burke and Brinkerhoff 1981; Labak 1972, 3), it nevertheless remains a clearly observable phenomenon in only a small number of people; Labak (1972) estimates approximately 7 percent of the population. When subjects are drawn from an extremely small subpopulation, a critical case research design may be the most useful research strategy (Patton 1980), at least in the initial stages of research. Subsequently a multiple case study format is desirable to permit several representatives of the subpopulation to be compared and contrasted (Bogdan and Biklen 1982).

Ultimately, however, the results of this study must be tested in the world. Beginning with the focus on a single charismatic individual and extending the focus to include a sample of subjects who appeared to be similar, the aim is finally to generalize to the most significant contemporary and historical prophets and their followers. However, when one is focusing so closely on a single trait or behavior, secondary variance may take many forms. Other traits or behaviors may overlap and contaminate; there may be changes over time; psychopathology may or may not be present, leading to problems of detection; and the act of studying a particular trait or behavior may produce factors that influence it in the manner of feedback, amplifying or attenuating it in unpredictable ways. When attempting to counter such effects, one is often reduced to using one's intuition in the face of varying possibilities. Perhaps no two interpretations will be the same. My status as an inside-outsider gave some native expertise in the employment of intuitive analysis, but clearly no method can be infallible and the approach taken herein must invariably contain some error.

It must, of course, be conceded that there are good arguments against the existence of a charismatic personality type (Strozier and Offer 1985, 307; Conger and Kanungo 1988), *and* that a variety of quite different kinds of prophets may be identified (Burridge 1969), and that the methodological problems encountered when trying to investigate such a notion may seem all but insurmountable. Nevertheless, in closely examining both the similarities and the differences between such figures, we may learn much. Only poor scientists seek or offer total explanations (Erikson 1958, 67), and only timid researchers remain within totally controlled environments. Clearly, the construction of an "ideal-typical natural history" of prophets (Robbins 1988, 66) will not satisfy theoretical "absolutists" (Conger and Kanungo 1988, 44). This study deals with "discernible regularities" (Barker 1984, 245) rather than rules, and like most explanations it is ultimately inadequate (Forgas 1986, 111); no single explanation can be correct in the social sciences, where exceptions *are* the rule (Barker 1984, 232, 245). One can never get at truth itself (Kohut 1980, 433), and the complexity of the world seems to surpass the limited capacity of the mind (Kohut 1985, 58–59). Further, a variety of effects of an attributional nature may be postulated as distorting the data of this study; the bias toward causality (Heider and Simmel 1944; Bassili 1976; Forgas 1986, 89) and "fundamental attribution error" (Ross 1977) spring immediately to mind. However, to attempt to identify and account for all the significant possible sources of secondary variance would require a separate study in itself.

The priorities that were set for this research concerned theory construction in a hitherto poorly researched area. The questions that loomed largest as the study progressed were not those concerning the subtleties of methodological purity; rather, they concerned the much more relevant issues of how and why charismatic movements behave in the ways they do. Undoubtedly the answers proposed herein will, at certain points, hinge upon possibilities of bias and error, either in the social milieus of the particular groups studied, in the contexts and details of the data-gathering process, or in the interpretations devised. Nevertheless, it seems unlikely that charisma can be substantially explained in terms of error and bias (although some studies do attach great weight to these effects, e.g., Festinger, Reicken, and Schachter 1956).

In conclusion, it has been said that the time a researcher best knows how a particular piece of research should be carried out is after its completion. The subject of this study is elusive—almost inaccessible—and the variability and unpredictability of field research permit few inflexible rules. Improvisation, compromise, moderation, and balancing were the *real* research strategies. Improvements await demonstration.

Appendix B | Leaders Studied

Leader	Marital status	Age	Educational status	ACL
Fred Thomson	Married	65	BA	Yes
Mary Spencer	Married	70	NFE	No
Leo Haley	Married	40	NFE	Yes
Swami Joe	Single	47	BA	No
Dr. Paul Clavell	Single	49	BA	Yes
Swami Divyananda	Single	48	BA/MA	No
Rev. William Hart[1]	Married	72[3]	BA	No
Wolf Schubart	Divorced	43	Matriculation	No
Joshua Einstein	Married	37	Matriculation	No
Harry Huntington[1]	Married	62[3]	Matriculation	No
Suzie Shiva	Single	40	Trade C.	Yes
Kit van Voon	Married	57	NFE	Yes
Charlie Tantra	Single	44	BA	Yes
"Bro" John	Divorced	44	NFE	Yes
Arnold Harper	Widowed	65	Trade C.	Yes
Frank Jansen	Divorced	44	BD	Yes
"Free-Love" Farley	Married	44	BA	Yes
Lindsey Amherst[1]	Married	78[3]	BA	No
Gary Melsop[2]	Divorced	55	BD	No
Golden Tara[2]	Married	52	Trade C.	No

Notes: [1]Deceased.
[2]No interviews were given by these leaders.
[3]Age at death.

Abbreviations: BA = Bachelor of Arts degree (MA = Master of Arts).
BD = Religious studies or divinity degree.
Trade C. = Trades certificate.
NFE = No formal educational qualifications.

Appendix B | Groups Studied

Group	Number of Followers[1]	LOT[2]	Ideology
Humanitas	280	12	HP
The Tribe	100	20	HP
Rastafarian	100	6	Rastafarian
Elysium	40	10	Hindu
Orgone Centre	40	10	HP
Deva Centre	30	5	Hindu
Church Christ Love	50	5	Christian
Bro'hood Strangers	35	(unknown)	Occult
(No name)	100	5	New Age
Oceanville	50	50	Christian
(No name)	6	<1	HP
(No name)	20	16	Ecology
(No name)	50	3	Hindu
New Ecstasy	20	12	Ecology
(No name)	200	20	Christian
(No name)	100	6	Christian
Sunshine Hill	40	15	Anarchist
Clear Lake	50	45	Christian
New Christ Chch.	100	25	New Age
Anima	50	20	Occult

Notes: [1]Estimates of maximum populations.
[2]Length of time in years the group has existed.

Abbreviation: HP = Human Potential.

Works Cited

Abse, D. W., and R. B. Ulman. 1977. "Charismatic Political Leadership and Collective Regression." In *Psychopathology and Political Leadership,* edited by R. S. Robins. New Orleans: Tulane Univ. Press.

Ainsworth, M. D. S., M. C. Blehar, E. Waters, and S. Wall. 1978. *Patterns of Attachment: A Psychological Study of the Strange Situation.* Hillsdale, N.J.: Erlbaum.

Allport, G. W. 1937. *Personality: A Psychological Interpretation.* London: Constable.

———. 1942. *The Use of Personal Documents in Psychological Science.* New York: Social Science Research Council.

———. 1950. *The Individual and His Religion.* New York: Macmillan.

Anderson, W. T. 1983. *The Upstart Spring: Esalen and the American Awakening.* Reading, Mass.: Addison-Wesley.

Anthony, E. J., and B. J. Cohler, eds. 1987. *The Invulnerable Child.* New York: Guilford Press.

Arend, R., F. Gove, and L. A. Sroufe. 1979. "Continuity of Individual Adaptation from Infancy to Kindergarten: A Predictive Study of Ego-Resilience and Curiosity in Pre-schoolers." *Child Development* 50, no. 4: 950–59.

Argyris, G. 1980. *The Inner Contradictions of Rigorous Research.* New York: Academic Press.

Arrowsmith, W. 1958. Introduction to *The Bacchae.* In *The Complete Greek Tragedies,* edited by W. Greene and S. Lattimore. Vol. 4. Chicago: Univ. of Chicago Press.

Bachrach, P. 1967. *The Theory of Democratic Elitism: A Critique.* Boston: Little, Brown.

Balay, J., and H. Shevrin. 1988. "The Subliminal Psychodynamic Activation Method: A Critical Review." *American Psychologist* 43, no. 3: 161–74.

Balch, R. W. 1980. "Looking Behind the Scenes in a Religious Cult: Implications for the Study of Conversion." *Sociological Analysis* 41, no. 2: 137–43.

Balint, M. 1965. "Early Developmental States of the Ego: Primary Object-Love." Chapter 5 in *Primary Love and Psycho-analytic Technique.* New York: Liveright.

Bandler, R., and J. Grinder. 1975. *Patterns of the Hypnotic Techniques of Milton Erickson, M.D.* Vol. 1. Palo Alto, Calif.: Meta Publications.

Barker, E. 1984. *The Making of a Moonie: Choice or Brainwashing.* Oxford: Basil Blackwell.

Barnes, D. F. 1978. "Charisma and Religious Leadership: An Historical Analysis." *Journal for the Scientific Study of Religion* 17, no. 1: 1–18.

Bartlett, A. F. 1988. *Profile of the Entrepreneur, or Machiavellian Management.* Southampton: Ashford Press.

Bartley, W. W. 1978. *Werner Erhard: The Transformation of a Man — the Founding of est.* New York: Clarkson Potter.

Bassili, J. N. 1976. "Temporal and Spatial Contingencies in the Perception of Social Events." *Journal of Personality and Social Psychology* 33: 680–85.

Bateson, G. 1936. *Naven.* London: Cambridge Univ. Press.

Batson, C. D., and W. L. Ventis. 1982. *The Religious Experience: A Social-Psychological Perspective.* Oxford: Oxford Univ. Press.

Becker, E. 1962. *The Birth and Death of Meaning: An Interdisciplinary Perspective on the Problem of Man.* New York: Free Press.

———. 1973. *The Denial of Death.* New York: Free Press.

Benseman, J., and M. Givant. 1975. "Charisma and Modernity: The Use and Abuse of a Concept." *Social Movements* 42, no. 4: 570–614.

Berger, A. L. 1981. "Hasidism and Moonism: Charisma in the Counterculture." *Sociological Analysis* 41, no. 4: 375–90.

Berger, P. L. 1963. "Charisma and Religious Innovation: The Social Location of Israelite Prophecy." *American Sociological Review* 28: 940–50.

———. 1969. *A Rumor of Angels.* New York: Doubleday.

———. 1980. *The Heretical Imperative: Contemporary Possibilities of Religious Affirmation.* New York: Anchor.

Berkowitz, L., ed. 1977. *Advances in Experimental Social Psychology.* New York: Academic Press.

Berne, E. 1961. *Transactional Analysis in Psychotherapy.* New York: Grove Press.

Bharati, A. 1976. *The Light at the Centre: Context and Pretext of Modern Mysticism.* London: East-West Publications.

Blau, P. M. 1963. "Critical Remarks on Weber's Theory of Authority." *American Political Science Review* 57, no. 2: 305–16.

Bloch, E. 1986. *The Principle of Hope,* translated by N. Plaice, S. Plaice, and P. Knight. Oxford: Basil Blackwell.

Bogdan, R. C., and S. K. Biklen. 1982. *Qualitative Research for Education: An Introduction to Theory and Methods.* Boston: Allyn & Bacon.

Bohm, D. 1993. Last Words of a Quantum Heretic. *New Scientist,* Feb. 27, 38–42.

Bord, R. J. 1975. "Toward a Social-Psychological Theory of Charismatic Social Change Processes." *Social Forces* 53, no. 3: 485–97.

Boring, E. G. 1961. *Psychologist at Large*. New York: Basic Books.

Boring, E. G., H. S. Langfeld, H. Werner, and R. M. Yerkes, eds. 1961. *A History of Psychology in Autobiography*. Vol. 4. Worcester, Mass.: Clark Univ. Press.

Bowen, E. S. 1954. *Return to Laughter*. New York. Harper.

Bowlby, J. 1969. *Attachment*. Harmondsworth: Penguin.

————. 1973. *Attachment and Loss*. Vol. 2, *Separation*. New York: Basic Books.

————. 1980. *Attachment and Loss*. Vol. 3, *Loss, Sadness, and Depression*. New York: Basic Books.

Braden, C. S. 1963. *Spirits in Rebellion: The Rise and Development of New Thought*. Dallas: Southwestern Univ. Press.

Bradley, R. T. 1987. *Charisma and Social Structure: A Study of Love and Power, Wholeness and Transformation*. New York. Paragon House.

Brenner, C. 1974. "On the Nature and Development of Affects: A Unified Theory." *Psychoanalytic Quarterly* 43, no. 4: 532–56.

Bretherton, I. 1985. "Attachment Theory: Retrospect and Prospect." In *Growing Points of Attachment Theory and Research,* edited by I. Bretherton and E. Waters. Monographs of the Society for Research in Child Development. Chicago: Univ. of Chicago Press.

Bretherton, I., and E. Waters, eds. 1985. *Growing Points of Attachment Theory and Research*. Monographs of the Society for Research in Child Development serial no. 209, 50, no. 1–2. Chicago: Univ. of Chicago Press.

Bucke, R. M. 1901. *Cosmic Consciousness*. New York: Dutton.

Buckingham, J. 1976. *Daughter of Destiny: Kathryn Kuhlman — Her Story*. Plainfield, N.J.: Logos.

Burke, K. L., and M. B. Brinkerhoff. 1981. "Capturing Charisma: Notes on an Elusive Concept." *Journal for the Scientific Study of Religion* 20, no. 3: 274–84.

Buros, O. E., ed. 1978. *Eighth Mental Measurements Yearbook*. Highland Park, N.J.: Gryphon Press.

Burridge, K. 1969. *New Heaven, New Earth: A Study of Millennarian Activities*. Oxford: Basil Blackwell.

Butler, E. 1948. *The Myth of the Magus*. Cambridge: Cambridge Univ. Press.

Camic, C. 1980. "Charisma: Its Varieties, Preconditions and Consequences." *Sociological Inquiry* 50, no. 1: 5–23.

Campbell, D. T. 1979. "Degrees of Freedom and the Case Study." In *Qualitative and Quantitative Methods in Evaluation Research,* edited by D. T. Cook and C. S. Reichart. Beverly Hills, Calif.: Sage.

Chaplin, J. P. 1968. *Dictionary of Psychology*. New York: Dell.

Clark, K. E., and M. B. Clark, eds. 1990. *Measures of Leadership*. West Orange, N.J.: Leadership Library of America.

Clark, M. S., and H. T. Reis. 1988. "Interpersonal Processes in Close Relationships." *Annual Review of Psychology* 39: 609–72.

Cohler, B. J. 1987. "Adversity, Resilience, and the Study of Lives." In *The Invulnerable Child*, edited by E. J. Anthony and B. J. Cohler. New York: Guilford Press.

Cohn, N. 1970. *The Pursuit of the Millennium: Revolutionary Millennarians and Mystical Anabaptists of the Middle Ages.* New York: Oxford Univ. Press.

Coles. 1989. *Conrad: Heart of Darkness: Notes.* Toronto: Coles Publishing.

Coles, R. W. 1973. "Football as a Surrogate Religion." *A Sociological Yearbook of Religion in Britain*, 61–77.

Conger, J. A., and R. N. Kanungo. 1988. *Charismatic Leadership: The Elusive Factor in Organizational Effectiveness.* London: Jossey-Bass.

Conrad, J. 1950. *Heart of Darkness* and *The Secret Sharer.* New York: Signet.

Constantine, L. L., and J. Constantine. 1973. *Group Marriage.* New York: Macmillan.

Cook, D. T., and C. S. Reichart, eds. *Qualitative and Quantitative Methods in Evaluation Research.* Beverly Hills, Calif.: Sage.

Crews, F. 1980. "Analysis Terminable." *Commentary* 70: 25–34.

Danziger, K. 1980. "Wundt and the Two Traditions in Psychology." In *Wilhelm Wundt and the Making of a Scientific Psychology*, edited by R. W. Rieber. New York: Plenum Press.

Davis, D., and B. Davis. 1984. *The Children of God: The Inside Story.* Grand Rapids, Mich.: Zondervan.

De Bono, E. 1970. *Lateral Thinking: A Textbook of Creativity.* London: McGraw Hill.

Denzin, N. K. 1970. *The Research Act in Sociology: A Theoretical Introduction to Sociological Methods.* London: Butterworth.

Derlega, V. I., M. S. Harris, and A. L. Chaikin. 1973. "Self-disclosure, Reciprocity, Liking, and the Deviant." *Journal of Experimental Social Psychology* 9: 277–84.

Dobson, J. 1981. Book review in *New Zealand Psychologist* 10, no. 1: 93.

Dow, T. E. 1978. "An Analysis of Weber's Work on Charisma." *British Journal of Sociology* 29: 83–93.

Duff, R. C., ed. 1979. *Memory, Organization and Structure.* New York: Academic Press.

Durkheim, E. 1915. *The Elementary Forms of the Religious Life.* London: George Allen and Unwin.

———. 1965. *The Elementary Forms of the Religious Life.* Translated from the French by Joseph Ward Swain. New York: Free Press.

Eacker, J. N. 1975. *Problems of Philosophy and Psychology.* Chicago: Nelson-Hall.

Edelson, M. 1988. *Psychoanalysis: A Theory in Crisis.* Chicago: Univ. of Chicago Press.

Eliade, M. 1964. *Shamanism: Archaic Techniques of Ecstasy*, translated by W. R. Trask. Princeton: Princeton University Press.

Ellwood, R. S. 1973a. *One Way: The Jesus Movement and Its Meaning.* Englewood Cliffs, N.J.: Prentice-Hall.

———. 1973b. *Religious and Spiritual Groups in Modern America.* Englewood Cliffs, N.J.: Prentice-Hall.

Ellwood, R. S., and H. B. Partin. 1988. *Religious and Spiritual Groups in Modern America,* 2nd ed. Englewood Cliffs, N.J.: Prentice-Hall.

Emmet, D. 1958. *Functions, Purpose and Powers.* London: Macmillan.

Emmons, N. 1988. *Manson in His Own Words.* New York: Grove Press.

Enroth, R. 1983. *A Guide to Cults and New Religions.* Downer's Grove, Ill.: Intervarsity Press.

Ericsson, K. K., W. G. Chase, and S. Faloon. 1980. "Acquisition of a Memory Skill." *Science* 208 (June 6): 1181–82.

Erikson, E. H. 1942. "Hitler's Imagery and German Youth." *Psychiatry* 5: 475–93.

———. 1958. *Young Man Luther.* New York: Norton.

———. 1963. *Childhood and Society,* 2nd ed. New York: Norton.

———. 1968. "On the Nature of Psycho-historical Evidence: In Search of Gandhi." *Daedalus* 97: 695–730.

Festinger, L., H. W. Reicken, and S. Schachter. 1956. *When Prophecy Fails.* Minneapolis: Univ. of Minnesota Press.

Filstead, W. J. 1979. "Qualitative Methods: A Needed Perspective in Evaluation Research." In *Qualitative and Quantitative Methods in Evaluation Research,* edited by T. D. Cook and C. S. Reichart. Beverly Hills, Calif.: Sage.

Firth, R. 1965. Introduction to "Religions of the Oppressed," by V. Lantenari, *Current Anthropology* 6, no. 4.

Flavell, J. H., and E. M. Markham, eds. *Handbook in Child Psychology.* Vol. 3, *Cognitive Development.* New York: Wiley.

Follesdal, D. 1979. "Hermeneutics and the Hypothetico-deductive Method." *Dialectica* 33, no. 3–4: 319–36.

Forgas, J. P. 1986. *Interpersonal Behaviour: The Psychology of Social Interaction.* Sydney: Pergamon Press.

———, ed. 1985. *Language and Social Situations.* New York: Springer-Verlag.

Foster, L. 1983. "A Personal Odyssey: My Encounter with Mormon History." *Dialogue* 16, no. 3: 87–98.

———. 1984a. *Religion and Sexuality: The Shakers, the Mormons, and the Oneida Community.* Urbana: University of Illinois Press.

———. 1948b. "Career Apostates: Reflection on the Works of Jerald and Sandra Tanner." *Dialogue* 17 (Summer): 35–60.

———. 1988. "The Rise and Fall of Utopia: The Oneida Community Crises of 1852 and 1879." *Communal Societies* 8: 1–17.

———. 1992. "The Psychology of Religious Genius: Joseph Smith and the Origins of New Religious Movements." Paper presented to the annual meeting of the Mormon History Association, Saint George, Utah, May 16.

Freud, A. 1966. *Normality and Pathology in Childhood*. Harmondsworth: Penguin.

Freud, S. 1900; 1965. *The Interpretation of Dreams*, translated by J. Strachey. New York: Avon.

———. 1912. *Totem and Taboo*, translated by J. Strachey. New York: Norton.

———. 1914. "On Narcissism." In *Standard Edition of the Complete Psychological Works of Sigmund Freud*, vol. 14, 73–102.

———. 1917. "A Childhood Recollection from *Dichtung und Wahrheit*." In *The Collected Papers of Sigmund Freud*, vol. 4, 357–67.

———. 1921. "Group Psychology and the Analysis of the Ego." In *Standard Edition of the Complete Psychological Works of Sigmund Freud*, vol. 18, 67–144.

———. 1930. "Civilization and Its Discontents." In *The Standard Edition of the Complete Psychological Works of Sigmund Freud*, vol. 21, 59–143.

———. 1931. "Libidinal Types." In *The Standard Edition of the Complete Psychological Works of Sigmund Freud*, vol. 21, 215–20.

———. 1939. *Moses and Monotheism*, translated by K. Jones. New York: Vantage.

———. 1953–75. *Standard Edition of the Complete Psychological Works of Sigmund Freud*, translated by J. Strachey. 24 Vols. London: Hogarth.

———. 1965. *The Collected Papers of Sigmund Freud*. London: Hogarth.

Friedland, W. 1964. "For a Sociological Concept of Charisma." *Social Forces* 43: 18–26.

Fromm, E. 1964. *The Heart of Man: Its Genius for Good and Evil*. New York: Harper.

———. 1973. *The Anatomy of Human Destructiveness*. Harmondsworth: Penguin.

Frosh, S. 1989. *Psychoanalysis and Psychology: Minding the Gap*. London: Macmillan.

Gaines, J. 1979. *Fritz Perls: Here and Now*. Millbrae, Calif.: Celestial Arts.

Galanter, M. 1979. "The Moonies: A Psychological Study of Conversion and Membership in a Contemporary Religious Sect." *American Journal of Psychiatry* 2: 36–42.

———. 1980. "Psychological Induction into a Large Group: Findings from a Modern Religious Sect." *American Journal of Psychiatry* 12: 137–50.

Garfinkel, H. 1967. *Studies in Ethnomethodology*. Englewood Cliffs, N.J.: Prentice-Hall.

Gedo, J. E., and G. H. Pollock, eds. 1976. *Freud: The Fusion of Science and Humanism. The Intellectual History of Psychoanalysis*. New York: International Universities Press.

George, C., and M. Main. 1979. "Social Interactions of Young Abused Children: Approach, Avoidance and Aggression." *Child Development* 50: 306–18.

Gergen, K. J. 1985. "The Social Constructionist Movement in Modern Psychology." *American Psychologist* 40: 266–75.

Gergen, K. J., and J. Morawski. 1980. "An Alternative Metatheory for Social Psychology." In *Review of Personality and Social Psychology*, edited by L. Wheeler. Beverly Hills, Calif.: Sage.

Gerth, H., and C. W. Mills, eds. 1946. *From Max Weber: Essays in Sociology*. London: Routledge and Kegan Paul.

Gilbert, G. M. 1950. *The Psychology of Dictatorship*. New York: Ronald Press.

Gilmour, R., and S. Duck, eds. 1980. *The Development of Social Psychology*. London: Academic Press.

Giovacchini, L., ed. 1972. *Tactics and Techniques in Psychoanalytic Therapy*. London: Hogarth Press.

Gitelson, M. 1954. "Therapeutic Problems in the Analysis of the 'Normal' Candidate." *International Journal of Psychoanalysis* 35: 174–83.

Glaser, B. G., and A. L. Strauss. 1967. *The Discovery of Grounded Theory: Strategies for Qualitative Research*. Chicago: Aldine.

Goldberg, A., ed. 1980. *Advances in Self-Psychology*. New York: International Universities Press.

Gordon, D. F. 1984. "Dying to Self: Self-control Through Self-abandonment." *Sociological Analysis* 45, no. 1: 41–56.

Gordon, J. S. 1987. *The Golden Guru: The Strange Journey of Bhagwan Shree Rajneesh*. Lexington, Mass.: Stephen Greene.

Gough, H. G., and A. B. Heilbrun. 1983. *The Adjective Checklist Manual*. Palo Alto, Calif.: Consulting Psychologists Press.

Grene, W., and S. Lattimore, eds. 1958. *The Complete Greek Tragedies*, vol. 4. Chicago: University of Chicago Press.

Haber, R. N., and R. B. Haber. 1964. "Eidetic Imagery: 1. Frequency." *Perceptual and Motor Skills* 19: 131–38.

Habgood, J. 1990. "Science and Religion: An Obsolete Gap." *New Scientist*, Dec. 8, 2.

Hall, L. K. 1983. "Charisma: A Study of Personality Characteristics of Charismatic Leaders." Ph.D. diss., Univ. of Georgia.

Hamilton-Byrne, S. 1995. *Unseen, Unheard, Unknown: My Life Inside the Family of Anne Hamilton-Byrne*. Ringwood, Australia: Penguin.

Hanly, C., and J. Masson. 1976. "A Critical Examination of the New Narcissism." *International Journal of Psychoanalysis* 57: 49–66.

Harre, R. 1985. "Situational Rhetoric and Self-presentation." In *Language and Social Situations*, edited by J. P. Forgas. Sydney: Pergamon Press.

Harrell, D. E. 1975. *All Things Are Possible: The Healing and Charismatic Revivals in Modern America*. Bloomington: Indiana Univ. Press.

Hartrup, W., and Z. Rubin, eds. 1985. *The Nature and Development of Relationships*. Hillsdale, N.J.: Erlbaum.

Hassan, S. 1988. *Combatting Cult Mind Control*. Rochester, Vt.: Park Street Press.

Heiber, H., ed. 1962. *The Early Goebbels Diaries: 1925–1926*. New York: Praeger.

Heidel, A., ed. trans. 1968. The Gilgamesh Epic. In *The Origins of Civilization*, edited by W. H. McNeill and J. W. Sedlar. London: Oxford Univ. Press.

Heider, F., and M. Simmel. 1944. "An Experimental Study of Apparent Behaviour." *American Journal of Psychology* 57: 243–49.

Heinberg, R. 1991. *Memories and Visions of Paradise*. Los Angeles: Jeremy Tarcher.

Hesse, J. 1970. "From Champion Majorette to Frank Sinatra Date." *Vancouver Sun*, Aug. 31.

Hiden, J., and J. Farquharson. 1988. "The Personality of Adolf Hitler." In *Explaining Hitler's Germany: Historians and the Third Reich*, edited by Hiden and Farquharson. 2nd ed. London: Batsford.

Hiden, J., and J. Farquharson, eds. 1988. *Explaining Hitler's Germany: Historians and the Third Reich*, 2nd ed. London: Batsford Academic and Educational.

Hinnells, J. R., ed. 1984. *The Penguin Dictionary of Religions*. Harmondsworth: Penguin.

Hodgkinson, S., R. Sherrington, H. Gurling, R. Marchebanks, S. Reeders, J. Mallet, M. McInnis, H. Petursson, and J. Brynjolfsson. 1987. "Molecular Genetic Evidence for Heterogeneity in Manic Depression." *Nature* 325 (Feb. 26): 805–06.

Hogan, R., R. Raskin, and D. Fazzini. 1990. "The Dark Side of Charisma." In *Measures of Leadership*, edited by K. E. Clark and M. B. Clark. West Orange, N.J.: Leadership Library of America.

Hood, R. W. 1970. "Religious Orientation and the Report of Religious Experience." *Journal for the Scientific Study of Religion* 9, no. 4: 285–91.

———. 1975. "The Construction and Preliminary Validation of a Measure of Reported Mystical Experience." *Journal for the Scientific Study of Religion* 14: 29–41.

———. 1977a. "Eliciting Mystical States of Consciousness with Semistructured Nature Experiences." *Journal for the Scientific Study of Religion* 16, no. 2: 155–63.

———. 1977b. "Differential Triggering of Mystical Experiences as a Function of Self-actualization." *Review of Religious Research* 18, no. 3: 264–70.

———. 1978. "Anticipatory Set and Setting: Stress Incongruities as Elicitors of Mystical Experience in Solitary Nature Settings." *Journal for the Scientific Study of Religion* 17, no. 3: 279–87.

Hood, R. W., and R. J. Morris. 1981. "Sensory Isolation and the Differential Elicitation of Religious Imagery in Intrinsic and Extrinsic Persons." *Journal for the Scientific Study of Religion* 20, no. 3: 261–73.

Horizon. 1989. *Playing with Madness*. BBC Horizon documentary.

Hostetler, J. A. 1980. *Amish Roots: A Treasury of History, Wisdom and Lore*. Baltimore: Johns Hopkins University Press.

House, R. J., J. Woycke, and E. M. Fodor. 1988. "Charismatic and Noncharismatic leaders: Differences in Behaviour and Effectiveness." In *Charismatic Leadership: The Elusive Factor in Organizational Effectiveness,* edited by J. A. Conger and R. N. Kanungo. London: Jossey-Bass.

Hummel, R. P. 1975. "The Psychology of Charismatic Followers." *Psychological Reports* 37: 759–70.

James, W. 1961. *Varieties of Religious Experience.* New York: Collier Macmillan.

———. 1950. *The Principles of Psychology.* New York: Dover.

Jamison, K. R. 1993. *Touched with Fire: Manic-Depressive Illness and the Artistic Temperament.* New York: Free Press.

Jarvie, I. C. 1964. *The Revolution in Anthropology.* New York: Routledge and Kegan Paul.

Johnson, D. P. 1979. "Dilemmas of Charismatic Leadership: The Case of the People's Temple." *Sociological Analysis* 40, no. 4: 315–23.

Jones, A. J., and R. M. Anservitz. 1975. "Saint-Simon and Saint-Simonism: A Weberian View." *American Journal of Sociology* 80, no. 5: 1095–1123.

Jones, E. E., and E. M. Gordon. 1972. "Timing of Self-disclosure and Its Effects on Personal Attraction." *Journal of Personality and Social Psychology* 24: 358–65.

Jourard, S. M. 1971. *Self-disclosure.* New York: Wiley.

Jourard, S. M., and L. A. Kormann. 1968. "Getting to Know the Experimenter, and Its Effect on Psychological Test Performance." *Journal of Humanistic Psychology* 8, no. 2: 155–59.

Jourard, S. M., and J. L. Resnik. 1970. "Some Effects of Self-disclosure Among College Women." *Journal of Humanistic Psychology* 10, no. 1: 17–22.

Jung, C. G. 1954. "The Mana Personality." Chapter 4 of *The Relations Between the Ego and the Unconscious.* In *The Collected Works of C. G. Jung,* vol. 7, 225–39.

———. 1965. *The Collected Works of C. G. Jung,* edited by Sir Herbert Read, Michael Fordham, and Gerhard Adler; translated by R. F. C. Hull. 20 Vols. Princeton, N.J.: Princeton Univ. Press.

———. 1976. *Psychology and the Occult,* translated by R. F. C. Hull. Princeton: Princeton University Press.

Kakar, S. 1981. *The Inner World: A Psycho-analytic Study of Childhood and Society in India.* Delhi: Oxford Univ. Press.

———. 1982. *Shamans, Mystics, and Doctors.* New York: Knopf.

Kanter, R. M. 1972. *Commitment and Community.* Cambridge, Mass.: Harvard Univ. Press.

Kantor, D. 1980. "Critical Identity Image: A Concept Linking Individual, Couple, and Family Development." In *Family Therapy: Combining Psychodynamic and Family Systems Approachs,* edited by J. K. Pearce and L. J. Friedman. New York: Grune and Stratton.

Kaplan, L. J. 1979. *Oneness and Separateness: From Infant to Individual*. London: Jonathan Cape.

Kernberg, O. 1974. "Barriers to Falling and Remaining in Love." *Journal of the American Psychoanalytic Association* 22, no. 4: 486–511.

Kilbourne, B. K., and J. T. Richardson. 1980. "People's Temple and Jonestown: A Corrective Comparison and Critique." *Journal for the Scientific Study of Religion* 19, no. 3: 239–55.

Klein, G. S. 1966. "The Several Grades of Memory." In *Psychoanalysis: A General Psychology. Essays in Honour of Heinz Hartmann*, edited by R. M. Loewenstein, L. M. Newman, M. Schur, and A. J. Solnit. New York: International Universities Press.

Klein, M. 1949. *The Psychoanalysis of Children*. New York: Delta.

Kohut, H. 1959. "Introspection, Empathy and Psychoanalysis." *Journal of the American Psychoanalytic Association* 7: 459–83.

———. 1960. "Beyond the Bounds of the Basic Rule." *Journal of the American Psychoanalytic Association* 8: 567–86.

———. 1966. "Forms and Transformations of Narcissism." *Journal of the American Psychoanalytic Association* 14: 243–72.

———. 1971. *The Analysis of the Self: A Systematic Approach to the Psychoanalytic Treatment of Narcissistic Disorders*. New York: International Universities Press.

———. 1972. "Thoughts on Narcissism and Narcissistic Rage." *Psychoanalytic Study of the Child* 27: 360–400.

———. 1976. "Creativeness, Charisma and Group Psychology: Reflections on the Self-analysis of Freud." In *Freud: The Fusion of Science and Humanism. The Intellectual History of Psychoanalysis*, edited by J. E. Gedo and G. H. Pollock. New York: International Universities Press.

———. 1977. *The Restoration of the Self*. New York: International Universities Press.

———. 1980. "Reflections on *Advances in Self-psychology*." In *Advances in Self-Psychology*, edited by A. Goldberg. New York: International Universities Press.

———. 1985. *Self-psychology and the Humanities: Reflections on a New Psychoanalytic Approach*, edited by C. Strozier. New York: W. W. Norton.

Kopp, S. B. 1971. *Guru*. Palo Alto, Calif.: Bantam.

———. 1972. *If You Meet the Buddha on the Road, Kill Him!* Palo Alto, Calif.: Science and Behavior Books.

Kris, E. 1952. *Psychoanalytic Explorations of Art*. New York: International Universities Press.

———. 1956. "The Personal Myth: A Problem in Psychoanalytic Technique." *Journal of the American Psychoanalytic Association* 5: 653–81.

Kung, H. 1974. *Does God Exist: An Answer for Today*, translated by E. Quinn. New York: Vintage.

La Barre, W. 1980. *Culture in Context: Selected Writings of Weston La Barre.* Durham, N.C.: Duke Univ. Press.

Labak, A. S. 1972. "The Study of Charismatic College Teachers." Ph.D. diss., Univ. of Northern Colorado.

Lamont, S. 1986. *Religion Inc.: The Church of Scientology.* London: Harrap.

Lane, D. C. 1989. *The Making of a Spiritual Movement.* Del Mar. Calif.: Del Mar Press.

Lankton, S. 1980. *Practical Magic.* Cupertino, Calif.: Meta Publications.

Lasswell, H. 1960. *Psychopathology and Politics.* New York: Viking.

Latkin, C., R. Hagen, R. Littman, and N. Sundberg. 1987. "Who Lives in Utopia? A Brief Report on Rajneeshpuram Research Project." *Sociological Analysis* 48: 73–81.

Laxmi, M. Y. 1980. *The Sound of Running Water.* Poona: Rajneesh Foundation.

Lazerfield, P. F. 1972. *Qualitative Analysis: Historical and Critical Essays.* Boston: Allyn & Bacon.

Leonard, G. 1992. "How to Have an Extraordinary Life: An Interview with Michael Murphy." *Psychology Today* (May/June): 42–90.

Lévi-Strauss, C. 1955. *World on the Wane,* translated by J. Russell. London: Hutchinson.

Levine, S. V. 1984. *Radical Departures: Desperate Detours to Growing Up.* New York: Harcourt Brace Jovanovich.

Levinson, D. 1978. *The Seasons of a Man's Life.* New York: Knopf.

Levy, O., ed. 1974. *The Complete Works of Friedrich Nietzsche,* vol. 2. New York: Gordon Press.

Lifton, R. J. 1961. *Thought Reform and the Psychology of Totalism.* New York: Norton.

Lindholm, C. 1990. *Charisma.* Cambridge, Mass.: Basil Blackwell.

Lings, M. 1986. *Muhammad: His Life Based on the Earliest Sources.* London: Unwin.

Little, G. 1980. "Leaders and Followers: A Psycho-social Prospectus." *Melbourne Journal of Politics* 12: 3–29.

———. 1985. *Political Ensembles: A Psycho-social Approach to Politics and Leadership.* Melbourne: Oxford Univ. Press.

Loehlin, J. C. 1982. "Are Personality Traits Differentially Heritable?" *Behaviour Genetics* 12, no. 4: 417–28.

Loewald, H. W. 1962. "The Superego and the Ego-Ideal. II: Superego and Time." *International Journal of Psychoanalysis* 43: 264–68.

———. 1972. "The Experience of Time." *Psychoanalytic Study of the Child* 27: 401–10.

Loewenstein, R. M., L. M. Newman, M. Schur, and A. J. Solnit, eds. 1966. *Psychoanalysis: A General Psychology. Essays in Honour of Heinz Hartmann.* New York: International Universities Press.

Long, B. N.d. *Barry Long's Journal: Number 2.* London: Barry Long Foundation.

MacKinnon, D. W. 1962a. "The Nature and Nurture of Creative Talent." *American Psychologist* 17, no. 3: 484–95.

———. 1962b. "The Personality Correlates of Creativity: A Study of American Architects." *Proceedings of the XIV International Congress of Applied Psychology. Copenhagen, 1961* 2: 11–39.

MacMillan, M. 1992. *Freud Evaluated: The Completed Arc.* New York: Elsevier.

Mahler, M., F. Pine, and A. Bergman. 1967. *The Psychological Birth of the Human Infant.* New York: Basic Books.

Mahrer, A. R. 1988. "Discovery-Oriented Psychotherapy Research: Rationale, Aims, and Methods. *American Psychologist* 43, no. 9: 694–702.

Main, M., N. Kaplan, and J. Cassidy. 1985. "Security in Infancy, Childhood and Adulthood: A Move to the Level of Representation." In *Growing Points of Attachment Theory and Research,* edited by I. Bretherton and E. Waters. Chicago: Univ. of Chicago Press.

Main, M., and D. R. Weston. 1981. "The Quality of the Toddler's Relationship to Mother and to Father Related to Conflict Behavior and the Readiness to Establish New Relationships." *Child Development* 52, no. 3: 932–40.

Malcolm, J. 1980. *Psychoanalysis: The Impossible Profession.* London: Picador.

Mandler, J. H. 1979. "Categorical and Schematic Organization in Memory." In *Memory, Organization and Structure,* edited by G. R. Duff. New York: Academic Press.

———. 1983. "Representation." In *Handbook in Child Psychology.* Vol. 3, *Cognitive Development,* edited by J. H. Flavell and E. M. Markham. New York: Wiley.

Marcus, J. T. 1961. "Transcendence and Charisma." *Western Political Quarterly* 14, no. 1 (Mar.): 236–41.

Maslow, A. H. 1954. *Motivation and Personality.* New York: Harper.

———. 1968. *Toward a Psychology of Being,* 2nd ed. New York: Van Nostrand Reinhold.

———. 1971. *The Farther Reaches of Human Nature.* New York: Viking.

May, R. 1975. *The Courage to Create.* New York: Norton.

McGuire, W. J. 1980. "The Development of Theory in Social Psychology." In *The Development of Social Psychology,* edited by R. Gilmour, and S. Duck. London: Academic Press.

McMullen, W. E. 1976. "Creative Individuals: Paradoxical Personages." *Journal of Creative Behavior* 10, no. 4: 265–75.

McNeill, W. H., and J. W. Sedlar, eds. 1968. *The Origins of Civilization.* London: Oxford Univ. Press.

Meehl, P. E. 1978. "Theoretical Risks and Tabular Asterisks: Sir Karl, Sir Ronald, and the Slow Progress of Soft Psychology." *Journal of Consulting and Clinical Psychology* 46: 806–34.

Melton, J. G. 1987. *Encyclopedia of American Religions,* 2nd ed. Detroit: Gale.

Melton, J. G., and R. L. Moore. 1982. *The Cult Experience: Responding to the New Religious Pluralism.* New York: Pilgrim Press.

Miller, R. 1987. *Bare-Faced Messiah: The True Story of L. Ron Hubbard.* London: Michael Joseph.

Millikan, D. 1991. *Imperfect Company: Power and Control in an Australian Cult.* Sydney: William Heinemann Australia.

Milne, H. 1986. *Bhagwan: The God That Failed,* edited by Liz Hodgkinson. London: Caliban.

Miyahara, K. 1983. "Charisma: From Weber to Contemporary Sociology." *Sociological Inquiry* 53, no. 4 (Fall): 368–88.

Mulgan, J. 1972. *Man Alone.* Auckland: Longman Paul.

Murphy, M. 1992. *The Future of the Body: Explorations into the Further Evolution of Human Nature.* Los Angeles: Jeremy Tarcher.

Murray, H. A. 1938. *Explorations in Personality.* New York: Oxford Univ. Press.

Nietzsche, F. 1961. *Thus Spake Zarathustra: A Book for Everyone and No One.* Translated, with an Introduction by R. J. Hollingdale. Harmondsworth: Penguin.

———. 1974. "Thus Spake Zarathustra." In *The Complete Works of Friedrich Nietzsche,* vol. 2, edited by O. Levy. New York: Gordon Press.

Norman, D. A., and D. E. Rumelhart. 1975. "Memory and knowledge." In *Explorations in Cognition,* edited by Norman and Rumelhart. San Francisco: W. A. Freeman.

Noy, P. 1969. "A Revision of the Psychoanalytic Theory of the Primary Process." *International Journal of Psychoanalysis* 50: 155–78.

Oakes, L. D. 1986a. "Religious Values and Encounter Groups." M.A. thesis, University of Auckland.

———. 1986b. *Inside Centrepoint: The Story of a New Zealand Community.* Auckland: Benton Ross.

———. 1988a. "Social Indicators Research into an Alternative Religious Commune." Address given to the Conference on Social Indicators and Social Policy, Sociology Department, University of Auckland.

———. 1988b. "Power and Finance in a Communal Psychotherapy Cult." In *Money and Power in New Religions,* edited by J. T. Richardson. New York: Edward Mellon Press.

———. 1989. *The Centrepoint Children at School.* Unpublished research report for the Centrepoint Community Growth Trust. Albany, New Zealand.

———. 1992. "A Psychology of Charisma: The Prophet." Ph.D. diss., University of Auckland.

Oakley, A. 1981. "Interviewing Women: A Contradiction in Terms." In *Doing Feminist Research,* edited by H. Roberts. London: Routledge and Kegan Paul.

Offer, D., and C. B. Strozier. 1985. "Reflections on Leadership." In *The Leader: Psychohistorical Essays,* edited by Strozier and Offer. New York: Plenum.

Olden, C. 1941. "About the Fascinating Effect of the Narcissistic Personality." *American Imago* 2: 347–55.

———. 1958. "Notes on the Development of Empathy." *Psychoanalytic Study of the Child* 13: 505–18.

Olin, S. C. 1980. "The Oneida Community and the Instability of Charismatic Authority." *Journal of American History* 67, no. 2 (Sept.): 285–300.

Olin, W. F. 1980. *Escape from Utopia: My Ten Years in Synanon*. Santa Cruz: Unity Press.

Ornstein, P. H., ed. 1978. *The Search for Self: Selected Writings of Heinz Kohut (1950–1978)*. 2 vols. New York: International Universities Press.

Osgood, C. 1953. *Winter*. New York: Norton.

Otto, R. 1958. *The Idea of the Holy*. London: Oxford Univ. Press.

Parens, H. 1972. "A Contribution of Separation-Individuation to the Development of Psychic Structure." *Psychoanalytic Study of the Child* 27: 360–400.

Parker, R. A. 1935. *A Yankee Saint: John Humphrey Noyes and the Oneida Community*. New York: G. P. Putnam. Parsons, T., E. Shils, K. Naegele, and J. Pitts, eds. 1961. *Theories of Society*. Glencoe, Ill.: Free Press.

Patton, M. 1980a. *Qualitative Research Methods*. Beverly Hills, Calif.: Sage.

———. 1980b. Foreword to W. F. Olin's *Escape from Utopia: My Ten Years in Synanon*. Santa Cruz: Unity Press.

Pearce, J. K., and L. J. Friedman, eds. 1990. *Family Therapy: Combining Psychodynamic and Family Systems Approaches*. New York: Grune and Stratton.

Peck, M. S. 1978. *The Road Less Travelled: A New Psychology of Love, Traditional Values, and Spiritual Growth*. London: Hutchinson.

Pervin, L. A. 1985. "Personality: Current Controversies, Issues, and Directions." *Annual Review of Psychology* 36: 83–114.

Piaget, J. 1961. Entry in *A History of Psychology in Autobiography*, edited by E. G. Boring, H. S. Langfeld, H. Werner, and R. M. Yerkes. Vol. 4. Worcester, Mass.: Clark Univ. Press.

Post, J. 1986. "Narcissism and the Charismatic Leader-Follower Relationship." *Political Psychology* 7, no. 4: 675–87.

Prather, H. 1970. *Notes to Myself: My Struggle to Become a Person*. Moab, Utah: Real People Press.

Pressman, S. 1993. *Outrageous Betrayal: The Dark Journey of Werner Erhard from est to Exile*. Melbourne: Bookman.

Rapp, T. 1972. *Beautiful Lies You Could Live in*. Reprise long-playing record, B-RS 6467.

Redl, F. 1942. "Group Emotion and Leadership." *Psychiatry* 5: 573–96.

Reichardt, C. S., and D. T. Cook. 1979. "Beyond Qualitative Versus Quantitative Methods." In *Qualitative and Quantitative Methods in Evaluation Research*, edited by Cook and Reichart. Beverly Hills, Calif.: Sage.

Reiterman, T., and J. Jacobs. 1982. *Raven: The Untold Story of the Rev. Jim Jones and His People*. New York: Dutton.

Richardson, J. T., ed. 1988. *Money and Power in New Religions.* New York: Edwin Mellon Press.

———. 1995. "Clinical and Personality Assessment of Participants in New Religions." *International Journal for Psychology of Religion* 5, no. 3: 145–70.

Richardson, J. T., M. W. Stewart, and R. B. Simmonds. 1979. *Organized Miracles: A Study of a Contemporary Youth Communal Fundamentalist Organization.* New Brunswick, N.J.: Transaction Books.

Ricks, M. H. 1982. "Origins of Individual Differences in Attachment: Maternal, Familial, and Infant Variables." Paper presented to the International Conference on Infant Studies, Austin, Texas.

———. 1983. "Individual Differences in Preschoolers' Competence: Contributions of Attachment History and Concurrent Environmental Support." Ph.D. diss., Univ. of Massachusetts, Amherst.

Rieber, R. W., ed. 1980. *Wilhelm Wundt and the Making of a Scientific Psychology.* New York: Plenum Press.

Robbins, T. 1988. "Cults, Converts and Charisma: The Sociology of New Religious Movements." *Contemporary Sociology* 36, no. 1 (Spring). (Entire issue)

Roberts, H., ed. *Doing Feminist Research.* London: Routledge and Kegan Paul.

Robins, R. S. 1986. "Paranoid Ideation and Charismatic Leadership." *Psychohistory Review* 15: 15–55.

———, ed. 1977. *Psychopathology and Political Leadership.* Tulane Studies in Political Science, vol. 16. New Orleans: Tulane Univ. Press.

Rogo, D. S. 1984. "Ketamine and the Near-Death Experience." *Anabiosis: The Journal for Near-Death Studies* 4, no. 1 (Spring): 87–95.

Rorer, L. G., and T. A. Widiger. 1983. "Personality Structure and Assessment." *Annual Review of Psychology* 34: 431–63.

Rose, G. J. 1972. "Fusion states." In *Tactics and Techniques in Psychoanalytic Therapy,* edited by P. L. Giovacchini. London: Hogarth Press.

Rosegrant, M. 1976. "The Impact of Set and Setting on Religious Experience in Nature." *Journal for the Scientific Study of Religion* 15, no. 4: 301–10.

Ross, L. 1977. "The Intuitive Psychologist and His Shortcomings: Distortions in the Attribution Process." In: *Advances in Experimental Social Psychology,* edited by L. Berkowitz. New York: Academic Press.

Ruether, R. R. 1981. *To Change the World: Christology and Cultural Criticism.* London: SCM Press.

Runyon, W. M. 1984. *Life Histories and Psychobiography: Explorations in Theory and Method.* New York: Oxford Univ. Press.

Russell, B. 1969. *The Autobiography of Bertrand Russell.* London: Allen and Unwin.

Sacks, O. 1985. *The Man Who Mistook His Wife for a Hat.* London: Picador.

Samuels, A., B. Shorter, and F. Plant. 1986. *A Critical Dictionary of Jungian Analysis.* London: Routledge and Kegan Paul.

Sass, L. A. 1988. "The Self and Its Vicissitudes: An " Archaeological" Study of the Psychoanalytic Avant-garde." *Social Research* 55, no. 4 (Winter): 551–607.

Savicki, V. 1972. "Outcomes of Nonreciprocal Self-disclosure Strategies." *Journal of Personality and Social Psychology* 23: 271–76.

Schachtel, E. G. 1947. "On Memory and Childhood Amnesia." *Psychiatry* 10: 1–26.

———. 1954. "The Development of Focal Attention and the Emergence of Reality." *Psychiatry* 17: 309–24.

Schank, R. C., and R. P. Abelson. 1977. *Scripts, Plans, Goals, and Understanding.* Hillsdale, N.J.: Erlbaum.

Schmalenbach, H. 1961. "Communion—A Sociological Category," translated by K. Naegele. In *Theories of Society,* edited by T. Parsons, E. Shils, K. Naegele, and J. Pitts. Glencoe, Ill.: Free Press.

Schooler, C. 1972. "Birth Order Effects: Not Here, Not Now." *Psychological Bulletin* 78, no. 3: 161–73.

Schweitzer, A. 1984. *The Age of Charisma.* Chicago. Nelson-Hall.

Sennett, R. 1975. "Charismatic De-legitimation: A Case Study." *Theory and Society* 2: 171–81.

Sharaf, M. 1983. *Fury on Earth: A Biography of Wilhelm Reich.* London: Hutchinson.

Sheehy, G. 1974. *Passages: Predictable Crises of Adult Life.* New York: Dutton.

Sheppard, M. 1976. *Fritz.* New York: Bantam.

Silverman, L. H., F. M. Lachman, and R. H. Milich. 1982. *The Search for Oneness.* New York: International Universities Press.

Silverman, L. H., and J. Weinberger. 1988. "Mommy and I Are One: Implications for Psychotherapy." *American Psychologist* 40, no. 12: 1296–1308.

Singer, P. 1961. "Hindu Holy Men: A Study in Charisma." Ph.D. diss., Syracuse University.

Slater, P. E. 1961. "Toward a Dualistic Theory of Identification." *Merrill-Palmer Quarterly* 7: 113–26.

Smith, W. C. 1962. *The Meaning and End of Religion.* London: SPCK.

———. 1979. *Faith and Belief.* Princeton: Princeton University Press.

Spitz, R. E. 1965. *The First Year of Life.* New York: International Universities Press.

Sroufe, L. A., and J. Fleeson. 1985. "Attachment and the Construction of Relationships." In *The Nature and Development of Relationships,* edited by W. Hartrup and Z. Rubin. Hillsdale, N.J.: Erlbaum.

Stace, W. T. 1960. *Mysticism and Philosophy.* Philadelphia: Lippincott.

Stark, S. 1968. "Toward a Psychology of Charisma. I: The Innovation Viewpoint of Robert Tucker." *Psychological Reports* 23: 1163–66.

———. 1969. "Toward a Psychology of Charisma. II: The Pathology Viewpoint of James C. Davies." *Psychological Reports* 24: 88–90.

———. 1977. "Toward a Psychology of Charisma. III: Intuitional Empathy, Vorbilder, Fuehrers, Transcendence Striving, and Inner Creation." *Psychological Reports* 40: 683–96.

Steiger, B. 1968. *In My Soul I Am Free*. Menlo Park, Calif.: IWP.

Stein, M. H. 1956. "The Marriage Bond." *Psychoanalytic Quarterly* 25: 238–59.

Stern, D. N. 1985. *The Interpersonal World of the Infant*. New York: Basic Books.

Stierlin, H. 1959. "The Adaptation to the Stronger Person's Personality." *Psychiatry* 22: 143–52.

Stonequist, E. V. 1937. *The Marginal Man: A Study of Personality and Culture Conflict*. New York: Russell and Russell.

Strelley, K., and R. D. San Souci. 1987. *The Ultimate Game: The Rise and Fall of Bhagwan Shree Rajneesh*. San Francisco: Harper & Row.

Streng, F. J. 1969. *Understanding Religious Man*. Belmont, Calif.: Dickenson.

Strozier, C. B. 1980. "Heinz Kohut and the Historical Imagination." In *Advances in Self-Psychology*, edited by A. Goldberg. New York: International Universities Press.

Strozier, C. B., and D. Offer. 1985. *The Leader: Psychohistorical essays*. New York: Plenum.

Teilhard de Chardin, P. 1959. *The Phenomenon of Man*, translated by B. Wall. London: Collins.

Thomas, R. D. 1977. *The Man Who Would Be Perfect: John Humphrey Noyes and the Utopian Impulse*. Pittsburgh: Univ. of Pittsburgh Press.

Thoreau, H. D. 1983. *Walden* and *Civil Disobedience*. Harmondsworth: Penguin.

Tillich, P. 1949. *The Shaking of the Foundations*. Harmondsworth: Penguin.

Trungpa, C. 1973. *Cutting Through Spiritual Materialism*. Berkeley: Shambhala.

Tucker, R. C. 1968. "The Theory of Charismatic Leadership." *Daedalus*. 97, no. 3: 731–56.

Turnbull, C. M. 1961. *The Forest People*. London: Methuen.

Turner, R. H., and J. Schutte. 1981. "The 'True Self' Method for Studying the Self-conception." *Symbolic Interaction* 4, no. 1: 1–20.

Turner, V. W. 1969. *The ritual Process: Structure and Anti-structure*. Chicago: Aldine.

———. 1974. *Dramas, Fields and Metaphors: Symbolic Action in Human Society*. Ithaca: Cornell Univ. Press.

Underhill, E. 1930. *Mysticism*. London: Methuen.

Ulman, R. B., and D. W. Abse. 1983. "The Group Psychology of Mass Madness: Jonestown." *Political Psychology* 4, no. 4: 637–61.

Valentine, E. R. 1982. *Conceptual Issues in Psychology*. London: George Allen and Unwin.

Waite, R. G. L. 1977. *The Psychopathic God: Adolf Hitler*. New York: Signet.

Wallace, A. F. 1956. "Acculturation: Revitalization Movements." *American Anthropologist* 58: 264–81.

Wallas, G. 1926. *The Art of Thought*. New York: Harcourt.

Wallerstein, R. S. 1988. "Psychoanalysis, Psychoanalytic Science, and Psychoanalytic Research—1986." *Journal of the American Psychoanalytic Association* 36, no. 1: 3–30.

Wallis, R. 1982. "The Social Construction of Charisma." *Social Compass* 29, no. 1: 25–39.

Wallis, W. D. 1943. *Messiahs: Their Role in Civilisation*. Washington, D.C.: American Council on Public Affairs.

Walter, J. A. 1985. "Achievement and Shortfall in the Narcissistic Leader: Gough Whitlam and Australian Politics." In *The Leader: Psychohistorical Essays*, edited by C. B. Strozier, and D. Offer. New York: Plenum.

Waters, E., J. Wippman, and L. A. Sroufe. 1979. "Attachment, Positive Affect, and Competencies in the Peer Group: Two Studies in Constant Validation." *Child Development* 50: 821–29.

Watts, A. 1961. *Psychotherapy East and West*. London: Jonathan Cape.

Weber, M. 1946. "The Sociology of Charismatic Authority." In *From Max Weber: Essays in Sociology*, edited and translated by H. Gerth and C. Wright Mills. New York: Oxford Univ. Press.

———. 1958. "The Three Types of Legitimate Rule." *Berkeley Publications in Society and Institutions* 4, no. 1 (Summer): 6–15.

———. 1964; 1947. *The Theory of Social and Economic Organization*, translated by A. M. Henderson and Talcott Parsons. New York: Oxford Univ. Press.

———. 1968a. *Economy and society*, edited by G. Roth and C. Wittich. 3 vols. New York: Bedminster Press.

———. 1968b. *On Charisma and Institution Building*, edited by S. N. Eisenstadt. Chicago: Univ. of Chicago Press.

Weber, Marianne. 1975; 1926. *Max Weber: A Biography*, translated by H. Zohn. New York: Wiley.

Welsh, G. S. 1975. *Creativity and Intelligence: A Personality Approach*. Chapel Hill: Institute for Research in Social Science, Univ. of North Carolina.

Westland, G. 1978. *Current Crises of Psychology*. London: Heinemann.

Westley, F. R., and H. Mintzberg. 1988. "Profiles of Strategic Vision: Levesque and Iacocca." In *Charismatic Leadership: The Elusive Factor in Organizational Effectiveness*, edited by J. A. Conger and R. N. Kanungo. London: Jossey-Bass.

Wheeler, L., ed. 1980. *Review of Personality and Social Psychology*. Beverly Hills, Calif.: Sage.

White, R. W., ed. 1963. *The Study of Lives: Essays in Honour of Henry A. Murray*. New York: Atherton Press.

Whiteside, M. 1981. "Rare Beasts in the Sheepfold." *Journal of Creative Behaviour* 15, no. 2: 189–98.

Wilkinson, L. 1975. "REGM: A Multivariate General Linear Hypothesis Program for Least Squares Analysis of Multivariate Data." *Behaviour Research Methods and Instrumentation* 7: 485–86.

Willner, A. R. 1968. *Charismatic Political Leadership: A Theory*. Center of International Studies, Woodrow Wilson School of Public and International Affairs, Research Monograph no. 32. Princeton: Princeton Univ. Press.

———. 1984. *The Spellbinders: Charismatic Political Leadership*. New Haven: Yale University Press.

Wilson, B. R. 1975. *The Noble Savages*. Berkeley: Univ. of California Press.

Winnicott, D. W. 1960. "The Theory of the Parent-Infant Relationship." *International Journal of Psychoanalysis* 41: 585–95.

Wolff, K. H. 1976. *Surrender and Catch: Experience and Enquiry Today*. Boston Studies in the Philosophy of Science, vol. 51. Boston: D. Reidel.

———. 1978. "Toward Understanding the Radicalness of Surrender." *Sociological Analysis* 39, no. 4: 397–401.

Wren-Lewis, J. 1991. "A Reluctant Mystic." *Self and Society* 16, no. 2: 4–11.

Wundt, W. M. 1916. *Elements of Folk Psychology: Outlines of a Psychological History of the Development of Mankind*. London: Allen and Unwin.

Wuthnow, R. 1976. *The Consciousness Reformation*. Berkeley: Univ. of California Press.

Young, S. 1989. "The Mini-explorers of Middle Earth." *New Scientist*, Sept. 30, 22–25.

Zablocki, B. 1980. *Alienation and Charisma: A Study of Contemporary American Communes*. New York: Free Press.

Zerzan, J. 1988. *Elements of Refusal*. Seattle: Left Bank Books.

Index